Rethinking Law and Religion

RETHINKING LAW

The Rethinking Law series is a forum for innovative scholarly legal writing from across all substantive fields of law. The series aims to enrich the study of law by promoting a cutting-edge approach to legal analysis.

Despite the old maxim that nothing is new under the sun, it is nevertheless true that laws evolve and contexts in which laws operate change. Law faces new and previously unforeseen challenges, responds to shifting motivations and is shaped by competing interests and experiences. Academic scrutiny and challenge is an essential component in the development of law, and the act of re-thinking and re-examining principles and precepts that may have been long-held is imperative.

Rethinking Law showcases authored books that address their field from a new angle, expose the weaknesses of existing frameworks, or 're-frame' the topic in some way. This might be through the introduction of a new legal framework, through the integration of perspectives from other fields or even other disciplines, through challenging existing paradigms, or simply through a level of analysis that elevates or sharpens our understanding of a subject. While each book takes its own approach, all the titles in the series use an analytical lens to open up new thinking.

For a full list of Edward Elgar published titles, including the titles in this series, visit our website at www.e-elgar.com.

Rethinking Law and Religion

Russell Sandberg

Professor of Law, Cardiff University, UK

RETHINKING LAW

Cheltenham, UK • Northampton, MA, USA

Cover image: 'Ruins of Margam Abbey, Wales UK', by Tony Martin Long

Published by
Edward Elgar Publishing Limited
The Lypiatts
15 Lansdown Road
Cheltenham
Glos GL50 2JA
UK

Edward Elgar Publishing, Inc.
William Pratt House
9 Dewey Court
Northampton
Massachusetts 01060
USA

A catalogue record for this book
is available from the British Library

Library of Congress Control Number: 2024934680

This book is available electronically in the **Elgar**online
Law subject collection
http://dx.doi.org/10.4337/9781800886193

ISBN 978 1 80088 618 6 (cased)
ISBN 978 1 80088 619 3 (eBook)

Printed and bound by CPI Group (UK) Ltd, Croydon, CR0 4YY

To Emma, with love

Contents

Preface

In many ways, this book is a follow-up to my first two books on law and religion: *Law and Religion* (Cambridge University Press, 2011) and *Religion, Law and Society* (Cambridge University Press, 2014). In the decade since my last full-length book on law and religion was published, my focus has shifted at least in part towards legal history. It is tempting to see this book as a return to law and religion. However, I am not going backwards; I am going forwards. This book draws upon but consolidates and recasts many of the arguments I have developed in publications and presentations in the last decade to 'rethink' much of what I assumed, created and perpetuated in those first two books and what the implications of this are in terms of developing the subject further. The punchline of this book is clear: we've got work to do.

The nature of this book means that I owe many debts to those who have engaged with my work over the years: the countless editors, peer reviewers, social media repliers and the occasional reader. Singling out individuals to name would be foolhardy. But I will do it anyway. My interest in law and religion dates back to lectures and classes studying under and then teaching with Professor Norman Doe. His influence is incalculable and my debt unquantifiable. I am also grateful to my numerous other co-authors over the years, including Frank Cranmer, Christopher Grout, Mark Hill KC and Dr Sharon Thompson. They have been responsible for the best aspects of our collaborations together and have usually tolerated and sometimes even laughed at my attempts at humour. Thanks are also due to my colleague Rebecca Riedel, whose research has sparked many critical thoughts about law and religion scholarship and who has indulged several conversations about ideas that have been developed here. I am also thankful to Amber Watts, who suggested writing for Edward Elgar's excellent Rethinking Law series when I emailed her some thoughts about what I was thinking of writing next. It has been a pleasure to work with her and the team at Edward Elgar. As ever, I owe the most, of course, to my family and especially to my wife Emma.

Russell Sandberg
Neath, South Wales
December 2023

1.   Navel battles

'There is an element of navel gazing over a minority interest.' That was the judgement of a recent peer review of one of my articles. The reference to 'navel gazing' bothered me the least. I think law writers do not spend enough time navel gazing; or to put it another way, we pay insufficient attention to the intellectual history and development of our fields of study.

One of the weaknesses in law as opposed to other disciplines is our tendency to downplay the work and role of scholars and commentators. While reference lists for other subjects typically comprise academic surnames with a sprinkling of primary materials, this ratio is typically reversed in much legal literature. Law writers (and law students in particular) tend to cite cases and pieces of legislation more than they do academic works. This is, of course, unobjectionable. If their role is to 'build up a systematic statement of the law on the relevant topic in a coherent form',[1] then this means that attention should be paid to primary legal sources.

However, what is objectionable is that way in which academic works are usually used in legal essays, articles and textbooks. We typically cite scholarly writings in law as part of the purpose of developing and critiquing a systematic statement of what the law is now on the particular topic. We treat them as an aid to interpretation without recognising that what they say is their interpretation. We do not really treat them like secondary sources. Unlike other subjects, we generally do not look further at the writer. We rarely ask why the writer developed that interpretation or critique, and we do not tend to step back and examine the values, assumptions and biases that shaped the author and therefore shaped the author's work.

We spend very little time exploring the intellectual history of areas of law. Courses and textbooks on contract law, land law, family law and so on rarely explain how the area in question developed as intellectual fields. They seldom provide an account of the leading writers and main works of the area and their influence in shaping how those fields are understood: what topics are included and excluded; how they are presented; how principles of law are articulated; what stories are told and not told. We tend to do this a bit more in relation to

---

[1]   Lord Goff of Chieveley, 'Judge, Jurist and Legislature' [1987] *Denning Law Journal* 79, 92.

interdisciplinary approaches such as jurisprudence, the sociology of law or legal history; but even there, the focus tends to be upon the classics – long dead, invariably white men who have been placed on a pedestal.[2] And in doctrinal subjects, there are some specialist works on their intellectual histories – book series that look at the philosophical underpinnings or leading works of particular areas.[3] But as ever, the exceptions to the rule prove the rule.

It may be countered that such navel gazing should not be our focus. Analysing names in footnotes is a side distraction from the task of developing and critiquing the systematic statement of what the law is and how it came to be. The conventional view is that the scribblings of scholars are not sources of law, with the possible exception of lauded jurists of the past whose glosses on the common law are now taken as authoritative statements of it. It has been said that until recently, there was a professional practice that judicial judgments would not cite living authors in case they subsequently changed their minds: the 'better read when dead' principle.[4] Even though academic writings are now regularly cited and discussed in judgments, especially in the higher courts, they are invariably seen as mere aids to interpretation.[5]

However, I think that downplays the actual role and significance of academic works on law, especially those textbooks that have become authoritative. Statutes and judgments only cover discrete legal issues. By contrast, academic and practitioner texts fill in the gaps.[6] They develop or at least finesse principles of law, especially those which are not subject to judicial or legislative analysis. And it is those works that are used to teach generations

---

[2] See, e.g., Richard A Cosgrove, *Scholars of the Law: English Jurisprudence from Blackstone to Hart* (New York University Press, 1996). Even critical scholarship tends to begin from the perspective of questioning the importance afforded to such figures within the canon: see Daniel Newman, 'Law and Philosophy' in Daniel Newman and Russell Sandberg (eds) *Law and Humanities* (Anthem Press, 2024) 115.

[3] See, e.g., Janet Halley, 'What is Family Law?: A Genealogy Part I' (2011) 23 *Yale Journal of Law and the Humanities* 1 and Janet Halley, 'What is Family Law? A Genealogy Part II' (2011) 23 *Yale Journal of Law and the Humanities* 189; James Goudkamp and Donal Nolan (eds), *Scholars of Tort Law* (Hart, 2019); and the Analysing Leading Works in Law series, published by Routledge.

[4] On which see Alexandra Braun, 'Burying the Living? The Citation of Legal Writings in English Courts' (2010) 58(1) *American Journal of Comparative Law* 27.

[5] For a summary and assessment from the perspective of the judiciary, see Lady Justice Carr, '"Delicate Plants", "Loose Cannons" or "A Marriage of True Minds"? The Role of Academic Literature in Judicial Decision-Making' (Harris Society Annual Lecture, Oxford, 16 May 2023).

[6] As Ian Ward has pointed out, if we wanted to 'trace the evolution of English constitutional law … we could do worse than plot our path through successive editorial introductions to Dicey's *Law of the Constitution*': Ian Ward, *Writing the Victorian Constitution* (Palgrave, 2018) 17.

of lawyers. There are dozens of student textbooks, for instance, on each area of law: their contents pages within each area are strikingly similar; the way they structure most topics is notably comparable; the principles of law they propound are markedly alike.

Emphasising the role of legal scholars may seem to be a bold claim. Yet it is not a novel one. AV Dicey noted in his inaugural lecture on 'Can English Law be Taught at the Universities?' that the role of legal scholarship in shaping the law is often more significant than we credit. He said that 'by teaching and by literature [we] can influence far more than is generally believed not the form only but the substance of the law'.[7] In addition to noting the 'ease by which judicial legislation is swayed by the pressure of authoritative opinion', Dicey noted the importance of the textbook tradition in shaping areas of law. As he put it: 'Particular authors have notoriously, even in recent times, modelled, one might almost say brought into existence, whole departments of law.'

The writer's articulation of law becomes what the law is for many readers. No court and no Act of Parliament or Code has ever sought to describe in detail the general principles of English criminal law, contract law, tort law and so on. It is the writers of the common law who have sought to synthesise and rationalise these and other bodies of law. Their work becomes what I have called elsewhere the 'common lore' that supplements and furthers the common law.[8] Over time, parts of this common lore – these syntheses – are referred to (and often not attributed to any one author) in primary legal materials. Their work stealthily becomes part of what we call 'the law'.

This is why I think we need to pay more attention to the intellectual history of the areas of law we study.[9] The textbook tradition disguises how the elucidation of general principles and of bodies of law is an act of construction. It is a work of interpretation and is therefore shaped by the assumptions, values and biases of the author. Yet the role of writers is often overlooked and their statements are not understood as being authored. Navel gazing, therefore, is about readdressing the balance: paying much needed attention to how fields have developed.

That said, as the term itself suggests, there can be too much navel gazing. I have spent a lot of time commenting on the development of the field of law and religion in England and Wales. Indeed, when I have not been writing about the development of law and religion, I have been performing a similar task in relation to the field of legal history. I hope that the book in your hands is my

---

[7] AV Dicey, *Can English Law be Taught at the Universities?* (McMillan, 1883).

[8] See further Russell Sandberg, *Subversive Legal History: A Manifesto for the Future of Legal Education* (Routledge, 2021) 202 *et seq.*

[9] See further ibid especially Chapters 3 and 8.

final statement on the issue at least for quite a while. It is important to analyse the intellectual development of fields of study: what is included; what is excluded; how it interacts with other fields both within its own discipline and elsewhere. But I am aware that there is a limit to such navel gazing. The risk is that otherwise you spend so much time analysing the field that you are in that you forget to engage with and actually contribute to developments in the field. You become an expert in the study of law and religion rather than in law and religion. Yet, as this book will argue, there is a pressing need to pay attention to the study of law and religion. We need to rethink it.

***

It was the reviewer's description of law and religion as a 'minority interest' that was not so easy to discount. I would argue that developing interests are exactly where navel gazing should be especially encouraged. That is, after all, where those initial and often long-lasting choices about inclusion and exclusion, about where and how the field sits in the academy, are made. It is also where there is a risk of constantly reinventing the wheel if writers are unaware of what each other is doing. So, creating a scholarly community and analysing the development of that is probably more important in up-and-coming fields. The same is true in relation to fields that are stagnating, where there is a need for diagnosis to pre-empt the post-mortem.

It was the implicit dismissal in the reviewer's phrase that bothered me. There seemed to be, at least implicitly, the suggestion that I was overanalysing something that did not merit such treatment. While I would imagine that the anonymous reviewer would readily recognise the value of an intellectual history of established legal fields, I inferred from the comments a feeling that law and religion was not worth such attention. It had not developed into a recognised legal field.

The worst thing about the comment was that I partly agreed with it. Law and religion in England and Wales has not developed in the way that I had expected. That was the focus of the article that the peer reviewer was dismissive of. That piece – and many of my other writings over the last decade or so – have explored why law and religion is 'not flourishing quite as it ought to flourish' in this jurisdiction.[10] Excellent research has been published but law and religion seems less visible now than it was in the first decade of the twenty-first century. Something seems to have gone astray – and I think this is

---

[10]   To quote Maitland's lament about the state of legal history in Frederic W Maitland, 'Why the History of English Law has not been Written' in HAL Fisher (ed) *Collected Papers of Frederic William Maitland, Downing Professor of the Laws of England* (Cambridge University Press, 1911) Vol 1, 480, 497.

in part due to the foundations that were built in the heyday of law and religion. This book explores why there is a need for a rethink and how the study of law and religion can be rethought. Hopefully, this excuses some further (and, with any luck, final) navel gazing. But one thing is for certain: the anonymous reviewer of that article would probably hate this book!

2.   Getting personal

This is not a book about law and religion. This book is about the study of law and religion. It focuses upon the development of law and religion as a field of studies in England and Wales.

My first book, *Law and Religion*, was published in 2011 following a decade in which questions concerning the place of religion in the public sphere were never far from the news headlines.[1] Moral panics occurred concerning the wearing of religious dress, the operation of religious courts and the clash between freedom of religion and free speech, as well as the need not to discriminate on grounds of sexual orientation. These controversies all had a legal component. In the years that followed the 9/11 terrorist attacks, a raft of legislation was passed and a tide of case law then sought to understand and contest the new legal framework. *Law and Religion* mapped the legal terrain, exploring how the new laws seeing freedom of religion and belief as a human right and forbidding discrimination on grounds of religion or belief sat with older laws protecting the Church of England as the established Church and merely tolerating other forms of religiosity. It was very much a book about law and religion. But it was also concerned with the study of law and religion.

Law and Religion reflected on how these developments had increasingly attracted scholarly attention from academic lawyers. It argued that law and religion was fast developing as a sub-discipline within law schools akin to family law or sports law. My second book – *Religion, Law and Society* – continued this analysis to argue that greater collaboration was needed between law and religion and the sociology of religion.[2] It painted both law and religion and the sociology of religion as sub-disciplines within the disciplines of law and sociology respectively. Focusing on the secularisation thesis as the main case study, the book made the case that a fuller understanding of the relationship between religion, law and society could be better understood by combining legal and sociological analyses of religion.

Yet, ten years on, law and religion remains nowhere near as developed as family law or even sports law. And it is by no means comparable to the sociology of religion as a field and in terms of how central the sociology of religion

---

[1]   Russell Sandberg, *Law and Religion* (Cambridge University Press, 2011).
[2]   Russell Sandberg, *Religion, Law and Society* (Cambridge University Press, 2014).

is to sociology as a discipline compared to how marginal law and religion is within law. Although the sociology of religion is less mainstream than it once was, it remains the case that it is an option on A Level sociology courses. By contrast, law and religion is only taught in a handful of British law schools, let alone on the A Level law syllabus – and crucially, the number of law and religion courses has actually declined in the last decade. Although excellent works of scholarship have been produced in the last decade, I am disappointed that the potential of law and religion as a field of studies has not been realised.

My first two books were both concerned with conceptualising law and religion as a sub-discipline and exploring its potential. The word 'rethinking' in this book's title refers to the way in which I will be rethinking my previous thoughts, actions and hopes for the development of law and religion. This draws upon much of my work published over the last decade. During that time, I have published two short books on particular law and religion areas where reform has been discussed or implemented,[3] as well as various edited collections[4] together with numerous articles and chapters. Although some of this work has focused on the challenges brought about by the legal framework on religion or belief, much has focused on how law and religion has developed as a field and has begun to reassess my earlier work – arguments that will be developed further here.

My research focus over the last decade has also shifted at least in part to examine legal history; but even in that context, a lot of my work has been occupied with how disciplines and sub-disciplines develop and the need for, but challenges of, interdisciplinary work. Focusing on legal history – a long-standing legal sub-discipline that had been characterised not entirely unfairly as 'slowly and inevitably dying', or being 'in a coma for the last 30 years, at least'[5] – shed light upon the development of law as a discipline and the emphases of the conventional law school curriculum. My book *Subversive*

---

[3] Russell Sandberg, *Religion and Marriage Law: The Need for Reform* (Bristol University Press, 2021); Russell Sandberg, *Religion in Schools: Learning Lessons from Wales* (Anthem, 2022).

[4] Russell Sandberg (ed), *Religion and Legal Pluralism* (Ashgate, 2015); Frank Cranmer, Mark Hill, Celia Kenny and Russell Sandberg (eds), *The Confluence of Law and Religion: Interdisciplinary Reflections on the Work of Norman Doe* (Cambridge University Press, 2016); Norman Doe and Russell Sandberg (eds), *Law and Religion – Critical Concepts* (Routledge, 2017); Russell Sandberg (ed), *Leading Works in Law and Religion* (Routledge, 2019); Russell Sandberg, Norman Doe, Bronach Kane and Caroline Roberts (eds), *Handbook of the Interdisciplinary Study of Law and Religion* (Edward Elgar Publishing, 2019); Daniel Newman and Russell Sandberg (eds), *Law and Humanities* (Anthem Press, 2024).

[5] Daniel Siemens, 'Towards a New Cultural History of Law' (2012) 2 *InterDisciplines* 18, 19.

Legal History: A Manifesto for the Future of Legal Education argued that legal
history needs to be at the beating heart of the legal curriculum as a method
that corrects the way in which law is presented as being universal, functional
and progressive.[6] My textbook *A Historical Introduction to English Law:
Genesis of the Common Law* facilitated this by providing law students with
a guide revisiting and reappraising the stories conventionally told about how
the common law had evolved.[7] It sought to plug the gap left by the absence of
history in many courses and textbooks as part of the wider project detailed in
Subversive Legal History, seeking to rejuvenate legal history by presenting
it as a method used by all legal scholars and students rather than a specialist
sub-discipline left to a select few.

This book is an attempt to bring together my work since *Religion, Law and
Society* and to examine how it all fits together, including insights from my
historical works. It adopts but completely rewrites aspects from my post-2014
publications in order to assess what I have learned along the way and what
I would do differently now.

***

I am not an objective bystander in the story that this book tells. Through
my publications and through developing research networks, book series and
taught modules, I have played an active role in shaping law and religion as
a field of studies in England and Wales. Academic fields of study are human
constructs. They are dynamic entities that are in a constant state of flux; being
continuously constructed, deconstructed and reconstructed. As Rosemary
Hunter and Ruth Fletcher noted in their introduction to a roundtable on the
field of law, gender and sexuality,[8] fields of study are 'in process, moving and
changing, rather than as a fixed, marked-out territory or state of being'; they
argued that 'the field is not, and perhaps never will be or ought to be "made",
but rather is one whose making is an activity in which we are all, in various
ways, engaged'.[9]

---

[6]   Russell Sandberg, *Subversive Legal History: A Manifesto for the Future of Legal
Education* (Routledge, 2021).
[7]   Russell Sandberg, *A Historical Introduction to English Law: Genesis of the
Common Law* (Cambridge University Press, 2023).
[8]   The roundtable discussion, organised by the Arts and Humanities Research
Council Research Centre for Law, Gender and Sexuality, was held at the University
of Westminster in March 2009 and subsequently appeared in printed form in *Feminist
Legal Studies.*
[9]   Rosemary Hunter and Ruth Fletcher, 'Law, Gender and Sexuality: The Making
of a Field – Introduction' (2009) 17 *Feminist Legal Studies* 289, 292.

The process of formulating a field is always an exercise in power. It is a means of inclusion and exclusion: deciding what is analysed and what is not and where the borders of the intellectual pursuit will be drawn. Moreover, this takes place even if attention is not being afforded explicitly to questioning the definition or ambit of the field. Every course lecturer, every textbook writer, every researcher, every journal or book series editor is constantly involved in this process – often unwittingly and frequently with significant effects. Joanne Conaghan highlighted this in her contribution to the roundtable, reflecting upon her experience assembling a four-volume anthology on feminist legal studies for the Critical Concepts in Law series[10] – an experience that I have also had in relation to law and religion.[11] Conaghan's recognition that the exercise of field-making in the micro-context of anthology assembling as well as in the macro-context of disciplinary formation was 'a far from neutral exercise' reflected my own experience.[12] As she put it:

> To delineate a field, to give it form, content, texture and depth, was an active not a passive interaction with the materials. It entailed the drawing up of boundaries by which the outer reaches of the field could be determined (essentially a process of inclusion and exclusion). It required the static, cartographic representation of a dynamic, multidimensional, spatially and temporally contingent sphere of ongoing intellectual and political engagement. It instituted a normative order which could then serve as a frame for interpretation and evaluation. Its effect, in other words, was unavoidably prescriptive.

This is perhaps why field-making occurs more implicitly than explicitly. The 'unavoidably prescriptive' nature of the endeavour allies it with a positivist approach to law that is out of vogue and under attack by critical approaches. This is perhaps why work focusing on the study of areas of law can be dismissed by some as navel gazing.

While field-making has the potential of highlighting these questions and highlighting inclusions and exclusions that are loaded with assumptions and biases, it also runs the risk of creating or at least perpetuating such disadvantages and blind spots. As Conaghan pointed out, the effect of field-making is political. She highlighted the way 'it lends strength to an intellectual tradition' and 'raises the visibility and enhances the authority of scholarship which

---

[10] Joanne Conaghan (ed), *Feminist Legal Studies: Critical Concepts in Law* (Routledge, 2009).

[11] Norman Doe and Russell Sandberg (eds), *Law and Religion: Critical Concepts in Law* (Routledge, 2017).

[12] Joanne Conaghan, 'The Making of a Field of the Building of a Wall? Feminist Legal Studies and Law, Gender and Sexuality' (2009) 17 *Feminist Legal Studies* 303, 304.

might otherwise be excluded or marginalised by the established conceptual or disciplinary infra-structure'. Field-making is a creative act, a deliberate act, a human act – and thus, as Conaghan reminds us, always a contestable act:

> To mark out a field, then, is never simply to describe what is already there; it is to create, to produce, to bring forth. Envisioning a field requires a vision, projection or plan, the execution of which involves selection, discrimination, and judgement making. Both the vision and the selection are contestable. Indeed, it is the nature of field-making to engender, often deliberately to provoke, contestation.[13]

This is why the act of field formulation and the analysis of this act are important; why they are not mere navel gazing. The act of field formulation has a significant and often unappreciated long-term effect by normalising a particular conception which not only becomes unquestioned in itself but also masks the very fact that the construction process is precisely that: a time and space-specific active process of choice.

The development of the field of study serves to stabilise that field. In so doing, this can also stabilise and normalise many aspects of the status quo. However if it exposes this, examining the development of fields of study has the capacity to challenge and to subvert. Exploring the development of fields can question orthodoxies and reveal the biases and power imbalances at the heart of academic fields and at the centre of the academy generally. As Conaghan puts it, 'field-making may serve as a technique of disruption or an act of resistance'.

This act of resistance can extend to questioning and disturbing the very idea of field formation and asking whether fields of study need to be developed as disciplines or sub-disciplines. Ruth Fletcher's contribution to the roundtable helpfully distinguished a field from a discipline and body of scholarship on the basis that a field is 'less than a discipline and more than a body of scholarship'.[14] For Fletcher, 'a field connotes an area of research and teaching, rather than a disciplinary mode of knowledge production, or a collection of academic scholarship'. She wrote of 'intellectual fields as distinguishing themselves from each other as they take on particular logics through the application of key concepts and methods to research terrain'.[15] It is no dusty administrative task akin to filing; rather, it is an active, dynamic and authored act of creativity. Fletcher emphasised the agency of those who work in and therefore construct the fields: 'Fields develop through critical practice as field-makers commu-

---

[13]   Ibid 305.
[14]   Ruth Fletcher, 'Embodied Practices' (2009) 17 *Feminist Legal Studies* 315.
[15]   Ibid 316.

nicate their findings and exchange over the significance of such findings.'[16] Fletcher paints fields as collective endeavours which develop as a result of and as part of 'embodied practices'.[17] As she put it:

> Fields are clearly sites on which agents put energy into the carving out of new research items. But fields are more than sites of intellectual agency it seems to me. Fields could not have these particular logics, critical practices and spheres of action unless they acquired them through the activity of those agents. Rather the making of the field happens through practice in a larger sense; through the embodied intellectual struggles that researchers have with logics and critiques, with their own energy and time, with each other.

Put another way, field construction is relational. It is affected by the relationships formed by those within the field relative to each other and relative to those outside the field. This underscores that the current construction of a field is neither fixed nor the end point, and also complicates the conventional lazy understanding that depicts the development of fields in a linear, progressive manner. As Fletcher puts it, 'thinking in terms of embodied practices helps us identify the ways in which [a field] grows organically in fits and starts, in cycles and flows, rather than in a top-down, even and linear fashion'.[18] This provides a way to critique the creation narratives that disciplines tell about themselves and which they use to constrain their development.

The contributions to the roundtable discussion on law, gender and sexuality also underscored that reflections about field construction need to be personal rather than institutional. A grounded analysis is very much a characteristic of feminist scholarship. Feminist theory is built 'from the ground up, from the shared experience of women talking from personal testimonies, story-telling, consciousness-raising, and other revelatory techniques aimed at highlighting perspectives ignored by traditional narratives'.[19] Feminist perspectives underscore that the personal is political.

This came to the fore in Alison Diduck's contribution to the roundtable, in which she pointed out that a field of study is more than just 'a place or space';

---

[16] Conaghan suggests that here Fletcher is thinking of the word 'field' as 'as a verb rather than as a noun (as in: to field a player in a sport or a fighter on a battlefield)', in that the focus 'is more on process (or practice in Ruth's conception) than on product, on doing rather than being': Joanne Conaghan, 'The Making of a Field of the Building of a Wall? Feminist Legal Studies and Law, Gender and Sexuality' (2009) 17 *Feminist Legal Studies* 303, 307.

[17] Ruth Fletcher, 'Embodied Practices' (2009) 17 *Feminist Legal Studies* 315, 316.

[18] Ibid 316.

[19] Joanne Conaghan, 'Reassessing the Feminist Theoretical Project in Law' (2000) 27(3) *Journal of Law and Society* 351, 364.

it is 'as much our actions as it is the products of those actions'.[20] For Diduck, this meant that offering a personal history was preferable to 'attempting an objective or even partial history of this intellectual field':

> It is important, I think, not to abstract out of existence the real people who do the work of actively constituting a field. The frame, walls and doors of any intellectual 'home' are not self-erecting and do not shift on their own. They are constructed, maintained and re-constructed by people, each of whom brings her or his life to the project.[21]

A personal history of the field is for Diduck an exploration of her intellectual 'home' and 'a set of embodied practices in and around a particular home that is undergoing constant renovation'. Understanding the developments of field in this way requires a change of focus from the usual presumed objective approach of telling and thus perpetuating the field's conventional narrative to a more subjective approach that looks at the agency of the field-makers. An embodied approach to field-making is interested in the 'stories' of those who work in fields, their experiences, their practices, their assumptions. Exploring the history of a field should therefore become an exercise in autoethnography: 'the use of self-reflection and personal experience to explore wider cultural, social and political meanings and understandings.'[22]

This is the approach taken by this book. Rethinking law and religion requires revisiting my own contributions to how the field was developed in England and Wales in the opening decade of the twenty-first century. In the pages that follow, I describe my own contributions, mistakes and the consequences of these. The following rethinks much of what I assumed, created and perpetuated in my earlier publications in light of my subsequent research and writings. It follows that, although this is not intended as a work of intellectual auto-biography, there will be a fair amount of self-reflection and introspection. It is, I suppose, a work of autoethnography.

Although this book is about the study of law and religion, it is also a personal story. The two are interlinked. As I explore the rise and fall of law and religion studies in England and Wales, I will reflect on my own experiences of the stories that I am telling and not shy away from my own role in what has happened. Our rethinking of law and religion will involve three stages and this autoethnographical approach will be particularly important in relation to the first stage. In identifying what has gone amiss with the development of

---

[20]   Alison Diduck, 'Doing Home' (2009) 17 *Feminist Legal Studies* 293, 295.
[21]   Ibid 293.
[22]   Carolyn Steedman, *History and the Law: A Love Story* (Cambridge University Press, 2020) 24.

the field of law and religion, I examine my own culpability. The first stage of rethinking law and religion is repentance, because I have a confession to make.

PART I

Repentance

In which the origins of and reasons for the decline of law and religion are explored, a life-changing moment is revisited, inspiration is sought from the land of the free and a confession is made.

3.   Creation myths

It is difficult to foresee those moments that change your life. Something trivial like a last-minute change of plans or even the choice of what to eat for breakfast can have life-altering effects. We do not know what would have happened in the counterfactual scenario where another choice was made; a different path taken; an altered timeline pursued. And often it is difficult to pinpoint with any sense of accuracy the moment when a life-changing event occurred. However, I know that one of my life-changing events happened in October 2002.

I was sitting in the lecture hall on the ground floor of the Cardiff Law School building. It is now a familiar setting but then was an alien new world. I was a new undergraduate, not accustomed to university life or the delights of the big city. I did not quite know what to expect. I had chosen to study law and sociology at Cardiff almost by default. I had wanted a university I could commute to and did not really know why I had chosen law. At A Level, I had studied sociology, history and religious studies, and had enjoyed interpreting and analysing texts; but I was most animated by studies that had a real-world application – that involved people.[1] I think this led me towards the law degree with the advantage that I could combine this with sociology, something I already knew a little about.[2]

The exact moment that changed my life came at the very start of my very first public law lecture. The lecture was due to be given by Dr Paul Robertshaw, the module leader. However, in his first lecture, he wanted to introduce the person who would be lecturing us over the first few weeks on constitutional principles. Dr Robertshaw looked exasperated that his colleague had not turned up. Unbeknown to him, the colleague in question was standing immediately behind him, pulling faces and enjoying the jape. That colleague was Professor Norman Doe.

In the weeks that followed, Doe's lectures stood out. For me, they underlined what a university education was about: not slavishly following the textbook accounts but exploring, analysing and questioning the law with erudition,

---

[1]   By contrast, I had never really taken to the sciences and to maths, while I showed no talent for the arts. Indeed, my art teacher decided not to put grades on my homework in case it would embarrass me.

[2]   Indeed, I had peppered my speech at my sixth form ball with thoughts from sociologist Talcott Parsons.

wit and a significant number of seemingly (and sometimes actually) irrelevant asides. Other lectures seemed staid and ordinary by comparison. He was clearly enjoying himself – one minute making profound points that went over the heads of his audience and the next trying to hoodwink them by correctly demonstrating that we would all write down whatever he said.

For the first time in my life, I saw someone I could relate to intellectually – someone who clearly relished learning and his subject but did not take it or himself entirely seriously. I had always felt that the way that I approached things differed from that of my peers. Even the arrogance of youth did not convince me that I was unique; but still, it hit me in those public law lectures that for the first time I was seeing someone like me. Doe was delivering the material in a way that I would like to think I would (ah, there was the arrogance of youth!). He was animated about his subject and life generally but wore his learning lightly.

By sheer luck, I was allocated Doe as my personal tutor and so arranged an introductory meeting. Fittingly, his room was not in the law school building but in the building opposite. At the top of the building, in a room with a turret, we met. Like his lectures, the meeting was far from conventional. Once we had bonded over our common Welshness, Doe was quick to show me his work on the Church in Wales. His enthusiasm was infectious. It was this more than the subject matter that engaged me. I suddenly felt that the university could be the place where I could be me. It would be no exaggeration to say that the seeds of my academic career were sown that October, but not my interest in law and religion. I had little idea of the role Doe had played in forging law and religion as an academic subject in England and Wales.

***

Paradoxically, law and religion is a new academic discipline which relates to an age-old interaction. Tensions between secular authorities and religious convictions are a constant throughout history. Laws have prohibited, constrained, tolerated, enabled, privileged and burdened both religious groups and the religious beliefs and actions of individuals. Yet the study of law and religion is a relatively new phenomenon, at least in England and Wales. And this is in part attributable to none other than Henry VIII.

Prior to the reign of Henry VIII (1509–47), England was a Catholic country. Although clerics often held positions of political authority, the Church had her own courts – the Courts Christian or ecclesiastical courts – which applied the canon law of Rome as modified by local provincial laws and developed by Church bodies. There were clashes between the canon law and the king's common law and areas where the common law took precedence. But by and large, the Courts Christian were left to their own devices and had a significant jurisdiction, covering not only matters that were clearly ecclesiastical but also a range of other matters such as wills, some criminal offences and what we would now call the law of marriage and divorce.

The Reformation – the move from Catholicism to Protestantism – differed in England as compared to the continental experience. The divorce from Rome in the 1530s under Henry VIII was not a religious upheaval that required political and constitutional reconstruction; it was rather a political and constitutional act that led in time to religious upheaval.[3] One often-overlooked effect of the English Reformation of the 1530s was the side-lining of religious law. The termination of papal jurisdiction was accompanied by a prohibition on the teaching of canon law at Oxford and Cambridge Universities.[4] The ban on the study of Catholic canon law did not result in the new law of the infant Church of England becoming a subject of study instead. Rather, it led to Church law not being formally taught.

Although lawyers in the Church courts continued to appeal to Roman canon law,[5] that and the developing new law of the English Church became solely subjects of professional training at a learned society which came to be known as the Doctors' Commons.[6] As the centuries passed, the law of the Church was occasionally the subject of professional texts but almost no attention was given to it as a field of law, let alone the general interaction between law and religion.[7] Even when alternative forms of religiosity became lawful following the slow and piecemeal march of toleration, there was no discrete law on religious freedom to comment upon and no identifiable social problem. As Maitland expressed it in his lectures subsequently published as *The Constitutional*

---

[3] Geoffrey R Elton, 'The Reformation in England' in Geoffrey R Elton (ed) *The New Cambridge Modern History Volume 2: The Reformation, 1520–1559* (2nd edition, Cambridge University Press, 1990) 262.

[4] Injunctions were issued in 1535 which substituted lectures in civil law for lectures in canon law, and in 1545 an Act (37 Henry VIII c 17) allowed judgeships in the ecclesiastical courts to be held by laymen who were doctors only of civil law.

[5] Richard Helmholz, *Roman Catholic Law in Reformation England* (Cambridge University Press, 1991). The Submission of the Clergy Act 1533 provided that the Roman canon law was to continue to apply unless it was 'contrariant or repugnant to the law, statutes or custom' of the realm or to the King's prerogative. See also Norman Doe, 'Pre-Reformation Roman Catholic Law in Post-Reformation English Ecclesiastical Law' (2022) 24(3) *Ecclesiastical Law Journal* 273.

[6] See George D Squibb, *Doctors' Commons: A History of the College of Advocates and Doctors of Law* (Clarendon Press, 1977); Paul Barber, 'The Fall and Rise of Doctors' Commons' (1996) 4(18) *Ecclesiastical Law Journal* 462; David Pocklington, 'The Continued Relevance of Doctors' Commons' (2011) 166 *Law and Justice* 52.

[7] See, e.g., in the twentieth century: W Dale, *The Law of the Parish Church* (Butterworths, 1932); Garth Moore, *Introduction to English Canon Law* (Clarendon, 1967).

History of England, 'religious liberty and religious equality [were] complete'.[8] The powers of the ecclesiastical courts of the Church of England had 'very much declined'.[9] And the feeling was that there was very little to say about the interaction between law and religion, at least in England.

This was still true by the mid to late twentieth century. Legal textbooks seldom mentioned religion.[10] Moreover, what little literature existed rarely extended beyond the study of the law of the established Church.[11] This changed, however, due to a curious mixture of personalities and politics. Developments in the 1980s and 1990s awakened interest in the law of the Church of England and treated it as the subject of academic analysis for the first time. In 1987, the Ecclesiastical Law Society was formed 'to promote the study of ecclesiastical and canon law particularly in the Church of England and those churches in communion with it'; and it began to publish its own journal, the *Ecclesiastical Law Journal*, and organise its own conferences.[12]

An attendee at one early conference was Doe, then a lecturer in law at Cardiff University who had just completed a doctorate on how legal ideas and philosophies had formed in the fifteenth century.[13] Doe was intrigued as to where all the canon law he had found in his historical research had gone. These thoughts and the encouragement and support of the Ecclesiastical Law Society led to the establishment of the LLM in Canon Law degree at Cardiff University in 1991, hailed as the first degree to study the laws of the Church of England and Catholic canon law since the Reformation.[14]

---

[8]   Frederic W Maitland, *Constitutional History of England* (Cambridge University Press, 1908) 520. It is worth noting that Maitland did dedicate a 20-page section to 'The Church' which examined the legal historical development of the Church of England, the history of toleration, the present condition and powers of the ecclesiastical courts and the status of the established church: ibid 506–26.

[9]   Ibid 523. On which see RB Outhwaite, *The Rise and Fall of the Ecclesiastical Courts, 1500–1860* (Cambridge University Press, 2006).

[10]   Julian Rivers, 'The Secularisation of the British Constitution' (2012) 14 *Ecclesiastical Law Journal* 371, 372.

[11]   The 1975 edition of the ecclesiastical law volume of *Halsbury's Laws of England* (4th edition, vol 14, London, 1975), for instance, dealt with 'other religious denominations' as an afterthought.

[12]   See Christopher Hill, 'The Genesis of the Society: Kemp, Moore, Routledge et al' (2012) 14 *Ecclesiastical Law Journal* 82.

[13]   Published as Norman Doe, *Fundamental Authority in Late Medieval Law* (Cambridge University Press, 1990).

[14]   Some canon law had been taught before 1991. From the late 1960s to 1981, Garth Moore offered a half-paper on the canon law of the Church of England as part of the law degree at Cambridge. At Oxford, seminars in canon law were conducted by Eric Kemp in the 1950s. See M Kotiranta, 'The Teaching and Study of Church–State Relations in the Nordic Countries, in the United Kingdom and in Ireland' in J Valle and

Throughout the 1990s, the focus of both the Ecclesiastical Law Society and the Cardiff postgraduate course broadened. In part, this was due to Doe's research.[15] Following an edited book on the law of the Church in Wales,[16] he published pioneering work comparing the laws of the Church of England and the Catholic Church. Such work, together with a pioneering practitioner text by Mark Hill – a barrister who had enrolled on the Cardiff LLM course[17] – saw the law of the Church of England being taken seriously as law for the first time.[18] The subtitle of Doe's book – 'A Critical Study in a Comparative Context' – is an apt shorthand description for Doe's prolific outputs. Later works placed the Church of England in the context of the wider Anglican Communion;[19] sought to extrapolate principles of law common to all Anglican churches;[20] placed the laws of Anglican churches in the wider Christian context;[21] and finally, placed the laws of Christian churches in the wider interfaith context.[22]

There were other publications too: an authoritative account of the law of the Church in Wales;[23] a comparative study of Church–State relations in Europe that innovated by comparing by topic rather than by country;[24] a study of cathedrals;[25] and more recently, works that have returned to his philosophical and

---

A Hollerbach (eds) *The Teaching of Church–State Relations in European Universities* (Peeters, 2005) 105, 153.

[15] For a further appraisal of Doe's contribution, see the essays in Frank Cranmer, Mark Hill, Celia Kenny and Russell Sandberg (eds) *The Confluence of Law and Religion: Interdisciplinary Reflections on the Work of Norman Doe* (Cambridge University Press, 2016); and John Witte Jr, 'Law at the Backbone: The Christian Legal Ecumenism of Norman Doe (2022) 24(2) *Ecclesiastical Law Journal* 192.

[16] Norman Doe (ed), *Essays in Canon Law: A Study of the Law of the Church in Wales* (University of Wales Press, 1992).

[17] Mark Hill, *Ecclesiastical Law* (Butterworths, 1995).

[18] Norman Doe, *The Legal Framework of the Church of England: A Critical Study in a Comparative Context* (Oxford University Press, 1996).

[19] Norman Doe, *Canon Law in the Anglican Communion* (Oxford University Press, 1998).

[20] Norman Doe, 'The Principles of Canon Law: A Focus of Legal Unity in Anglican–Roman Catholic Relations' (1999) 5 *Ecclesiastical Law Journal* 221; Norman Doe, 'Canon Law and Communion' (2002) 6 *Ecclesiastical Law Journal* 241; Norman Doe, *An Anglican Covenant* (Canterbury Press, 2008).

[21] Norman Doe, *Christian Law: Contemporary Principles* (Cambridge University Press, 2013).

[22] Norman Doe, *Comparative Religious Law: Judaism, Christianity, Islam* (Cambridge University Press, 2018).

[23] Norman Doe, *The Law of the Church in Wales* (University of Wales Press, 2002).

[24] Norman Doe, *Law and Religion in Europe* (Oxford University Press, 2011).

[25] Norman Doe, *The Legal Architecture of English Cathedrals* (Routledge, 2020).

historical roots.[26] But overall, Doe's research saw religious law as being subject to the same if not greater rigour as other areas of law, and saw the development of law and religion as a field. The success of the LLM programme and the work of Doe and his students led Cardiff University to establish its Centre for Law and Religion in 1998.[27] And the growing canvas of law and religion scholarship was reflected in the development of the *Ecclesiastical Law Journal* into a law and religion journal in content if not in name, publishing articles on the laws of other religions and faith communities and on national and international laws affecting religion.

There were, of course, works being produced outside of Cardiff. There were practical guides to Church law[28] and occasional works on particular topics that would later be seen as coming under the umbrella of law and religion.[29] As Anthony Bradney has noted, such work was 'spasmodic and disjointed'; there was 'no concrete and sustained debate about the proper relationship between religion and legal rules', and 'such articles and books as were produced failed to have any impact upon other more established areas of academic discourse'.[30] There were no specialist journals other than the *Ecclesiastical Law Journal* (which at this point was privately published by the Ecclesiastical Law Society); no book series; and no research groups or centres in England and Wales other than the then-infant Centre for Law and Religion at Cardiff, which began to interact with international groupings such as the European Consortium for Church and State Research (founded in 1989). The focus was Christian-centric, largely exploring historical remnants that continued to have legal effect.

By the late 1990s, law and religion was beginning to exist not only as an object of study for practitioners of Church law – as seen by the activities of the Ecclesiastical Law Society and its journal – but also as an academic

---

[26] E.g., Norman Doe (ed), *Christianity and Natural Law: An Introduction* (Cambridge University Press, 2017); Norman Doe (ed), *A New History of the Church in Wales* (Cambridge University Press, 2020); Norman Doe and Stephen Coleman (eds), *The Legal History of the Church of England* (Hart, 2024).

[27] See Norman Doe, 'The First Ten Years of the Centre for Law and Religion, Cardiff University' (2008) 10(2) *Ecclesiastical Law Journal* 222.

[28] See, e.g., William Dale, *The Law of the Parish Church* (Butterworths, 1932); Garth Moore, *Introduction to English Canon Law* (Clarendon, 1967); Garth Moore, Timothy Briden and Kenneth MacMorran, *Handbook for Churchwardens and Parochial Church Councillors* (Mowbray, 1989); John Pitchford, *An ABC for the PCC* (Wyche, 1980).

[29] C Crowther, *Religious Trusts* (Oxford University Press, 1954).

[30] Anthony Bradney, 'Politics and Sociology: New Research Agenda for the Study of Law and Religion' in Richard O'Dair and Andrew Lewis (eds) *Law and Religion* (Oxford University Press, 2001) 65, 66.

research interest. The prolific publications of Doe and his LLM students meant that increased attention was beginning to be given not just to the law of the Church, but also to how the law of the land affected religion. These questions also animated occasional research outputs by academic authors from outside Cardiff – most notably the monographs by Robilliard, Bradney and Hamilton.[31] However, this emerging literature very much focused on the interaction between religion and a series of discrete legal topics. It did not develop the idea of the existence of law and religion as a legal sub-discipline.

This is where the academic study of law and religion may have stayed. It could have remained as an esoteric subject for those interested in the laws of their religious groups who would be occasionally joined by a wayward academic adventurer. Yet it did not. In the first decade of the twenty-first century, there was a dramatic increase in law and religion scholarship. It is tempting to attribute this to wider social trends – specifically, the way in which the place of religion in the public sphere became increasingly controversial. The expansion of law and religion as a legal sub-discipline can be attributed and dated back to the aftermath of the terror attacks in New York on 11 September 2001. However, lines of cause and effect are rarely as straightforward and linear as they invariably appear given the benefit of hindsight. Regarding law and religion as a by-product of 9/11 may be overly simplistic.

***

As Anver Emon has observed:

> Depending on where one lives, calling September 11, 2001 an epic moment in world history is either cliché or hubris. Horrifying in its flash-bang scale and scope, 9/11 sits amidst a distressing spectrum of violence, pogroms, and genocides – the 1994 Rwanda genocide of Tutsis (approx. 800,000–1,000,000 dead); the July 1995 Srebrenica massacre (approx. 8000 dead); and the 2002 Gujarat riots (approx. 1044 dead, 223 missing) – to list a few examples. But unlike these other incidents of violence, the 9/11 attacks unleashed on an enormous scale state-coordinated military and national security campaigns against non-state actors, namely some paradigmatic 'Muslim extremists', in the service of the 'War on Terror'. For students and researchers we cannot ignore how 9/11 had has the effect (whether deserved or not) of signalling a sea change in what is researched, who did the research, and how that research was deployed.[32]

---

[31]   St John A Robilliard, *Religion and the Law* (Manchester University Press, 1984); Anthony Bradney, *Religions, Rights and Laws* (Leicester University Press, 1993); Carolyn Hamilton, *Family, Law and Religion* (Sweet & Maxwell, 1995).

[32]   Anver Emon, 'Islamic Law and the State' in Mariana Valverde et al (eds) *The Routledge Handbook of Law and Society* (Routledge, 2021) 174.

The events of and following 9/11 clearly had an impact upon the development of law and religion in England and Wales. The resulting controversies had a key legal component. There was a significant increase in interest in questions concerning religion and the law – a number of new laws were enacted and a plethora of high-profile cases were heard – and this animated the rapid development of law and religion as an academic sub-discipline with the associated institutional trappings. Some of this came from the political desire to attract votes from Muslim communities in the context of anti-terror rhetoric and laws that were likely to repel such communities.

Yet political tensions about religion and racial integration were increasing long before the events of 9/11. Maitland's assumption that religious freedom was 'complete' was questioned way before 9/11. Tensions between secular authorities and religious convictions are a constant throughout history. Moral panics that once concerned Catholicism have been superseded by moral panics about Islam. Moreover, tensions had come to the boil significantly before the attack on the Twin Towers. Concerns about morality and differentness had accelerated following the liberalisation brought about as a result of what Charles Taylor has referred to as the 'individuating revolution' of the 1960s,[33] as shown by the moral panics following the publication of the *Satanic Verses* a couple of decades later.

In the last couple of decades of the twentieth century, the place of religion in the public sphere began to be questioned. As the historian Callum Brown argued, 'in the midst of overall decline in popular religiosity, British religion showed signs of increasing seriousness and militancy'.[34] This was a sign of weakness, not strength: British Christianity became more militant as it contracted.[35] For instance, in addition to the rise of religious pressure groups and charismatic movements, 'British Catholicism showed a radically different approach to its position in British life': after the visit of Pope John Paul II to the UK in 1982, the domestic Church stopped 'keeping its head down' and 'established a new spirit of political and ecumenical engagement by the Church in Britain', which was 'nurtured through media contact'.[36] The growth of the Internet helped to foster the 'growing opportunities for vigorous minorities' – both liberal and conservative – to 'argue their cases, achieve success and push forward agendas'.

---

[33]   Charles Taylor, *Varieties of Religion Today* (Harvard University Press, 2002) 80. See further Russell Sandberg, *Religion, Law and Society* (Cambridge University Press, 2014), Chapter 5.

[34]   Callum G Brown, *Religion and Society in Twentieth-Century Britain* (Pearson, 2006) 297.

[35]   Ibid 314, 298.

[36]   Ibid 309.

As Brown pointed out, 'this was an uneven and in some ways imperceptible process and one that only became really noticeable in the early twenty-first century'.[37] While previously religious fundamentalism was 'widely considered as almost irrelevant' in mainland Britain, by the close of the century 'a swing from racism to religious bigotry' meant that on the streets of English cities such as Bradford, 'what were formerly classed as racist attacks were being re-counted as anti-religious attacks'.[38] The Al-Qaeda terrorist attacks in New York on 11 September 2001 and in London on 7 July 2007 provided a watershed moment. It was not the fear of religious extremism that was new: as sociologist Linda Woodhead noted, 'religiously-inflicted terrorism by the IRA had ... been a much more serious threat in Britain for much longer than anything done in the name of Islam – yet this did not shake secular certainties'.[39] What was new was that these fears occurred against a backdrop of wider uncertainty: the motivations behind the terror were largely unknown and the fear of terrorism became indistinguishable from wider notions distrusting 'otherness'. Although, as Woodhead argued, attributing 'the atrocities in the name of Islam as the turning point' whereby religion was placed back on the agenda is too simple an answer,[40] the events of September 2001 changed the way in which the West thought and spoke about not only Islam but religion *per se*. The notion that religions were an invariably benign force for good became questioned and the fact that religious believers were loyal to forms of authority other than the State became to be seen as a problem.

This new context shaped the way in which religions operated in public life. Religion became seen as a social problem and attention was afforded to it. It also contributed to the creation of new laws – most significantly, those formally regarding religion as a human right actionable in domestic courts and laws expressly specifically prohibiting discrimination on grounds of religion or belief.[41] This abundance of new laws regulating religion was followed by a multitude of cases seeking to define the contours of the new religious rights and how the new laws interact (or not) with earlier provisions and older understandings. Several of these cases, especially those concerning the wearing of religious dress and symbols at schools and workplaces, became newsworthy. Meanwhile, a lecture by the then Archbishop of Canterbury, Dr Rowan Williams – in which he acknowledged the existence of religious laws

---

[37] Ibid 297.
[38] Ibid 298, 313.
[39] Linda Woodhead, 'Introduction' in Linda Woodhead and Rebecca Catto (eds) *Religion and Change in Modern Britain* (Routledge, 2012) 1, 9.
[40] Ibid 8.
[41] By virtue of the Human Rights Act 1998, the Employment Equality (Religion or Belief) Regulations 2003 and the Equality Act 2006 (now see the Equality Act 2010).

and religious courts such as shariah councils – became headline news, with the main television news programmes graphically illustrating the item with footage of a stoning.[42] These legal changes and the headlines they provoked naturally led more law academics to pay attention to the interaction between law and religion, or aspects of that interaction.

The development of law and religion as a field of study can therefore be regarded as a post-9/11 phenomenon. As Julian Rivers has noted, there has been 'a new loss of consensus about the role and significance of religion'.[43] This resulted in legal changes and unease at existing legal situations, and law and religion developed in order to study this further. There are numerous causes of this loss of consensus.[44] It was clear, however, that the assumption of religion as a benign force was challenged in an age when all authority was questioned; when populations were more diverse than ever before; when individuals' identities were more multifaceted; and when acts of terror in the name of religion dominated the news headlines. The early years of the twenty-first century, in particular, saw a number of moral panics about the place of religion in the public sphere: media and political heat roasted such topics as religious dress and symbols, the operation of religious tribunals and the clash of rights between religion on the one hand and freedom of expression and homosexual rights on the other. Given this backdrop, the growth in scholarly literature on issues concerning religion and the law was perhaps inevitable. The rise in scholarly writing and teaching on religion in law schools in England and Wales coincided with significant changes which have challenged conventional assumptions that predicted the social decline of religion. The conventional account has drawn a line of causation between these political and social developments and the rise of law and religion studies. It has been commonly assumed that law and religion blossomed as an area of study as its subject matter has become more controversial.

However, it may be overly convenient and simplistic to regard the post-9/11 tide of legislation and litigation as the main cause of this development of interest in law and religion; to say that the sub-discipline of law and religion was created by new laws.[45] The increase in academic writing might be attributable to changes within law schools whereby research has become more central to

---

[42]   The lecture was subsequently published as: Rowan Williams, 'Civil and Religious Law in England: A Religious Perspective' (2008) 10 *Ecclesiastical Law Journal* 262.

[43]   Julian Rivers, 'The Secularisation of the British Constitution' (2012) 14 *Ecclesiastical Law Journal* 371, 385.

[44]   See further Russell Sandberg, *Religion, Law and Society* (Cambridge University Press, 2014), Chapter 5.

[45]   The causal link between the legal changes and 9/11 may also be questioned.

their mission and where there has been a move towards interdisciplinary work as a result. Yet much of the work produced on law and religion in England and Wales suggests that there is some truth in this creation narrative. And this has shaped how law and religion has developed. As Anthony Bradney has observed, law and religion scholarship has tended to assume and characterise the relationship between law and religion 'as a problem that is capable of solution'.[46] The moral panics of the early twenty-first century have meant that the focus has often been narrow, with much attention being afforded to particular spots of conflict. While early works on the subject tended to be shaped around particular legal issues (such as how religion interacts with employment and charity law),[47] much work now focuses either on one area in particular (such as, religious discrimination in isolation from other laws on discrimination or laws affecting religion)[48] or develops an argument that law and religion (or aspects of it) constitutes a distinct field of study – an emerging sub-discipline in its own right.[49] Particular topics have dominated the field: an initial fixation with the law on religious dress and symbols has partially given way to new obsessions.[50] Patrick Nash has commented that there is no need for 'another rehearsal of dull material on done-to-death areas such as Muslim marriage and sharia councils'[51] – which made me feel slightly bad about sending him a draft of my book on the topic for his comments!

Law and religion's creation narrative – some might say myth – has played a key role in how law and religion scholarship has developed. By focusing on immediate changes and issues, by regarding them as discrete problems to be solved, by linking itself too firmly with the news agenda, law and religion has not developed a level of permanence or maturity within academia. It has developed as a legal interest – and, ironically, the very developments that

---

[46]   Anthony Bradney, 'Politics and Sociology: New Research Agenda for the Study of Law and Religion' in Richard O'Dair and Andrew Lewis (eds) *Law and Religion* (Oxford University Press, 2001) 65, 68.

[47]   Epitomised by St John Robilliard, *Religion and the Law: Religious Liberty in Modern English Law* (Manchester University Press, 1984).

[48]   E.g., Lucy Vickers, *Religious Freedom, Religious Discrimination and the Workplace* (2nd edition, Hart Publishing, 2016).

[49]   See Julian Rivers, *The Law of Organized Religions* (Oxford University Press, 2010) and Russell Sandberg, *Law and Religion* (Cambridge University Press, 2011) for slightly different examples of this.

[50]   However, some authors have shown that there remains more to be said on the issue: Sylvie Bacquet, *Religious Symbols and the Intervention of the Law* (Routledge, 2019); Erica Howard, *Law and the Wearing of Religious Symbols in Europe* (2nd edition, Routledge, 2021).

[51]   Patrick S Nash, *British Islam and English Law: A Classical Pluralist Perspective* (Cambridge University Press, 2022) 1.

have fostered and accelerated the field as a specialism (such as the number of specialist research groups, journals, conferences and book series) have resulted in its marginalisation. Instead of dialogue with the legal mainstream, law and religion has developed at the margins of law schools, and the focus has been mainly on the pragmatic question of the extent to which and how religious difference should be accommodated by law. Its often headline-following focus, coupled with the related haste in which law and religion has developed institutionally, has resulted in short-term gain only. Law and religion has developed as a specialism on the margins of legal studies; and the very activities that have helped to constitute law and religion as a distinct entity have curtailed its development by cutting it adrift from the legal mainstream.

The post-9/11 expansion in interest in law and religion transformed an academic legal interest in religion that had already begun to grow in the last decade of the twentieth century. It allowed law and religion to solidify as a legal sub-discipline, with the usual institutional trappings of specialist conferences, journals, research groupings and so on. However, this process was too quick and the foundations were not properly built. Law and religion became attached to the headline controversies and was understood narrowly. The rise of law and religion in the first decade of the new millennium proved to be a false dawn – and I played a significant role in that.

4.   A false dawn

In the second half of the first decade of the twenty-first century, the revival of celebrated television series *Doctor Who* and its spinoff *Torchwood* put Cardiff on the map. Both series were filmed near Cardiff and often featured locations from the Welsh capital, with the adult-themed spinoff being set in Cardiff.[1] At the same time, another (much lower-profile) development was taking place: Cardiff was fast becoming *the* place for the study of law and religion. Cardiff University's Centre for Law and Religion established itself a hub for the sub-discipline, which had quickly grown during that period as questions concerning the place of religion in the public sphere increasingly made headline news.

Aside from their Cardiff connection, it would appear that there is little to connect the growth of law and religion and *Torchwood* – which was, after all, a fictional programme about a small and mostly dysfunctional team dealing with extra-terrestrial incidents. It would be pushing it to say that both were concerned with tackling otherworldly matters that were controversially clashing with ordinary daily life. Yet there were similarities between the two. The scholarly communities that developed under the auspices of the Centre for Law and Religion and the fictional Torchwood Institute were both outsiders: operating at the margins, developing their own identities and often refusing to conform. Moreover, the quote that began episodes of the first series of *Torchwood* provides a neat summary of the development of law and religion as a field of studies: 'The twenty-first century is when everything changes. And you've got to be ready.'

While *Torchwood* depicted the turn of the millennium as the starting point when alien invasions and the like became the norm, law and religion scholarship saw the new millennium as a similar starting point: the events of 9/11 resulted in a changed climate concerning religion, with a number of pieces of legislation and court cases concerning religious rights. The twenty-first

---

[1]   The programmes were made by BBC Wales with a number of senior figures – most notably, showrunner Russell T Davies – being Welsh. This was not, however, the first link between the series and Cardiff. The writer of the first Dalek serial in 1963, regarded as being pivotal to the series' success, was Cardiff-born screenwriter Terry Nation, who also penned a number of mostly Dalek-related scripts up until 1979.

century saw the juridification of religion – and a new scholarly community was more than ready for the change.[2]

***

By the close of the first decade of the new millennium, law and religion had become established as a legal sub-discipline. A literature had blossomed. A bibliography I compiled for the Ecclesiastical Law Society's silver jubilee in 2012 indicated that while on average, two to three books on law and religion matters were published each year between 1987 and 1997, this figure grew to an average of six books between 1997 and 2000 and to ten books after 2007.[3] This rise was even more accelerated in the case of edited books. An academic industry devoted to law and religion had sprung into existence.[4] There quickly developed a plethora of law and religion journals and book series; many specialist conferences and symposiums; numerous centres and research groups; several prolific national and international networks. To a lesser extent, there were a few courses and textbooks dedicated to the subject – although it remained largely true that legal textbooks on areas such as public law, family law and employment law seldom mentioned religion; and while some work was published in mainstream general legal journals, scholarship in this field tended to be published in specialist journals, edited collections and monographs.

Many of these developments were led by the Cardiff Centre for Law and Religion, which had celebrated its tenth anniversary in 2008 by formulating new networks that focused more on the interaction between religions and the state: namely, the Interfaith Legal Advisers Network (ILAN) and the Law and Religion Scholars Network (LARSN).[5] In particular, LARSN sought to bring together academics who identified their teaching or research interest as being law and religion (variously subjectively defined). The first meeting, held at Cardiff Law School, brought together around 30 academics, with a further 20 sending their apologies.[6] While that meeting focused on participants intro-

---

[2] For discussion of the term 'juridification of religion', see Russell Sandberg, *Law and Religion* (Cambridge University Press, 2011) 193–95; and Russell Sandberg, *Religion, Law and Society* (Cambridge University Press, 2014), Chapter 1.

[3] Russell Sandberg, 'Silver Jubilee Bibliography: Ecclesiastical Law Publications 1987–2011' (2012) 14 *Ecclesiastical Law Journal* 149.

[4] The language of 'industry' is derived from Ralph Grillo, *Muslim Families, Politics and the Law* (Ashgate, 2015).

[5] These sat alongside the pre-existing and differently focused Colloquium of Anglican and Roman Catholic Canon Lawyers.

[6] The second and third meeting (in 2009 and 2010) had around 50 delegates, while the fourth in 2011 had almost 100 people present.

ducing themselves and their interests in an attempt to avoid us all reinventing the wheel, subsequent meetings took the form of a one or two-day academic conference with papers being presented on substantive topics.[7]

By this point, I was actively involved in the life of the Centre and its development into the wider interaction between religion and the state, being the co-creator with Doe of the ILAN and LARSN networks. My early academic career coincided with the significant increase in attention on law and religion matters. The foundations were laid in the academic year 2004–05, the final year of my LLB degree. In my second year, I had not seen much of Doe, except the occasional personal tutee meeting; the highlight of that year was undoubtedly studying the English legal history module taught by Professor Thomas Watkin. However, I saw quite a lot of Doe in my final year.

During that year, I wrote a dissertation under Doe's supervision on the legal and constitutional position of the civil service (for which I convinced myself that binge-watching *Yes Minister* and *The Thick of It* was required), and also studied a module that he led entitled 'Comparative Law of Religion'. What struck me about this module was how free it was. While other modules had shelves full of textbooks prescribing their content and approach (similar to those in most law schools up and down the country), this module had no set texts. Instead, the lectures and seminars were accompanied by a diverse list of reading materials, as well as notes drafted by those teaching on the module. The subject matter instantly felt more alive, more fluid and more experimental. The actual legal materials discussed (cases and statutes) were rather thin on the ground. Much emphasis was given to history and to the law of the Church of England; and when the focus eventually shifted to religious freedom, there was precious little substantive law to discuss – though this was rectified by discussion of international legal instruments and some comparative analysis.

The paucity of legal material added, however, to the excitement. Doe had begun the module by saying that we were studying something new, something at the start of its development; and this feeling intensified throughout the course, making other modules seem staid and passé by comparison. The discussion of the new religious freedom laws made the subject appear cutting-edge, but this sat oddly with the emphasis on history and the focus on the law of the Church of England. It felt that there were numerous subjects competing for attention, none of which quite justified being a module of study in its own right. Despite its imperfections, the module provided a ground-breaking introduction into not only a new subject but also a new way of studying law, away from the

---

[7]   The conference was held annually in person in most years with an online version being introduced for a few years as a result of the Covid-19 pandemic.

mainstream modules that were animated by a series of textbooks perpetuating and thus dictating their contents.

This was particularly true of the second lecture delivered on the course. Boldly, this was devoted to the topic of 'Religion, Law and Society', and saw Doe basically deliver a summary of the text of an article he had recently submitted to *Law and Justice* proposing the development of a new field: a sociology of law on religion.[8] This article was the concluding reflection in a special edition which recounted the findings of an Arts and Humanities Research Board-funded project, *Legal Responses to Religious Pluralism in European Society*, which had brought together scholars from the UK, Ireland, France, Italy, Spain and Greece to interview religious leaders, policymakers and academics. This had led Doe to speculate that collaboration between lawyers and sociologists of religion might be fruitful; so the article and lecture elaborated principles and ideas from the sociology of religion, which Doe then used legal examples as evidence to support or refute. For most of the audience, just one week into the course, the discussion no doubt went over their heads or seemed irrelevant. The lecture handout Doe was supposedly speaking to was over 5,000 words long and included 147 footnotes (which I was to learn was low by his standards). This was not a typical undergraduate lecture: it broke almost all the rules. But for me, that lecture in the autumn of 2004 was a watershed moment. Not only did it show what academic research really looked like, but for the first time the two halves of my degree in law and sociology made sense. It also – though I was unaware of this at the time – introduced me to the idea of disciplines and sub-disciplines, pulling open the curtain closed during most undergraduate studies to show that the modules we were studying were constructs with an intellectual history.

However, it was the experience of writing my dissertation that convinced me that a PhD and hopefully a career in academia were for me. I flirted with the idea of developing my dissertation into a doctoral-level examination of constitutional law.[9] The one thing I was sure about was that I wanted Doe to supervise it. By now, we had clicked both personally and intellectually, and there was no one else I wanted to work with. Not only was his teaching style inspiring, if unorthodox, but his scholarship showed a mastery of the detail and the ability to reach erudite and often audacious conclusions. Although the appeal of writing more about Whitehall did not fade, I kept having flashbacks to the 'Religion, Law and Society' lecture and the revelatory effect that it had

---

[8]   Norman Doe, 'A Sociology of Law on Religion – Towards a New Discipline: Legal Responses to Religious Pluralism in Europe' (2004) 152 *Law and Justice* 68.

[9]   One of the chapters was subsequently revised for publication as Russell Sandberg, 'A Whitehall Farce? Defining and Conceptualising the British Civil Service' (2006) *Public Law* 653.

had on me. I decided that I wanted this to be the focus of my PhD study and I wanted to develop further the ideas presented in that lecture, with my background in sociological theory complementing and being complemented by black-letter legal analysis. I was also taken by the dynamism of the subject: the law on religious freedom seemed to be in flux and this excited me.

In September 2005, generously funded by Cardiff Law School, I began work on my PhD, only to become distracted by other exciting matters. The doctorate was to be a study of the interface between the law and religion and the sociology of religion. However, while the sociology of religion was an established field of study,[10] law and religion by this point was still in its infancy. Indeed, I often asked myself whether the subject of my study actually existed: I pondered whether there was such a thing as law and religion, let alone whether it was comparable to the sociology of religion. Even if it did exist, it was clearly in a state of flux. During the years of my PhD research, a significant amount of new legislation and case law on religious matters not only added legal meat to topics, but also brought the subject matter into the glare of the news agenda. This was incredibly exciting. The land was moving under my feet and more often than not, the legal earthquakes were attracting media and public interest. And there I was, free of any other commitments with a front-row seat, watching and commenting.

This was the making of my academic career because it provided an opportunity to publish short articles and comments in journals. This began with an invitation from a friend of Doe's, Mark Hill (who was then the editor of the *Ecclesiastical Law Journal* and who was to become a close friend), to speedily write two comments for the journal on the new Equality Act and on human rights challenges to the law on exhumation respectively.[11] After this, I had caught the bug: writing for journals had become normalised. It was not something I did with any career plan in mind – just a natural activity every time there was a notable legal development on religion. Over the next few years, often co-authoring with Doe or Hill, I wrote a number of (usually short) pieces which sought to contextualise and analyse specific developments and predict their likely significance.[12] I traipsed through many traditional legal

---

[10] Though often at the margins of the discipline, at least in higher education institutions. See Samuel L Perry, '(Why) is the Sociology of Religion Marginalized? Results from a Survey Experiment' (2023) 54 *The American Sociologist* 485.

[11] Russell Sandberg, 'To Equality and Beyond: Religious Discrimination and the Equality Act 2006' (2006) 8 *Ecclesiastical Law Journal* 470; Russell Sandberg, 'Human Rights and Human Remains: The Impact of *Dödsbo v Sweden*' (2006) 8 *Ecclesiastical Law Journal* 453.

[12] E.g., Russell Sandberg, 'Flags, Beards and Pilgrimages: A Review of the Early Case Law on Religious Discrimination' (2007) 9 *Ecclesiastical Law Journal* 87;

sub-disciplines; I would write about anything legal as long as it affected religion. My mind sometimes wandered to how these various interactions fitted together and this became an important preliminary question for my PhD.

These early pieces shaped how I understood the field: although I covered a wide range of areas, as time went on, my work identified the growing importance of human rights and discrimination laws affecting religion and their increasing interdependence. An article in *Public Law* authored with Hill proved pivotal.[13] 'Is Nothing Sacred? Clashing Symbols in a Secular World' – or, as one set of offprints mistakenly put it, 'Is Nothing Scared?' – provided a trenchant critique of the English courts' interpretation of Article 9 of the European Convention on Human Rights, benefiting tremendously by being co-written by a barrister at the top of his game. However, what we did not realise at the time was that we were also writing the narrative. Our elucidation of how Article 9 had been interpreted (or, in our view, misinterpreted) became accepted as 'the story'; and our narrative that the Human Rights Act had ushered in a new era in the history of religious freedom quickly became widely accepted.

I began to develop the view that there was now a body of English law affecting religion. And unwittingly, the work I was producing was helping to provide the building blocks for this. Implicitly, I began to accept and to argue that law and religion was not just about specific interactions between religion and areas of law such as employment law, human rights law and criminal law. Rather, those interactions interrelated with one another and led to common principles and understandings. Cases on religious discrimination could not be read separately from discussion of the jurisprudence on Article 9; cases on the definition of 'religion' under charity law referred to and used registration law decisions affecting religion; and so on. Some of these overlaps had long existed, but I argued that the importance being placed on freedom of religion as a human right and discrimination on grounds of religion by new legal provisions gave increased impetus to the unifying effect. I unconsciously subscribed to, created and perpetuated the idea that law and religion was a separate body

---

Norman Doe and Russell Sandberg, 'Religious Exemptions in Discrimination Law' (2007) 66(2) *Cambridge Law Journal* 302; Russell Sandberg, 'Controversial Recent Claims to Religious Liberty' (2008) 124 *Law Quarterly Review* 213; Russell Sandberg, 'Gods and Services: Religious Groups and Sexual Orientation Discrimination' (2008) 10 *Ecclesiastical Law Journal* 20; Norman Doe and Russell Sandberg, 'The Strange Death of Blasphemy' (2008) 71(6) *Modern Law Review* 971; Russell Sandberg, 'Underrating Human Rights: *Gallagher v Church of Jesus Christ of the Latter-Day Saints*' (2009) 11 *Ecclesiastical Law Journal* 75.

[13]   Mark Hill and Russell Sandberg, 'Is Nothing Sacred? Clashing Symbols in a Secular World' (2007) *Public Law* 488.

of study; and that a key focus – if not the key focus – of the study was upon national and international laws on religious freedom and discrimination. This situated the field very much within the doctrinal legal tradition found within law schools.

This was shaped by my own background and place. Being in Cardiff and at the Centre for Law and Religion shaped the way that I saw and contributed to this. It also provided me with the opportunity to develop initiatives to develop and entrench this understanding of law and religion as a field of study, through themed conference sessions and most notably through the establishment of LARSN in 2008. It was beginning to be recognised that law and religion was an emerging field of study; that this study was based within law schools; and that the audience for papers on religious discrimination law comprised legal scholars with an interest in religion rather than an interest in discrimination. Of course, papers were also presented at other conferences and scholarly events; but there was a dramatic growth in the number of law and religion-specific journals and book series, as well as online blogs and news sites. LARSN was not the cause of this development, though it was often cited as evidence for the increase in attention. Moreover, LARSN and associated developments also unwittingly limited the interactions so that they took place within the field rather than outside it. The papers presented at LARSN conferences also reflected the focuses of the news agenda. Even when legal change slowed, certain topics dominated. Attending a law and religion conference or reading a law and religion journal meant being subjected to many papers on Article 9 alongside other areas where the cases kept coming, such as the clashes between freedom of religion and the prohibition of discrimination on grounds of sexual orientation and – oddly enough – the employment status of minsters of the clergy.

***

Even at this early stage, some doubts had begun to creep in. I began to suspect that law and religion was being too narrowly understood. But at this point, my concern was just that, aside from the work of the Cardiff Centre for Law and Religion and the Ecclesiastical Law Society, most of the 'new' work on law and religion neglected religious law. Being in Cardiff (where I had now secured a permanent academic position) shaped this conviction. This background heightened my awareness that the literature on law and religion focused upon developments in national and international laws affecting religion. Little if any attention was paid to the rules and norms within religious groups. This became

evident the more I taught our module on law and religion.[14] It struck me that
not enough attention was being afforded to the study of religious law and in
particular how it interacted with State law.

My first opportunity to reflect upon and comment on this came in the
introduction and conclusion to an edited collection based on papers originally
delivered at a law and religion stream that Doe and I had organised at the
Socio-Legal Studies Association Annual Conference at Canterbury in April
2007. Many of the papers were eventually published in a collection entitled
Law and Religion: New Horizons, for which Doe and I wrote a short introduction and a lengthy conclusion.[15] The introduction provided the first opportunity
to provide a detailed definition of what we meant by 'law and religion', in
which we articulated a distinction between what we termed 'religion law' and
'religious law'. This passage from the introduction is worth quoting in full:

> Given this collection's focus upon both the substantive law and the scholarly study
> of that law, it seems appropriate to reflect briefly at the outset about what we con-
> ceive of as 'law and religion'. For us, to study law and religion is to study both:
>   The 'external' national and international laws affecting religious individuals and
>   collectives, which may be styled 'religion law'; and
>   The 'internal' laws or other regulatory instruments created by religious collec-
>   tives themselves, which may be styled 'religious law'.
> 'Religion law' and 'religious law' are two complementary and overlapping entities.
> The distinction is made to stress their interconnected state and to allow closer anal-
> ysis to be paid to the proper ambit of the discipline. Many works on religion law
> routinely exclude the study of religious law and many studies on religious law fail
> to place it within the wider environment of State law on religion and society. This
> seems misguided, especially given the establishment of the Church of England. The
> prime question for most law and religion academics in England and Wales is how
> law does and does not (or should and should not) accommodate religious difference.
> We submit that the word "law" in this question should be interpreted to include both
> the laws that apply to religious groups and also the laws created by those religious
> groups. It includes the study of how State law accommodates religious difference
> manifest in religious law. The study of law and religion is actually the study of *laws*
> and *religions*.[16]

---

[14]   The word 'comparative' being dropped at some point from its title, though we
ironically increased discussion of the legal place of religion in European legal systems,
especially following the publication of Norman Doe, *Law and Religion in Europe:
A Comparative Introduction* (Oxford University Press, 2011).
[15]   Norman Doe and Russell Sandberg (eds), *Law and Religion: New Horizons*
(Peeters, 2010).
[16]   Norman Doe and Russell Sandberg, 'Introduction' in Norman Doe and Russell
Sandberg (eds) *Law and Religion: New Horizons* (Peeters, 2010) 9, 11. Reading this
back, I regret that I did not emphasise the final sentence more in subsequent work.

The contents page of that volume similarly indicated that law and religion was being understood, if not defined, as the study of international and national laws affecting religious freedom, with some (rather separate) analysis of religious law. The late publication of the *New Horizons* book meant that by the time it had arrived, further work on developing law and religion as a field had taken place.[17] An invitation to Hill had led him, Doe and I to contribute the British monograph in the Religion Law series of the *International Encyclopaedia of Laws*.[18] The use of the term 'religion law' in the title was notable but undefined. However, as we wrote to a prescribed table of contents, it became increasingly clear what a body of religion law looked like in an English context.[19] The prescribed order of the contents was to allow comparison with other books in the series but at times frustrated the flow and coherence of the text. It convinced me, however, that something was needed that outlined the new legal framework on religion in England and Wales in a way that was more accessible and which gave some attention to religious law in general and the place of the established Church in particular. This something was to become my textbook for Cambridge University Press, boldly titled *Law and Religion*.[20]

I received the contract for the textbook the day before my PhD viva. The plan was to extract the work I had done for and in the PhD about the development of the new legal framework into the textbook, and then to reflect upon how to develop the PhD's argument about the need for a sociological approach to law and religion in a subsequent publication. Telling the story of how the law had developed felt more pressing and was also becoming increasingly necessary for the purposes of teaching the law and religion module. The various articles written over the course of the PhD did not really add up to a coherent whole and so there were gaps on the reading lists. The plan was to quickly collate my existing materials and notes to write the textbook before then paying attention to getting the PhD thesis into print. Half of the plan came into operation. From March 2010 to September 2010, I wrote the textbook.[21] The contents of the book had evolved during the process of putting together the proposal and changed further during its writing. The speed with which I wrote meant that

---

[17]   Doe and I joked that it had become 'old horizons' by the time it was published.

[18]   Mark Hill, Russell Sandberg and Norman Doe, *Religion and Law in the United Kingdom* (Kluwer Law International, 2011). A second edition followed in 2014 and a third edition in 2021, by which time Christopher Grout had joined the writing team.

[19]   Although the title referred to the 'United Kingdom', we excluded Northern Ireland from our coverage and paid little attention to Scotland, relying on the goodwill of Frank Cranmer to help with this.

[20]   Russell Sandberg, *Law and Religion* (Cambridge University Press, 2011).

[21]   I wrote out of order so that I could do the most straightforward chapters while teaching. This led to quite a lot of notes about stuff I was referring to but had yet to write. I resolved never to write a book out of sequence again!

I paid little attention to the significance of the task. The absence of textbooks in the field meant that I was defining the sub-discipline. I was distilling the main topics, the canon and the approach.

Law and Religion expressed what I considered to be the core of the sub-discipline. The religion law/religious law distinction was expanded into the first chapter. I nuanced the previous formulation by stressing that 'the study of law and religion is at least the study of religion law and religious law', somewhat labouring the point to state that: 'This conceptualisation does not mean that the study of law and religion is only the study of religion law and religious law.'[22] Yet the book gave no further indication of what law and religion also included, simply noting that the term 'law and religion' was itself 'problematic' in that it 'simply describes' the interaction between religion and the law rather than referring to 'an identified legal subject'.[23] My explicit focus was on identifying 'whether laws affecting religion can now be understood as forming a single coherent sub-discipline: in short, whether it is now possible to speak of something particular called "religion law" as well as a general interaction called "law and religion"'.[24]

Law and Religion recognised that the question of defining a field is a means of inclusion or exclusion. However, I did not seek to explain or justify my own choices in terms of inclusion and exclusion. An initial conversation with the publishers led to the plan that the book would be small and selective in the first edition and could then subsequently grow in coverage. To date, however, only one edition has been produced. Notwithstanding the intention to subsequently expand, the choice of topics in *Law and Religion* notably reflected my focus on what I called 'religion law' and within that fixated upon matters of religious freedom. In addition to an introduction and conclusion, chapters included 'Historical Development', 'Legal Definitions of Religion', 'The Legal Position of Religious Groups', 'Religious Freedom as a Human Right', 'Discrimination on Grounds of Religion', 'Religious Offences', 'Religion in Schools' and 'Religious Law'. Coverage was given to Church–State relations but almost as background early on; and a penultimate chapter was devoted to religious law, which addressed questions of definition and status and so examined the topic from a State-centric approach. The emphasis throughout was upon State law, providing a doctrinal account of how the legal framework affecting religion now stood. The book focused on constitutional law, human rights law, discrimination law (with a particular emphasis on employment and education law) and criminal law. Interactions between religion and the law in miscella-

---

[22]   Russell Sandberg, *Law and Religion* (Cambridge University Press, 2011) 6.
[23]   Ibid 9. I am now not sure what I meant by that!
[24]   Ibid 10.

neous legal areas were omitted. Indeed, the chapters deliberately did not refer to other areas of law: so, for instance, the chapter on religion and criminal law was entitled 'Religious Offences'. Rather, the intent was to demarcate the main contours of religion law. This meant that there was no room for discussion of religion under charity law, employment law or family law.[25]

Despite the book's general title, my focus was on particular laws that dealt explicitly with religious rights. I remember a colleague at the time suggesting that the book might have been better titled 'Religious Rights'. I dismissed this at the time, on the basis that the field had become known as 'law and religion'. However, in so doing, I made the error of conflating the field with the selective and limited coverage given in my book. The benefit of hindsight shows that at the very least, I was operating under a 'religious rights'-driven understanding of my subject matter. This would not have happened had I been writing – and perhaps had I been educated – a decade previously. The lens through which I saw the subject was shaped and constrained by the new laws on religion and their rights-based nature. The book now stands as an attempt to portray law and religion as a subject similar to other doctrinal areas of law in law school. It was not about an interaction between two social institutions: it was about the detail of how the legal system governed religion at the time of writing.

This was true of other law and religion works published at around this time; though my book alone committed the sin of having this focus in a book with the title of *Law and Religion*, clearly suggesting that this was what the study of law and religion entailed.[26] Most works stated that their theme was 'religious freedom': these included several works on religion in the context of international human rights laws,[27] as well as books by Hamilton and Ahdar and

---

[25] The contents of *Law and Religion* can be contrasted with St John A Robilliard's ground-breaking monograph: St John A Robilliard, *Religion and the Law* (Manchester University Press, 1984). On which see Anthony Bradney, 'Religion and the Law: An Unconventional Path Maker' in Russell Sandberg, *Leading Works in Law and Religion* (Routledge, 2019) 32. In *Religion and the Law*, for instance, following an introductory chapter on 'General Protections of Religious Belief', chapters were devoted to: 'Blasphemy', 'Sunday Laws', 'Charitable Status, Taxation Advantages and Related Matters', 'Freedom of Movement', 'Freedom of Association', 'Clashing with the Criminal Law', 'Prisons and the Armed Services', 'Religion, Medicine and the Law', 'Public Education', 'The Workplace' and 'Family Matters'.

[26] Despite the title of Robilliard's book, it includes no claims about a legal field developing and at the time in which he wrote there was no field of note that his focus could have constrained.

[27] Most notably Carolyn Evans, *Freedom of Religion and the European Convention on Human Rights* (Oxford University Press, 2002); Malcolm Evans, *Religious Liberty and International Law in Europe* (Cambridge University Press, 1997); and Paul M Taylor, *Freedom of Religion – UN and European Human Rights Law and Practice* (Cambridge University Press, 2005).

Leigh. Hamilton's *Family, Law and Religion* 'examines a number of themes relating to religious freedom';[28] while the focus of Ahdar and Leigh's work was clear from its title, *Religious Freedom in the Liberal State*.[29] Other works referred to religious rights as being their focus;[30] while others noted that they were exploring certain aspects of the interaction between religion and the law. Peter W Edge's seminal 450-page *Legal Responses to Religious Difference* begins with the wise recognition that: 'Any survey of an area as the interaction between law and religion must be selective.'[31]

Julian Rivers' 2010 monograph *The Law of Organized Religions* sought to provide a systematic study of English law as it related to organised religions.[32] Substantive chapters following a historical introduction entitled 'The Changing Law of Church and State' included 'The Human Rights of Religious Associations', 'The Constitution of Religious Bodies', 'Ministers of Religion', 'Public Religion' (dealing with requirements under charity and registration law), 'Regulated Rites', 'Chaplaincies', 'Faith Schools', 'Faith Based Welfare' and 'Access to Public Discourse'. While other works focused on an interaction between religion and a series of discrete legal topics, Rivers' *The Law of Organized Religions* – like my *Law and Religion* – assumed the existence of law and religion as a field of study. The two books did so in different ways, however. *Law and Religion* explored the various ways in which laws interact with religion but claimed that the similarities between these interactions produced a whole that is worthy of study. *The Law of Organized Religions* provided an account of a body of law relating to religious groups. Both of these texts, however, were based on the assumption that it was possible to identify a discrete body of law applying to religions.

In the years that followed, few books took such an approach. They tended once more to focus on particular aspects of law and religion: specific areas of law (most notably human rights and employment laws) or particular problem areas (most notably the wearing of religious dress in the public sphere and the operation of religious courts and tribunals). Such authors often positioned their work within law and religion as a sub-discipline, while others seemed weary at

---

   28   Carolyn Hamilton, *Family, Law and Religion* (Sweet & Maxwell, 1995) vii.
   29   Rex Ahdar and Ian Leigh, *Religious Freedom in the Liberal State* (Oxford University Press, 2005). A second edition was published in 2013.
   30   This is true of Anthony Bradney's early monograph on the subject which is similarly stated to focus on 'the relationship between religion, rights and legal rules within Great Britain': Anthony Bradney, *Religions, Rights and Laws* (Leicester University Press, 1993) 3, 8. No definition is given in his later monograph: Anthony Bradney, *Law and Faith in a Sceptical Age* (Routledge, 2009).
   31   Peter W Edge, *Legal Responses to Religious Difference* (Kluwer Law, 2002) 3.
   32   Julian Rivers, *The Law of Organized Religions* (Oxford University Press, 2010).

the limits of such a framing. Javier Garcia Oliva and Helen Hall – who organ-ised a number of LARSN conferences – used the words 'law' and 'religion' in their jointly authored monograph and published that book within a series dedicated to law and religion. Yet in *Religion, Law and the Constitution: Balancing Beliefs in Britain*, they maintained that:

> Our book does not sit primarily within the blossoming topic of Law and Religion, and our focus has been quite different from that of scholars concentrating on questions within this subject. We are considering an aspect of the UK Constitution namely its religious dimension, and see this book as addressing the mainstream audience within the public law world.[33]

This suggestion that law and religion was a marginal rather than a mainstream phenomenon sits oddly with the paragraph before this in Oliva and Hall's introduction, which observed that 'in the last few decades British academia has witnessed the development of the study of Law and Religion as a distinct discipline'; and that we had 'now reached the stage where Law and Religion can claim to be an independent field, with strong links to core legal subjects, such as public law, contract law and family law'.[34] It is also curious that while they regarded law and religion scholars as concentrating on distinct (but unidentified) questions, they also referred to the 'very heterogeneous' membership of LARSN as being 'a testimony to the number of areas which the discipline touches, as well as its widespread appeal'.[35] Their decision not to position their work within the wider umbrella of law and religion studies, and their suggestion that law and religion could be distinguished as a narrower field with a particular focus, seem to suggest a degree of wariness towards the vision of law and religion as sub-discipline formulated in *Law and Religion* and perpetuated in LARSN and other developments.

There are numerous further signs of this growing concern. *Law and Religion* was intended to help increase the number of university courses on the topic, establishing it as a legal sub-discipline like sports law or even family law. Yet although some courses continued and new ones were created, many of these developments proved to be short-lived.[36] *Law and Religion* did not inspire the

---

[33] Javier Garcia Oliva and Helen Hall, *Religion, Law and the Constitution: Balancing Beliefs in Britain* (Routledge, 2018) 6.

[34] Ibid 5–6.

[35] Ibid 6.

[36] Oliva and Hall claim that the 'subject is now taught in more than thirty univer-sities across the country' (ibid 5) but provide no evidence for this. Most of the courses that I am aware of – including the undergraduate module and LLM at Cardiff – have been discontinued, despite a significant rise in the number of law students in the same period.

publication of other textbooks or teaching related materials; indeed, requests to update the materials on its accompanying website stopped and no further editions were commissioned. Indeed, even I began to have my doubts.

***

My research interests diverged following the publication of *Law and Religion*. The academic year 2010–11 was spent working on a project funded by the Arts and Humanities Research Council/Economic and Social Research Council (AHRC/ESRC) Religion and Society Programme on 'Social Cohesion and Civil Law: Marriage, Divorce and Religious Courts' with Doe, Gillian Douglas (then a family law professor at Cardiff Law School) and Sophie Gilliat-Ray (the director for the Centre for the Study of Islam in the UK at the School of History, Archaeology and Religion at Cardiff University). My state-centric understandings of law were beginning to dilute and I was beginning to appreciate the gender dimensions of the issue.[37] This animated a long-term interest in the recognition of religious law – particularly in relation to family law matters, an area of law upon which *Law and Religion* had been silent.

While on study leave in the academic year 2012–13, I returned to the long-postponed task of converting my PhD (now minus the account of the development of law and religion that had provided the core of *Law and Religion*) into a monograph, entitled *Religion, Law and Society* to accommodate the publisher's desire to ensure that the book would be visible in search engine results and the like.[38] I basically spent the year on study leave writing the PhD I would have written had I started again at the end of the viva. Although some of the arguments had been hinted at in previous publications,[39] the monograph was where I explored at length the need for a sociological approach to law and religion. This book also betrayed my implicit perception of what law and religion was. Crucially, it still regarded this as a sub-discipline of law that was comparable to the sociology of religion, understood as a sub-discipline of sociology. The desirability of regarding law and religion as a sub-discipline was not questioned.

---

[37]   Especially in Russell Sandberg, Gillian Douglas, Norman Doe, Sophie Gilliat-Ray and Asma Khan, 'Britain's Religious Tribunals: "Joint Governance" in Practice' (2013) 33(2) *Oxford Journal of Legal Studies* 263.

[38]   Russell Sandberg, *Religion, Law and Society* (Cambridge University Press, 2014).

[39]   Particularly pivotal was a chapter co-authored with a sociologist of religion: Russell Sandberg and Rebecca Catto, 'Law and Sociology: Toward a Greater Understanding of Religion' in Norman Doe and Russell Sandberg (eds) *Law and Religion: New Horizons* (Peeters, 2010) 275.

Yet, curiously, in the sixth and final chapter of *Religion, Law and Society*, where I revisited Doe's call for a 'sociology of law on religion' (as made in that early undergraduate lecture and as published in *Law and Justice*),[40] I found myself supporting his argument but not his need for a new discipline. At this stage, I did not question the usefulness and effect of understanding the development of law and religion as a sub-discipline, but an argument was beginning to develop that self-contained sub-disciplines could limit the ambit of legal studies. Further, developing a throwaway suggestion in Doe's work that the sociology of law had a role to play in bringing law and religion and the sociology of religion together, I was critical of the way in which the sociology of law had been regarded as a specialism and so its ideas, concepts and methods had remained the preserve of a select few. While I had made a career of arguing that law and religion ought to be seen as a sub-discipline in its own right, I now argued that the sociology of law ought not to be a sub-discipline, since that meant that its insights were being limited to specialists rather than being part of the toolkit of all academic lawyers, to be used whenever they were exploring the social context of law. And in four pages towards the end of the chapter, I tentatively applied this argument to historical approaches to law too. Criticising the way in which both sociological and legal accounts of social and legal change paid scant attention to history, I argued that:

> Both the sociology of law and legal history should not be regarded as separate sub-disciplines but rather as an integral part of the study of law (and therefore every legal sub-discipline) alongside the doctrinal study of the current legal position. They are better regarded, not as sub-disciplines, but as methods. To an extent, this is already the case. All legal sub-disciplines are concerned to some extent with historical and sociological matters even if this amounts only to a vague aim to understand law within its context. However, the problem with this informal approach is it is not systematic. The literatures, methods and approaches of the sociology of law and legal history do not tend to become part of the toolkit of each sub-discipline. Seeing the sociology of law and legal history as methods which complement and build upon doctrinal approaches would allow this to occur.[41]

In the years that followed, my work developed this insight in relation to legal history.[42] Moreover, when I dipped a toe back into law and religion matters,

---

[40] Norman Doe, 'A Sociology of Law on Religion – Towards a New Discipline: Legal Responses to Religious Pluralism in Europe' (2004) 152 *Law and Justice* 68.

[41] Russell Sandberg, *Religion, Law and Society* (Cambridge University Press, 2014) 262.

[42] Russell Sandberg and Norman Doe, 'Textual and Contextual Legal History' in Norman Doe and Russell Sandberg, *Law and History – Critical Concepts in Law* (Routledge, 2017) 1; Russell Sandberg, *Subversive Legal History: A Manifesto for the Future of Legal Education* (Routledge, 2021).

my publications and utterances on the topic (much of which have been adapted to form this current book) slowly began to apply this realisation back to the context of law and religion itself. I began to feel that the prevailing focus in law and religion scholarship was too State-centric and too legalistic. I started to wonder whether the criticisms I had made of the sociology of law and of legal history could also be made of law and religion, and whether I had unwittingly helped to create the very situation that I was being critical of. With hindsight, I can see that the sin I committed was my unquestioning conceptualisation of law and religion, by the religion law/religious law distinction, through the contents pages of my textbook and through the arguments made about it being a sub-discipline. The focus of law and religion as I presented it was narrow: the emphasis was on religious freedom (and this did not even include non-religious beliefs until employment tribunals and courts began to grapple with the issue of defining belief). The approach was legalistic and State-centric: even the study of religious law in my work largely focused on how it interacted with State laws and norms.

Of course, this confession might be seen as overemphasising the influence of my scribblings. The point is, however, that the understandings of the subject implicit in my work animated further developments that I helped to lead. *Law and Religion*, LARSN, the development of new specialist book series and other institutional developments flowed from my assumptions. In England and Wales, law and religion developed as a specialism largely located in law schools that was mostly fixated on the problem of how and to what extent the State could and should accommodate religious difference. And I was at least partly to blame for that.

This narrow conceptualisation of law and religion and the way in which a significant amount of its scholarship was motivated by the moral panics of the day meant that the early years of the twenty-first century were something of a false dawn. Although good work continued to be done, interest in law and religion petered out. This was at least in part due to the way in which law and religion had been constructed as a legal sub-discipline, but it was also attributable to political and legal factors. Politically, the focus on social justice and the concerns about Islamic terrorism which had dominated under the Labour government of 1997–2010 were superseded by the longer-term effects of the 2008 global financial crisis and the policy of austerity pursued by the Conservative government that came to power in 2010. Legally, as the next chapter will reveal, the new religious rights proved to be rather limited, with cases showing that they were interpreted narrowly and claimants relying on the Article 9 freedom of religion clause rarely succeeding.

5.   A paper tiger

Since 1968, Iftikhar Ahmad had been employed as a primary school teacher by the Inner London Education Authority. As a devout Muslim, he was under a religious duty to offer prayers on a Friday and, if considerations of distance permitted, to attend a mosque. He had been employed at a number of schools: those that were too far from a mosque offered him a prayer room, while others permitted him to attend a mosque or at least tolerated this by facilitating cover. However, in 1975, while employed at a Catholic school, Ahmad was refused permission to leave work to go to a mosque but was provided with a prayer room. He left to attend the mosque anyway, resulting in a letter from the local authority stating that his contract would be varied from being full-time to being part-time. Ahmad replied that he would rather be dismissed. He subsequently resigned and took the matter to an industrial tribunal,[1] which dismissed his case on the basis that 'as a matter of contract the applicant was bound to be in school on Friday afternoons', and that he was required 'to work full-time'. Ahmad then applied for a part-time teaching post while he appealed the decision to the Industrial Appeal Tribunal and the Court of Appeal, both of which rejected the appeal.[2]

At the Court of Appeal, Lord Denning MR and Orr LJ rejected the appeal, with Scarman LJ dissenting. Scarman LJ paid particular attention to the argument concerning Article 9 of the European Convention on Human Rights (ECHR), to which the UK is a party. Article 9 provides that:

> (1) Everyone has the right to freedom of thought, conscience and religion; this right includes freedom to change his religion or belief and freedom, either alone or in community with others and in public or private, and to manifest his religion or belief, in worship, teaching, practice and observance.
> (2) Freedom to manifest one's religion or beliefs shall be subject only to such limitations as are prescribed by law and are necessary in a democratic society in the interests of public safety, for the protection of public order, health or morals, or for the protection of the rights and freedoms of others.

---

[1]   Now known as an employment tribunal, with appeals going to the Employment Appeal Tribunal.
[2]   *Ahmad v Inner London Education Authority* [1976] ICR 461; [1978] QB 36.

Scarman LJ held that society and the law had changed since the enactment of the Education Act 1944.[3] Religions such as Islam and Buddhism now had 'substantial followings' and 'room has to be found for teachers and pupils of the new religions in the educational system, if discrimination is to be avoided. This calls not for a policy of the blind eye but for one of understanding'. Such a policy was further warranted because since 1944, 'the United Kingdom has accepted international obligations designed to protect human rights and freedoms, and has enacted a series of statutes designed for the same purpose in certain critical areas of our society'. In particular, under the ECHR,[4] legal provisions now had to be construed and applied 'not against the background of the law and society of 1944 but in a multi-racial society which has accepted international obligations and enacted statutes designed to eliminate discrimination on grounds of race, religion, colour or sex'. Even where treaty obligations had not been made part of domestic law, courts were still required to 'pay very serious regard to them: in particular, they will interpret statutory language and apply common law principles, wherever possible, so as to reach a conclusion consistent with our international obligation'. For Scarman LJ, this meant that a wide interpretation of the law was required, since a narrow construction 'would mean that a Muslim, who took his religious duty seriously, could never accept employment as a full-time teacher, but must be content with the lesser emoluments of part-time service'.[5] He concluded that:

> In modern British society, with its elaborate statutory protection of the individual from discrimination arising from race, colour, religion or sex, and against the background of the European Convention, this is unacceptable, inconsistent with the policy of modern statute law, and almost certainly a breach of our international obligations.

The other members of the Court of Appeal disagreed. Lord Denning – now invariably fondly remembered by law students as a maverick judge – dismissed the appeal on grounds of contract law:

> The school time-table was well known to Mr. Ahmad when he applied for the teaching post. It was for the usual teaching hours from Monday to Friday, inclusive. If he wished to have every Friday afternoon off for his prayers, *either* he ought not to

---

³   [1978] QB 36 at 48. Lord Scarman was referring in particular to Section 30 of the Act, which provided that teachers were to be disadvantaged because of their 'religious opinions' or by attending or omitting to attend religious worship and were not to be required to give religious instruction (as long as they worked in a non-faith school).

⁴   Signed November 1950: in force since 3 September 1953.

⁵   [1978] QB 36 at 50.

have applied for this post: *or* he ought to have made it clear at the outset and entered into a 4-day engagement only. This was the sensible thing for him to do.[6]

Although he noted that he had 'no doubt that all headmasters will try to arrange their time-table so as to accommodate devout Muslims like Mr. Ahmad', Lord Denning held that such head teachers should not 'be compelled to do so, if it means disrupting the work of the school and the well-being of the pupils'.[7] For Lord Denning, Article 9 did not assist matters. He held that:

> The convention is not part of our English law, but, as I have often said, we will always have regard to it. We will do our best to see that our decisions are in conformity with it. But it is drawn in such vague terms that it can be used for all sorts of unreasonable claims and provoke all sorts of litigation. As so often happens with high-sounding principles, they have to be brought down to earth. They have to be applied in a work-a-day world. I venture to suggest that it would do the Muslim community no good—or any other minority group no good—if they were to be given preferential treatment over the great majority of the people. If it should happen that, in the name of religious freedom, they were given special privileges or advantages, it would provoke discontent, and even resentment among those with whom they work. As, indeed, it has done in this very case. And so the cause of racial integration would suffer.

This ignored the fact that Ahmad was not seeking 'special privileges.' He was seeking the same right to manifest religion that his co-religionists already enjoyed by the fact that the school calendar already accommodated Christian holy days and the Jewish Sabbath. Lord Denning concluded:

> So, whilst upholding religious freedom to the full, I would suggest that it should be applied with caution, especially having regard to the setting in which it is sought. Applied to our educational system, I think that Mr. Ahmad's right to 'manifest his religion in practice and observance' must be subject to the rights of the education authorities under the contract and to the interests of the children whom he is paid to teach. I see nothing in the European Convention to give Mr. Ahmad any right to manifest his religion on Friday afternoons in derogation of his contract of employment: and certainly not on full pay.

It is difficult to see how this constitutes 'upholding religious freedom to the full', unless religious freedom means very little indeed. The phrasing of Lord Denning's judgment made it seem that freedom of contract would always trump freedom of religion. This was also the conclusion of Orr LJ, who held that Article 9 'cannot be construed as entitling an employee to absent himself, for the purpose of religious worship, from his place of work during working

---

6 At 40.
7 At 41.

hours and in breach of his contract of employment'.[8] Indeed, Orr LJ went further to insist that this remained so even if the absence for Friday prayers only caused a small inconvenience in the school because such a legal right would 'involve detailed investigation in each case as to the degree of difficulty involved', and would be in any case 'unacceptable in principle since absence without leave in school hours would be a breach of contract even if the inconvenience involved were slight'.

The Court of Appeal did not give permission to appeal to what was then the Judicial Committee of the House of Lords.[9] Ahmad therefore took his case to the European Court of Human Rights at Strasbourg. He contended that the way in which the domestic courts had interpreted the law was contrary to Article 9. In March 1981, the European Commission of Human Rights declared the application inadmissible.[10] The Commission observed that Ahmad had, 'of his own free will, accepted teaching obligations' that prevented him from attending the mosque during school time and had not 'convincingly shown that, following his transfer in 1974 to a school "nearer to mosques", he was required by Islam to disregard his continuing contractual obligation'.[11] Moreover, even if such a religious obligation were assumed, the application would have been dismissed.[12] Freedom of religion under Article 9 is not absolute.[13] It not only is 'subject to the limitations set out in Article 9(2)', but also 'may, as regards the modality of a particular religious manifestation, be influenced by the situation of the person claiming that freedom'. The Commission noted that it had recognised this in the case of a detained person (*X v United Kingdom*[14]) and in the case of a person with special contractual obligations (*X v Denmark*[15]). Referring to *X v United Kingdom*, the Commission observed:

> In the case of a person at liberty, the question of the 'necessity' of a religious manifestation, as regards its time and place, will not normally arise under Article 9. Nevertheless, even a person at liberty may, in the exercise of his freedom to manifest his religion, have to take into account his particular professional or contractual position.[16]

---

[8]   At 45.
[9]   From 2009, the same body with the same powers became known as the UK Supreme Court.
[10]   *Ahmad v United Kingdom* (1982) 4 EHRR 126. At this point, the Commission served as a filter prior to cases going to the Court.
[11]   Para 9.
[12]   Para 10.
[13]   Para 11.
[14]   *X v United Kingdom* (1974) 1 D & R at 41–42.
[15]   *X v Denmark* (1976) 5 D & R at 157–58.
[16]   *Ahmad v United Kingdom* (1982) 4 EHRR 126 at para 7.

In *X v Denmark* – which concerned a member of the clergy who contended that a requirement by his church to abandon a certain practice of christening breached his freedom of religion – the Commission stated that a cleric's freedom of religion was 'exercised at the moment they accept or refuse employment as clergymen, and their right to leave the church guarantees their freedom of religion in case they oppose its teachings'.[17] In relation to *Ahmad*, the Commission considered that, although its reasoning in *X v Denmark* could not be automatically applied, it could be 'adapted to its particular circumstances'.[18] The Commission held that throughout his employment, Ahmad 'remained free to resign if and when he found that his teaching obligations conflicted with his religious duties' and did in fact do so.[19] The school authorities 'had to have regard not only to his religious position, but also to the requirements of the education system as a whole'.[20] The Commission applied what was to become known as the 'margin of appreciation'. It held that it was 'not called upon to substitute for the assessment by the national authorities of what might be the best policy in this field'.

In addition to holding that there was 'no interference with the applicant's freedom of religion under Article 9',[21] the Commission further held that there was no breach of Article 14 in conjunction with Article 9. It noted that 'Article 14 safeguards individuals or groups of individuals, place in comparable situations, from all discrimination in the enjoyment of the rights and freedoms set forth in the other normative provisions of the Convention'.[22] The Commission concluded that Ahmad had not proved that he 'was either individually or as a member of his religious community treated less favourably by the education authorities than individuals or groups of individuals placed in comparable situations'.[23] This was despite arguments concerning how the school calendar already accommodated certain religions:

> The Commission further observes in respect of the general question of religious and public holidays, discussed in the parties' submissions, that, in most countries, only the religious holidays of the majority of the population are celebrated as public holidays. Thus Protestant holidays are not always public holidays in Catholic countries and vice versa.[24]

---

[17] Quoted at para 11.
[18] Para 13.
[19] Para 15.
[20] Para 19.
[21] Para 23.
[22] Para 26.
[23] Para 27.
[24] Para 28.

The Commission seemed relaxed about the discrimination that this resulted in. It concluded that the application – both if considered under Article 9 and if examined under Article 14 in conjunction with Article 9 – was 'manifestly ill-founded'.[25] Freedom of contract outweighed freedom of religion. The religious rights under the ECHR provided no protection for Ahmad.

***

Since September 2000, Shabina Begum had attended Denbigh High School in Luton, a school outside the catchment area where her family lived. The school uniform policy had been specifically designed to ensure that it satisfied the requirement of modest dress for Muslim girls. Begum wore the *shalwar kameez* – a sleeveless, smock-like dress worn to between knee and mid-calf length – for the first two years at the school. However, on the first day of term in September 2002, she turned up at school wearing a *jilbab*: a long, shapeless dress ending at the ankle and designed to conceal the shape of the wearer's arms and leg. She was accompanied by her brother and another young man who asked to see the head teacher and insisted that she be allowed to wear to school what she was wearing that day, talking of human rights and legal proceedings. When she was told to go home and change, the family took the case to the High Court, contending that she had been 'excluded/suspended' from the school in breach of her right to manifest her religion under Article 9.

While Begum was unsuccessful at first instance, on the basis that her refusal to follow the school uniform policy was merely 'motivated by religious beliefs' and not a manifestation of them,[26] that decision was reversed by the Court of Appeal.[27] The Court of Appeal held that there had been interference with Article 9(1), and that it was not justified under Article 9(2) because the school had not used an ECHR-compliant decision-making structure. This decision rested upon a basic error: the Human Rights Act 1998, which largely incorporated the ECHR into domestic law, does not require that decision-makers follow a particular approach to their own decision-making. It does, however, require that the outcome of the decision-making process be ECHR compliant. The Human Rights Act requires courts to interpret domestic legislation so far as is possible in a manner compatible with the rights outlined in the ECHR;[28]

---

[25]   Para 29.
[26]   *R (on the application of Begum) v Headteacher and Governors of Denbigh High School* [2004] EWHC 1389.
[27]   [2005] EWCA Civ 199.
[28]   Section 3(1).

and in so doing, they must take into account[29] – though not necessarily follow[30] – the decisions of the European Court of Human Rights at Strasbourg.[31] The Act also made it unlawful for public authorities to act in a way which is incompatible with an ECHR right.[32]

At the House of Lords in 2006, the judges were unanimous that the appeal was allowed and that Begum's claim was dismissed.[33] However, the reasoning of the judges differed. Lord Nicholls and Lady Hale held that there had been an interference with Article 9(1) but that it had been justified under Article 9(2). In contrast, Lords Bingham, Hoffmann and Scott held that there had been no interference with Article 9(1).[34]

Lords Bingham, Hoffmann and Scott proclaimed that interference with the right to religious freedom was 'not easily established'.[35] They declared that the right to manifest one's religion or belief did 'not require that one should be allowed to manifest one's religion at any time and place of one's own choosing'.[36] Rather, 'people sometimes have to suffer some inconvenience for their beliefs'. They said that for religious believers, there was an 'expectation of accommodation, compromise and, if necessary, sacrifice in the manifestation of religious beliefs'.[37] For Lord Bingham:

> The Strasbourg institutions have not been at all ready to find an interference with the right to manifest religious belief in practice or observance where a person has voluntarily accepted an employment or role which does not accommodate that practice or observance and there are other means open to the person to practise or observe his or her religion without undue hardship or inconvenience.[38]

Lord Bingham held that the Article 9 case law of the European Court of Human Rights showed that 'there remains a coherent and remarkably con-

---

[29]   Section 2(1).

[30]   *R (Alconbury Developments Ltd) v. Secretary of State for the Environment, Transport and the Regions* [2001] UKHL 23, para 26.

[31]   In the event of the courts issuing a declaration of incompatibility, the domestic legislation prevails subject to a 'fast-track' system of executive action to bring English law into line with the ECHR. See Human Rights Act 1998, Section 4 (declaration of incompatibility) and Section 10 (remedial action).

[32]   Section 6.

[33]   *R (on the application of Begum) v Headteacher and Governors of Denbigh High School* [2006] UKHL 15.

[34]   Lord Bingham did note that Article 9 was 'engaged or applicable', but by this he seemed to simply recognise that the claimant was sincere: para 21.

[35]   Lord Bingham, para 24.

[36]   Lord Hoffmann, para 50.

[37]   Lord Hoffmann, para 54.

[38]   Para 23.

sistent body of authority which our domestic courts must take into account and which shows that interference is not easily established'.[39] However, it is questionable whether this overstated the Strasbourg jurisprudence. Lord Bingham's elucidation of the rule suggested that two requirements must be met for the rule to apply. First, the claimant must have 'voluntarily accepted an employment or role which does not accommodate' the religious manifestation they seek to exercise. Second, there must be 'other means open to the person to practise or observe his or her religion without undue hardship or inconvenience'. However, their Lordships seem to have placed greater emphasis upon this second requirement. They focused upon the issue of whether Begum could have gone to another school and gave rather less attention to the question of whether she voluntarily submitted to the system of norms.[40] By contrast, the Strasbourg case law focused on the first requirement.[41] As noted in *Ahmad v United Kingdom*,[42] the rule typically applied in relation to employment and similar situations where the claimant has voluntarily submitted themselves to a system of norms. Since *Ahmad v United Kingdom*, it had been applied in relation to those who voluntarily submit to military service,[43] those who voluntarily enter into a contract of employment[44] and those who voluntarily enrol at a university.[45]

In a series of writings around the time of the House of Lords judgment, often co-written with Mark Hill KC,[46] we referred to this as the 'specific situation rule'.[47] We expressed concern that the judgment in *Begum*, by focusing on the second part of the rule, had given the 'specific situation rule' general effect: there was no interference with Article 9 'where the individual is left with a viable and voluntary choice to put themselves in a position where they can manifest their religion, even if this requires some personal sacrifice'.[48] For

---

[39]   [2006] UKHL 15, para 24.

[40]   Note, by contrast, the speech of Baroness Hale which suggested this is a significant issue based on the facts given that 'that the choice of secondary school is usually made by parents or guardians rather than by the child herself' at para 92.

[41]   There is some limited support for this wider interpretation in *Jewish Liturgical Association Cha'are Shalom Ve Tsedek v France* (2000) 9 BHRC 27. However, this has not been followed in subsequent Strasbourg judgments.

[42]   (1982) 4 EHRR 126.

[43]   *Kalaç v Turkey* (1997) 27 EHRR 552.

[44]   *Stedman v United Kingdom* (1997) 5 EHRLR 544.

[45]   *Karaduman v Turkey* (1993) 74 DR 93.

[46]   See, most notably, Mark Hill and Russell Sandberg, 'Is Nothing Sacred? Clashing Symbols in a Secular World' (2007) *Public Law* 488.

[47]   These culminated in Chapter 5 of Russell Sandberg, *Law and Religion* (Cambridge University Press, 2011).

[48]   Maleiha Malik, 'Judgment: *R (SB) v Denbigh High School*' in Rosemary Hunter et al (eds) *Feminist Judgments: From Theory to Practice* (Hart, 2010) 336, 339.

Lords Bingham, Hoffmann and Scott, this was sufficient to dismiss the claim: the school's refusal to allow Begum to wear a *jilbab* did not interfere with her religious freedom. This was objectionable in that it did not recognise the religious freedom of the child given that the choice of schooling is a matter for the parents and not the child. It was also illogical: the refusal to allow Begum to attend school wearing the *jilbab* clearly prevented her from manifesting her religion in practice or observance. Moreover, deciding the case in this way meant that little attention was paid to the question of justification where a nuanced, fact-specific judgment could be reached. The approach of Lord Nicholls and Lady Hale focusing on Article 9(2) was to be preferred.

Unfortunately, the approach of Lords Bingham, Hoffmann and Scott proved to be influential. A series of lower-court decisions concerning school uniforms regarded the *Begum* precedent as an 'insuperable barrier' to religious rights claims, which has erected 'a high threshold before interference can be established'.[49] Moreover, lower-court decisions went even further than Lord Bingham by applying the 'specific situation rule' where only his second requirement was met.[50] In *X v Y School*,[51] Silber J stated held that there was no interference with Article 9 where the claimant was free to go to another school. The same conclusion was reached by the High Court in *Playfoot*,[52] where the court deemed itself competent to determine questions of Christian doctrine to develop an even more restrictive version of the manifestation test. Supperstone QC, sitting as a High Court judge, held that although the claimant believed that she was wearing a 'purity ring' at school as a sign of her sexual restraint, this was not protected under Article 9: she was not manifesting her Christian beliefs because she 'was under no obligation, by reason of her belief, to wear the ring; nor does she suggest that she was so obliged'.[53] Moreover, Supperstone QC held that, even if the wearing of the ring was deemed to be a manifestation, the school's refusal to allow it to be worn did not represent an interference with Article 9 given that there were 'other means by which the Claimant [could] express her belief', such as by attaching the ring to her bag,

---

[49]   *R (on the application of X) v Y School* [2006] EWHC (Admin) 298, para 38, 100.

[50]   Under this interpretation, the rule may be more accurately referred to as the 'contracting out doctrine'; see Maleiha Malik, 'Judgment: *R (SB) v Denbigh High School*' in Rosemary Hunter et al (eds) *Feminist Judgments: From Theory to Practice* (Hart, 2010) 336, 338.

[51]   *R (on the application of X) v Y School* [2006] EWHC (Admin) 298.

[52]   *R (on the Application of Playfoot (A Child)) v Millais School Governing Body* [2007] EWHC Admin 1698.

[53]   Para 23.

wearing a badge or sticker instead, contributing to personal and social health education classes on the topic or transferring to another school.[54]

The result of the extension of the specific situation rule was that Article 9 would rarely be of help. It was now established that there was no interference with Article 9 where it was possible for the claimant to manifest their religion elsewhere, even in ways which would be inconvenient and require significant upheaval. If a believer could go to another school, resign their job or take their custom elsewhere, then they could not rely on Article 9. Even the Equality and Human Rights Commission expressed concern at this, concluding in its 2012 Human Rights Review that: 'Courts are setting too high a threshold for establishing "interference" with the right to manifest a religion or belief, and are therefore not properly addressing whether limitations on Article 9 rights are justifiable.'[55]

This restrictive interpretation discouraged litigants from bringing Article 9 claims under the Human Rights Act 1998.[56] Instead, for a while, claims were made under new discrimination law provisions. A plethora of employment tribunal decisions followed on the right not to be discriminated against for employment purposes in relation to religion or belief, all of which would have been dismissed had they been argued on Article 9 grounds due to the 'specific situation rule'. However, while some claims succeeded under religious discrimination laws, others were unsuccessful, and it became suspected that the restrictive legalistic approach found in the human rights case law had started to cross over to the religious discrimination decisions too.[57]

***

From 1999, Nadia Eweida had worked as a member of the check-in staff at British Airways (BA). Up until 2004, her uniform included a high-neck blouse which allowed her to conceal her silver cross. In 2004, a new uniform was introduced consisting of an open-neck blouse. Originally Eweida wore her cross but concealed it under her cravat; but from May 2006 she began wearing it openly in breach of BA's then uniform policy, which prohibited visible religious symbols unless their wearing was mandatory. She was sent home without pay and then offered a different non-customer facing role, which she refused. She

---

[54]   Para 30.
[55]   At page 315. The full report is available at http://www.equalityhumanrights.com/human-rights/our-human-rights-work/human-rights-review.
[56]   There were occasional exceptions, however – most notably *R (on the Application of Bashir) v The Independent Adjudicator and HMP Ryehull and the Secretary of State for Justice* [2011] EWHC 1108 (Admin).
[57]   See Russell Sandberg, *Law and Religion* (Cambridge University Press, 2011), Chapter 5.

took the case to an employment tribunal and subsequently to the Employment Appeal Tribunal (EAT) alleging religious discrimination but lost.[58] The test for indirect religious discrimination requires a provision, criterion or practice to be applied generally that put or would put people who share the claimant's religion or belief at a particular disadvantage, actually put the claimant at that disadvantage and was not a proportionate means of achieving a legitimate aim.[59] The test is therefore conceptually similar to that under Article 9, in that the first stage is a technical legal analysis to establish disadvantage/interference; while the second stage is a contextual, policy-driven investigation concerning questions of proportionality and justification. The employment tribunal and the EAT rejected the claim at the first stage. In particular, they held that there was no evidence that the uniform policy disadvantaged those who shared Eweida's religion or belief. For Elias J, 'the whole purpose of indirect discrimination is to deal with the problem of group discrimination'. The Court of Appeal agreed. There was no evidence that practising Christians considered the visible display of the cross to be a requirement of the Christian faith and no evidence that the provision created a barrier to Christians employed at BA.[60] Sedley LJ held that solitary disadvantage was not sufficient.[61] Quoting from *Begum*,[62] he suggested that 'the jurisprudence on [Article] 9 does nothing to advance the claimant's case'.[63]

Since 1981, Shirley Chaplin had worked as a nurse and had worn her crucifix to work. In 2007, a new V-necked uniform was introduced and in 2009 she was asked by her manager to remove her 'necklace'. After approval to wear it was denied, Chaplin was moved to a non-nursing temporary position that ceased to exist in July 2010. Her claims were also rejected by an employment tribunal on the same ground as Eweida's.[64] Despite evidence that another nurse – Mrs Babcock – had been asked to remove her cross and chain,[65] the employment tribunal held that Mrs Babcock had not been put at a particular disadvantage since the word 'particular' meant that the disadvantage suffered needed to be 'noteworthy, peculiar or singular', and this criterion had not been

---

58   *Eweida v British Airways* [2008] ET Case Number 3306998/2018 (26 October 2018); *Eweida v British Airways* (2008) UKEAT/0123/08LA (20 November 2008).
59   The law is now to be found in Section 19 of the Equality Act 2010 but was previously found in the Employment Equality (Religion or Belief) Regulations 2003 (SI 2003/1660).
60   *Eweida v British Airways* [2010] EWCA Civ 80, para 8.
61   [2010] EWCA Civ 80, para 15.
62   Para 23.
63   Para 22.
64   *Chaplin v Royal Devon & Exeter NHS Foundation Trust* [2010] ET Case Number: 17288862009 (6 April 2010).
65   See para 15.

met since Mrs Babcock's religious views were not so strong as to lead her to refuse to comply with the policy.[66] This was 'sufficient to dispose of the case', since the test for indirect discrimination referred 'to "persons" in the plural rather than the singular and here we have evidence that only one person, the claimant, was placed at a particular disadvantage'.[67]

Lillian Ladele had been employed by the London Borough for Islington since 1992, becoming a registrar in 2002. In 2005, when the Civil Partnership Act 2004 came into force, she refused on grounds of conscience to perform civil partnership ceremonies. Initially she was able to make informal arrangements to avoid such work; but following a disciplinary action, she was asked to sign a new job description requiring her to carry out straightforward signings of the civil partnership register and administrative work in connection with civil partnerships, but with no requirement to conduct ceremonies. Her resulting employment tribunal case was successful.[68] The tribunal held that there had been direct and indirect discrimination and harassment, and that the local authority had 'placed a greater value on the rights of the lesbian, gay, bisexual and transsexual community than it placed on the rights of [Ms Ladele] as one holding an orthodox Christian belief'. Both the EAT[69] and the Court of Appeal[70] disagreed, however, and the original tribunal decision was reversed, holding that there had been a disadvantage but that it had been justified. The Court of Appeal held that the Council's policy decision to designate all registrars as civil partnership registrars had a legitimate aim: fulfilling the Council's policy to combat discrimination on grounds of sexual orientation.[71] For Dyson LJ, the aim of the Council's 'Dignity for All' policy:

> was of general, indeed overarching, policy significance [having] fundamental human rights, equality and diversity implications, whereas the effect on Ladele of implementing the policy did not impinge on her religious beliefs: she remained free to hold those beliefs, and free to worship as she wished.[72]

---

[66]   Para 27. This was the decision of the majority. Mr Parkhouse, by contrast, held that both nurses had been placed at a disadvantage.

[67]   Para 28. Article 9 was only mentioned in passing in the judgment when it was noted that Article 9 was 'incorporated' into the Employment Equality Regulations: para 6. Presumably the intention was to say that the Regulations were compatible with Article 9.

[68]   *Ladele v London Borough of Islington* [2008] ET Case Number 2203694/2007 (20–23 May 2008).

[69]   *Ladele v London Borough of Islington* (2008) UKEAT/0453/08/RN (10 December 2008).

[70]   *Ladele v London Borough of Islington* [2009] EWCA (Civ) 1357.

[71]   [2009] EWCA (Civ) 1357.

[72]   At para 51.

Further, Ladele was employed in a public job and was being 'required to perform a purely secular task, which was being treated as part of her job'.[73] Dyson LJ held that this conclusion was reinforced by Article 9.[74] Citing *Begum* and a number of Strasbourg decisions which had upheld the specific situation rule,[75] he concluded that:

> Ladele's proper and genuine desire to have her religious views relating to marriage respected should not be permitted to override Islington's concern to ensure that all its registrars manifest equal respect for the homosexual community as for the heterosexual community.[76]

In 2003, Gary McFarlane began working as a counsellor at Relate. His initial concerns about providing counselling services to same-sex couples was allayed by his acceptance that his counselling of a homosexual couple did not involve endorsement of such a relationship and he was therefore prepared to continue. However, following completion of a diploma in psychosexual therapy in 2007, MacFarlane confirmed that he had difficulty in reconciling working with couples on same-sex sexual practices and his duty to follow the teaching of the Bible. In 2008, MacFarlane was dismissed for gross misconduct, his employer having concluded that McFarlane had said he would comply with Relate's policies and provide sexual counselling to same-sex couples without having any intention of doing so. The employment tribunal,[77] the EAT[78] and the Court of Appeal[79] all dismissed the claim, finding *Ladele* to be definitive on this point. As Laws LJ noted, the two cases 'cannot sensibly be distinguished'.[80] It was held that although McFarlane had been disadvantaged, the employer's actions had had a legitimate aim (the provision of counselling services to all sections of the community regardless of their sexual orientation) and was proportionate.

In all four cases, the claimants lost at the highest domestic court or tribunal that heard their case. This in itself is not necessarily problematic. It was not so much the outcome but rather the way in which the domestic courts and tribunals dealt with the claims that was of concern. It was the speed with which

---

[73] Para 52.

[74] See paras 54–61.

[75] *Pichon and Sajous v France* Application 49853/99 (2 October 2001); *C v United Kingdom* App No 10358/83, 37 ECHR Dec & Rep 142; *Sahin v Turkey* (2007) 44 EHRR 5.

[76] [2009] EWCA (Civ) 1357, para 55.

[77] *McFarlane v Relate Avon Ltd* (5 January 2009).

[78] *McFarlane v Relate Avon Ltd* [2009] UKEAT 0106/09/3011 (30 November 2009).

[79] *McFarlane v Relate Avon Ltd* [2010] EWCA Civ 880.

[80] [2010] EWCA Civ 880, para 27.

they rejected the religious rights argument and their unwillingness to concede the relevance of the claimants' Article 9 rights that were problematic. The treatment of all four claims underlined how, following *Begum*,[81] the specific situation rule was applied to cancel out any consideration of Article 9 in the workplace. Indeed, it might be questioned whether some of the claimants had voluntarily agreed to policies that restricted their religious rights. In particular, it is questionable whether Ladele had voluntarily agreed to a contract of employment that included civil partnerships. When she applied for her job, there was no such thing as civil partnerships; and – unlike other Councils – Islington had not been willing to compromise but had designated all registrars as civil partnership registrars.[82] Although the approach in *Ladele* and *McFarlane* was preferable to that in *Eweida* and *Chaplin*, in that the indirect religious discrimination claims were dismissed on the basis of justification rather than disadvantage, in both *Ladele* and *McFarlane* it is regrettable that in determining the question of justification, the courts and tribunals took a one-sided approach which paid little attention to religious rights. The courts and tribunals were correct in emphasising the importance of preventing sexual orientation discrimination but were incorrect in underplaying the importance of preventing religious discrimination.

It was therefore unsurprising that the treatment of these four claims by domestic courts and tribunals raised the question of whether the UK's approach breached its obligations under Article 9 of the ECHR. It is this question which the Strasbourg decision in *Eweida v UK*[83] was concerned with. That decision was an important landmark, in that it represents the first time that Strasbourg institutions found the UK to be in breach of Article 9.[84] The Court's statement of 'General Principles under Article 9 of the Convention' not only corrected the approach taken in the UK post-*Begum*, but also provided an expansive new

---

[81]   *R (on the application of Begum) v Headteacher and Governors of Denbigh High School* [2006] UKHL 15.

[82]   As Dyson LJ noted (*Ladele v London Borough of Islington* [2009] EWCA (Civ) 1357, para 6), Section 29(2) of the Civil Partnership Act 2004 required each 'registration authority to ensure that there is a sufficient number of civil partnership registrars for its area to carry out the functions of civil partnership registrars'. See further paras 75–76.

[83]   (2013) 57 EHRR 8.

[84]   This is particularly noteworthy given that Strasbourg 'seems to have been fairly reluctant to overturn local decisions about religious practice or religious symbols in relation to Article 9 rights – particularly in employment': Javier Garcia Oliva and Frank Cranmer, 'Education and Religious Symbols in the United Kingdom, Italy and Spain: Uniformity or Subsidiarity?' (2013) 19(3) *European Public Law* 555, 561.

interpretation of Article 9 that had the potential to transform the understanding of religious freedom across the Council of Europe.[85]

The UK's interpretation of Article 9 was rejected by the Strasbourg Court. In its elucidation of the 'general principles' that apply under Article 9, the Court rearticulated that although 'religious freedom is primarily a matter of individual thought and conscience', the text of Article 9(1) made it plain that 'freedom of religion also encompasses the freedom to manifest one's belief, alone and in private but also to practice in community with others and in public'.[86] The Court stressed that Article 9 protects 'views that attain a certain level of cogency, seriousness, cohesion and importance'; and that provided that this threshold was satisfied, 'the State's duty of neutrality and impartiality is incompatible with any power on the State's part to assess the legitimacy of religious beliefs or the ways in which those beliefs are expressed'.[87] Although most of these general principles were not new, this reference to the fact that the State had no role in assessing the ways in which beliefs are expressed can be seen as being corrective to the tendency of domestic courts to do just that in deciding that expressing belief in idiosyncratic ways are not protected. The Court was even clear, however, in its rearticulation of the manifestation requirement and the 'specific situation rule'.

In clarifying the manifestation requirement, the Court accepted that it could not be said that 'every act which is in some way inspired, motivated or influenced by it constitutes a "manifestation" of the belief'.[88] This meant that 'acts or omissions which do not directly express the belief concerned or which are only remotely connected to a precept of faith fall outside the protection of Article 9'.[89] The Court rearticulated that in order to be a 'manifestation', the act must be 'intimately linked' to the applicant's religion or belief.[90] It was noted that an example of such a manifestation would be 'an act of worship or devotion which forms part of the practice of a religion or belief in a generally recognised form'. However, the Court stressed that 'the manifestation of religion or belief is not limited to such acts'; rather, 'the existence of a sufficiently close and direct nexus between the act and the underlying belief must be determined on the facts of each case'. Strasbourg was clear that 'there is no requirement on the applicant to establish that he or she acted in fulfilment of a duty mandated

---

[85] Paras 79 *et seq.*
[86] (2013) 57 EHRR 8, para 80.
[87] Para 81.
[88] (2013) 57 EHRR 8, paras 81–82.
[89] Para 82.
[90] This formulation of the rule had been laid out by the Court before, eg, in *C v UK* (1983) 37 DR 142, 144; *Hasan and Chaush v Bulgaria* (2002) 34 EHRR 55.

by the religion in question'.[91] The Strasbourg Court therefore made it clear that statements in the domestic case law which required actions to be obliged by the religion in question to be manifestations were incorrect. The judgment suggested that the manifestation requirement will fail to be met only if the action does not directly express the belief concerned or if the connection between the action and the belief is remote. The first limb of this test is easier to interpret than the second. It is difficult to find a clear example of an action which would fail the 'remote connection' test, especially where the 'direct expression' test has been met (given that the word 'or' is used in the judgment). This suggested that courts would now have to assess 'remoteness'.

In clarifying the ambit and role of the specific situation rule, the Court observed that the submission for the UK government had been correct to point out that – as Lord Bingham observed in *Begum* – the case law of the Strasbourg institutions had indicated that there would be no interference with Article 9(1) where 'a person is able to take steps to circumvent a limitation placed on his or her freedom to manifest religion or belief'; and that in several employment cases, it had been held that 'the possibility of resigning from the job and changing employment meant that there was no interference with the employee's religious freedom'.[92] However, it was noted that this approach had not been taken by the Strasbourg Court in employment cases concerning other ECHR rights and so this principle was no longer to be followed 'given the importance in a democratic society of freedom of religion'.[93] Now:

> where an individual complains of a restriction on freedom of religion in the workplace, rather than holding that the possibility of changing job would negate any interference with the right, the better approach would be to weigh that possibility in the overall balance when considering whether or not the restriction was proportionate.

This meant that the specific situation rule would no longer form part of the part of the Article 9(1) analysis but would be a factor – and not a definitive one – in weighing up the Article 9(2) question of justification. This would mean that cases such as *Begum* would in future be decided on Article 9(2) grounds. It is also striking that the Strasbourg Court's interpretation of the 'specific situation rule' exclusively referred to the context of employment; this seems to suggest that the *Begum* reasoning overstated the case law by applying the rule outside

---

[91]   (2013) 57 EHRR 8, para 82. The same point was expressed clearly in the partly dissenting opinion of Judges Bratza and Björgvinsson, para 2.

[92]   (2013) 57 EHRR 8, para 83.

[93]   Para 83. The same point was expressed clearly in the partly dissenting opinion of Judges Bratza and Björgvinsson, para 2.

its original contractual setting, as Hill KC and I had argued in a number of publications.[94] Now, the fact that a child could go to another school to manifest their religion will be a factor that falls for consideration under Article 9(2), if it is relevant at all.

The elucidation of general principles suggested that the focus was being moved from the Article 9(1) issue of interference to the Article 9(2) question of justification. As Hill KC noted, this new approach 'will not necessarily lead to a seismic shift in litigation outcomes' because 'shifting the theatre of dispute from Article 9(1) to Article 9(2) might well create produce identical results but for different and more sophisticated reasoning'.[95] However, he also noted that 'there is a greater subjective element to Article 9(2)' and this has the effect that 'judicial outcomes may become less predictable'. This unpredictability is furthered, however, by the way in which the judgment gives little guidance on how this balancing act is to be performed. While the discussion of the general principles that animate Article 9 suggested that Strasbourg was ushering in a new era for religious rights, the way in which the Court applied these principles to the four cases before it would suggest that this initial impression might be overly optimistic.

The claim in *Eweida* was the only one of the four that succeeded. Unlike the domestic courts, Strasbourg held that there had been an interference with her Article 9 right and that a fair balance had not been struck under Article 9(2).[96] Although the national courts operated within a margin of appreciation, they had afforded too much weight to the employer's wish to project a certain corporate image and not enough to the applicant's desire to manifest her religious belief.[97] For the majority,[98] there was a breach of Article 9 since inadequate attention had been given to whether the interference was proportionate. By contrast, in relation to *Chaplin*, the Court held that while there had been an interference with Article 9, this was justified because of the need to protect health and safety on a hospital ward, and that this 'was inherently of a greater magnitude than that which applied in respect of Ms Eweida'.[99] This was a field where a 'wide margin of appreciation' was allowed since the

---

[94] As argued, for example, by Mark Hill and Russell Sandberg, 'Is Nothing Sacred? Clashing Symbols in a Secular World' (2007) *Public Law* 488; and Russell Sandberg, *Law and Religion* (Cambridge University Press, 2011) 91.

[95] Mark Hill, 'Religious Symbolism and Conscientious Objection in the Workplace' (2013) 15 *Ecclesiastical Law Journal* 191, 199, 200.

[96] Para 94.

[97] Para 94.

[98] The partly dissenting opinion of Judges Bratza and Björgvinsson dissented from the majority's opinion in relation to Eweida on the basis that they disagreed that they considered that the domestic courts had struck a fair balance: para 5.

[99] Para 99.

'hospital managers were better placed to make decisions about clinical safety than a court, particularly an international court which has heard no direct evidence'. However, this ran the risk of writing a blank cheque whenever health and safety concerns are invoked – especially since the discussion of this issue had been *obiter* in the domestic decisions, which dispensed with the case by saying that there was no disadvantage. Moreover, the Court's judgment left unanswered the question of whether the test for indirect religious discrimination breaches Article 9 in requiring proof that the claimant's particular belief is shared by their co-religionists.[100] The logic of the Court's elucidation of general principles is that an individual's belief, which is shared by no-one else, will still be protected under Article 9. This would suggest that a rule under indirect discrimination law which requires evidence that the belief is shared would breach Article 9.[101]

The claims in *Ladele* and *McFarlane* were also dismissed on grounds of justification under Article 9(2). In respect of *Ladele*, the Strasbourg Court held that the council's actions had a legitimate aim and the means pursued was proportionate.[102] It was noted that the Court 'generally allows the national authorities a wide margin of appreciation when it comes to striking a balance between competing Convention rights'.[103] This wide margin of appreciation had not been exceeded in this case. However, the Court did note that the specific situation rule was not fatal to the claim. The majority opinion stated that:

> it cannot be said that, when she entered into her contract of employment, the applicant specifically waived her right to manifest her religious belief by objecting to participating in the creation of civil partnerships, since this requirement was introduced by her employer at a later date.

This suggests that the weight of the specific situation rule as a factor under Article 9(2) will be higher where the actions that the claimant complains of were part of their contractual duties when they became an employee, and so they can be said to have specifically waived their Article 9 rights. The claim in *McFarlane* was dismissed in a similar manner. The Court again stressed that a wide margin of appreciation was afforded to States where 'the employer's action was intended to secure the implementation of its policy of providing

---

[100] This point is noted but not dealt with in paragraph 9 of the partly dissenting opinion of Judges Bratza and Björgvinsson.

[101] This does not necessarily mean that the statutory test is incorrect but rather the judicial interpretation of it. Emphasis should be placed on the word 'would' in order to recognise – contrary to the Court of Appeal's decision in *Eweida* – that solitary disadvantage can be sufficient: [2010] EWCA Civ 80, para 15.

[102] Paras 105–06.

[103] Para 106.

a service without discrimination' and that this had not been exceeded in the present case.[104] The Court also emphasised again the new role of the specific situation rule as a factor under Article 9(2) rather than being determinative under Article 9(1).[105] It is noticeable that, even in regarding *McFarlane* as a case in which Article 9 rights were specifically waived by contract, the Court seemed adamant to stress that this is only a minor factor to be taken into account for the purposes of justification.[106]

However, it is of note that, despite the Court downplaying the importance of the specific situation rule, both of these claims were lost because they were constructed as involving the balancing of rights, with more weight being afforded to the need to combat discrimination on grounds of sexual orientation rather than on the complained case of religious discrimination. The wide deference given to the domestic courts was problematic given that the domestic courts were operating under a restrictive understanding of Article 9 following *Begum* which meant that the case was not argued on Article 9 grounds and that no real balancing of rights took place. The reliance on the margin of appreciation meant that the part of the judgment which applies the law was of little practical use to domestic courts and to employees. It would have been useful to see discussion of when and how employers might be expected to balance the rights not to discriminate on grounds of sexual orientation with the right to religious freedom.

The decade following the *Eweida* judgment at Strasbourg has shown that my initial observation that religious freedom 'died' as a result of *Begum* and was 'reborn' following *Eweida* was clearly overstated.[107] The decision has not had a dramatic effect: it has not led to a string of successful cases on religious freedom or the clear articulation of what is and what is not protected by Article 9. Indeed, the post-*Begum* drought of Article 9 cases seems to have continued. The cases that have been heard by the higher courts over the last decade suggest that *Eweida* has not been a watershed moment.

On the one hand, *Eweida* has often been cited – typically as a part of the court or tribunal's articulation of what Article 9 protects. For instance, *Eweida* was cited in *R (On Application of Harrison) v Secretary of State for Justice*[108]

---

[104] Para 109.

[105] See para 109.

[106] In contrast, the partly dissenting opinion of Judges Vučinić and De Gaetano at para 5 commented that 'the reason why there was no violation of Article 9 in respect of the fourth applicant is that he effectively signed off or waived his right to invoke conscientious objection when he voluntarily signed up for the job'.

[107] It was deliberately provocative at the time: Russell Sandberg, *Religion, Law and Society* (Cambridge University Press, 2014) 1, 217.

[108] [2020] EWHC 2096 (Admin) at para 69.

to support the conclusion that the current non-recognition of humanist marriage interfered with the applicant's human rights.[109] The *Eweida* rejection of the specific situation rule has been accepted and followed by domestic courts. The Supreme Court in *Bull v Hall*[110] stated that in *Eweida*, 'the Strasbourg court abandoned its previous stance that there was no interference with an employee's right to manifest her religion if it could be avoided by changing jobs', and that this was now to be taken into account in the overall proportionality assessment.[111] The legacy of *Eweida* is that cases are not being dispensed with on grounds of the specific situation rule. However, the absence of cases applying the rule might suggest that the decline in such cases arguing Article 9 following *Begum* has continued.

In most cases, *Eweida* has been cited rather than applied. However, in *Higgs v Farmor's School*,[112] the EAT allowed the appeal and remitted the case back to an employment tribunal since the original decision had failed to engage with the interpretation of Article 9 identified in *Eweida*; had it done so, the tribunal would have concluded that there was a close or direct nexus between the Facebook posts that a school administrator had posted about relationships education and her protected beliefs. Although some decisions have applied *Eweida*, this has not always led to the religious argument winning.[113] A strong example of this is the employment tribunal decision in *Gareddu v London Underground*,[114] which concerned the claim that a policy stating that employees could not have more than 15 days off consecutively in August constituted indirect religious discrimination due to the claimant's religious belief that he was required to return to Sardinia for a period of approximately five weeks around the month of August each year to attend and participate in religious festivals with his family. The tribunal held that the claim was not made in good faith and that the motive for wanting the time off work related to family arrangements.[115] There would be an intimate link between participating in

---

[109] It was held, however, that this was justified by the fact that the law was currently under review by the Law Commission. *Eweida* was similarly cited in *Re Smyth's Application for Judicial Review* [2018] NICA 25 to hold that humanist beliefs were within the ambit of Article 9 in the context of marriage law in Northern Ireland.

[110] [2013] UKSC 73 at para 47.

[111] *Eweida* has also been cited by the EAT to insist that the Article 9 understanding of belief is used for the purpose of discrimination law: *Harron v Chief Constable of Dorset Police* [2016] UKEAT/0234/15/DA.

[112] [2023] EAT 89.

[113] See also *R (on the Application of Cornerstone) v Office of Standards in Education* [2020] EWHC 1679 (Admin) paras 297 and 298.

[114] [2015] Case Number: 2201116/2015.

[115] Para 33.

each individual festival and his religious beliefs, but there was no such nexus between the five-week period as a whole and his underlying beliefs.[116]

Some decisions have ignored *Eweida*. Perhaps most notably, this was true of the leading UK Supreme Court decision about the balancing of the rights of discrimination on grounds of religion and sexual orientation, *Lee v Ashers Baking Company*,[117] which does not mention *Eweida*. Other decisions have explicitly said that *Eweida* was not relevant.[118] In *Kuteh v Dartford and Gravesham Trust*,[119] concerning an appeal by a nurse sacked for gross misconduct as a result of her initiating inappropriate conversations about religion with patients, counsel submitted the *Eweida* section on general principles, but the Court of Appeal did 'not find anything of assistance in those passages, important though they are in setting out the general principles which apply in Article 9 cases'. Other cases have cited *Eweida*, but to support statements and conclusions that are not compatible with the Strasbourg decision. In *Core Issues Trust v Transport for London*,[120] *Eweida* was cited as summarising the manifestation requirement; but it was then questionably held that Article 9 was not engaged because:

> even if the advertisement sought to be placed by the Trust was motivated by a religious belief, it did not actually express that belief. Nor was the Trust required by religious belief to communicate these views by way of advertisement on London buses.

The second sentence, at least, is not compatible with *Eweida*. The most detailed consideration of the impact of *Eweida* can be found in the Court of Appeal decision in *Mba v Mayor and Burgess of the London Borough of Merton*,[121] concerning whether Sunday working constituted indirect discrimination on grounds of the claimant's Christian beliefs. The employment tribunal had dismissed the claim on the basis that to be protected, the belief must be a core component of Christianity. The Court of Appeal unanimously dismissed the claimant's appeal because although there had been errors of law in the employment tribunal's decision, its ultimate conclusion that the disadvantage had been proportionate was plainly and unarguably right.[122] The judges considered that the requirement that the manifestation be core was an error of law but did not see *Eweida* as being the catalyst for this conclusion.

---

[116] Para 34.
[117] [2018] UKSC 49.
[118] *Page v NHS* [2019] UKEAT/0183/18/DA at para 37.
[119] [2019] EWCA Civ 818 at para 54.
[120] [2013] EWHC 651 (Admin) at paras 162, 165 and 166.
[121] [2013] EWCA Civ 1562.
[122] Paragraphs 23–24.

Maurice Kay LJ held that the claimant's case was not strengthened by *Eweida* because that decision 'was entirely fact sensitive'.[123] Elias J held that the need for a core component could be a relevant factor in the justification discussion for indirect discrimination claims that were not against a public body.[124] He noted that although Article 9 did not require group disadvantage to be proved,[125] 'Article 9 cannot be enforced directly in employment tribunals because claims for breaches of Convention rights do not fall within their statutory jurisdiction' – a point he said that the Strasbourg Court had not seemed to appreciate.[126] He further held that although domestic law needed to be read in a way that was compatible with ECHR rights, it was 'simply not possible to read down the concept of indirect discrimination to ignore the need to establish group disadvantage'. Maurice Kay LJ, although adopting different reasoning, also agreed that while Article 9 does not require group disadvantage, this did not justify reading down the domestic law on indirect discrimination.[127] Subsequent cases have not required manifestations to be core to the religion in order to be protected, but it is unclear whether this is due to the legacy of *Eweida*.[128] It is clear, however, that *Eweida* has not led to the abandonment of the group disadvantage requirement in indirect discrimination claims.[129]

There are echoes here of Lord Denning's comments in *Ahmad v Inner London Education Authority*[130] that while courts will do their best to see that their decisions confirm with Article 9, the high-sounding principles of the ECHR nevertheless need to be brought down to earth. However, this goes further than a simple reminder that cases are fact specific.

Although interpretations of Article 9 have changed, it remains questionable whether the ECHR right does much to assist matters. This is not to say that claimants making religious rights claims always need to succeed. Yet there is a sense that Article 9 claims are not being brought and that Article 9 is not being argued in cases where they could be expected to be. That there has not

---

[123]   Para 20.
[124]   Para 33.
[125]   Paras 34 and 36.
[126]   Para 35.
[127]   Para 21.
[128]   *Eweida* was followed in *Sethi v Elements Personnel Services* [2019] Case Number: 2300234/2018.
[129]   See *Page v NHS* [2019] UKEAT/0183/18/DA at para 48. While this book was in press, the High Court in *R (on the Application of TTT) v Michaela School* [2024] EWHC 843 (Admin) applied *Begum* to hold that a ban on ritual prayer by a school did not amount to an interference under Article 9. See Russell Sandberg, 'Say a Prayer for Article 9? *R (on the Application of TTT) v Michaela School* and the Question of Interference' (2024) *Law and Justice*, forthcoming.
[130]   [1978] QB 36 at 41.

been an avalanche of Article 9 claims is not necessarily a sign that the law is ineffective. It may actually point to increased awareness of human rights by employers. Moreover, the focuses of senior courts do not necessarily reflect the day-to-day issues of litigation. Religious discrimination claims not only continue to come regularly before employment tribunals but also have an unpredictable success rate. Yet for all these caveats, a concern remains that despite the significant legal changes of the last 40 years – the enactment of the Human Rights Act 1998, the new law on religious discrimination, the rearticulation of general principles in *Eweida* – Article 9 has not blossomed. This is shown in the way that it receives less discussion and sometimes no discussion in human rights textbooks for undergraduates and presumably taught modules.

The stories of the claimants discussed in this chapter and the general lack of success of their Article 9 arguments may provide a further explanation for why the field of law and religion has not flourished as an area of study in England and Wales. Yet the marginal position of religious rights in general and Article 9 in particular does not only apply to England and Wales. The jurisprudence of the European Court of Human Rights generally on religious matters has been much criticised for its dependence on the margin of appreciation and the way in which Article 9 is often not argued even in cases seemingly concerning religious rights. Reviewing the Court's case law on religious symbols, Frank S Ravitch observed that the Court 'is simply reifying majoritarian biases that find their ways into the laws of nation states'.[131] For Ravitch, this 'renders Article 9 a paper tiger in many circumstances and disadvantages the religious freedom of religious minorities or unpopular religions'.[132] He concluded that this is interestingly 'quite similar to the situation in the US, albeit through different analysis and concepts'. This suggests that the impotence of religious rights claims does not necessarily correspond with the development of an academic literature on law and religion matters because law and religion has flourished as a field of study in other European jurisdictions and in the US. The lack of such a link is to be expected not only given that unsuccessful religious rights claims provide law and religion academics with something to write about,[133] but also because law and religion as a subject is larger than the discussion of religion as a human right. The often quick rejection of religious rights by the judiciary may be part of the reasons why the initial interest in law and religion studies petered out, but it cannot be the main reason – as the successes of law and religion in other jurisdictions have shown.

---

[131] Frank S Ravitch, *Advanced Introduction to Law and Religion* (Edward Elgar Publishing, 2023) 77.

[132] A 'paper tiger' comes from a Chinese phrase and refers to something that appears to be powerful but is actually ineffective.

[133] Though this is not true where the lack of success of such claims leads to a paucity of litigation or at least reported decisions.

6.   The American dream

The early years of the twenty-first century saw law and religion studies blossom around the world. In continental Europe and the US, where aspects of law and religion have long been studied and taught, recent years have seen the topic become increasingly controversial and the focus evolve beyond the study of Church and State. In other jurisdictions – such as the UK, Australia and South Africa – law and religion became established as an area of study for the first time, with research clusters and courses being set up and academics defining themselves as law and religion scholars. International and regional associations have been established, most notably the International Consortium for Law and Religion Studies.

In the English-speaking world at least, it is in the US that law and religion scholarship is at its most advanced, with two prolific and world-leading research centres: the Center for the Study of Law and Religion, founded at Emory University in 1982; and the International Center for Law and Religion Studies, established at Brigham Young University in 2000. The Emory Center is responsible for more than 350 books on the topic, with its Director, John Witte Jr, himself having published 40 books.[1] Witte has described how 'a new interdisciplinary movement has emerged in the US dedicated to the study of the religious dimensions of law, the legal dimensions of religion and the inter-action of legal and religious ideas and institutions, norms and practices'.[2] In the words of Witte, this requires acceptance of a 'dialectical interaction' between law and religion:

> This study is predicated on the assumptions that religion gives law its spirit and inspires its adherence to ritual and justice. Law gives religion its structure and encourages its devotion to order and organisation. Law and religion share such ideas as fault, obligation and covenant and such methods as ethics, rhetoric and textual interpretation. Law and religion also balance each other by counterpoising justice

---

[1]   For an appraisal of Witte's contribution see Norman Doe, 'Faith, Freedom and Family: An Introduction to the Work of John Witte Jr' (2022) 24(2) *Ecclesiastical Law Journal* 175. See also John Witte Jr, *Table Talk: Short Talks on the Weightier Matters of Law and Religion* (Brill, 2023).

[2]   John Witte, Jr, 'The Study of Law and Religion in the United States: An Interim Report' (2012) 14 *Ecclesiastical Law Journal* 327.

and mercy, rule and equity, discipline and love. This dialectical interaction gives these two disciplines and dimensions of life their vitality and their strength.[3]

For Witte, 'law and religion are distinct spheres and sciences of human life, but they exist in dialectical interaction, constantly crossing over and cross-fertilising each other'.[4]

Witte's schema suggests that there is a need to study law and religion as two distinct spheres not only in how they interact with one another, but also in how they see and reconstruct one another on their own terms. Understood as an interdisciplinary endeavour, law and religion involves both reading law religiously and understanding religion legally. Witte's interdisciplinary conceptualisation of law and religion studies has much in common with work on law and literature, where a distinction has been drawn between scholarship on literature as law – examining literature from a legal standpoint – and law as literature, which examines law from a literature standpoint. However, before returning to Witte's work, further attention needs to be paid to this common demarcation – what may be referred to as the 'X as law'/'law as X' distinction.

***

The 'X as law'/'law as X' distinction refers to the way in which the interdisciplinary study of law includes two objects of study and two frames of analysis which cross over. The study of 'X as law' refers to the study of the non-legal discipline (such as literature, music, politics, religion) from a legal standpoint; while the study of 'law as X' covers the study of law from the standpoint of the other discipline. The 'X as law'/'law as X' distinction is most often attributed to the law and literature movement. However, the original and most common distinction is actually phrased slightly differently as being between 'law in literature' (which examines 'the possible relevance of literary texts ... as texts appropriate for legal scholars') and 'law as literature' (which 'seeks to apply the techniques of literary criticism to legal texts').[5]

This distinction shows the two objects of study and the frames of analysis. Law and literature includes the study of literature through the frame of law ('law in literature') and the study of law through the frame of literature ('law as literature'). The study of law in literature includes analysis of 'the appearance of legal themes or the depiction of legal actors or processes in fiction or

---

[3]   Ibid 327–28.

[4]   Ibid 328.

[5]   Ian Ward, *Law and Literature: Possibilities and Perspectives* (Cambridge University Press, 1995) 3.

drama;[6] this involves 'looking at how legal issues, legal institutions, and legal actors are portrayed in literature, as well as symbolic uses of law in literary texts'.[7] The study of law as literature involves the 'parsing of such legal texts as statutes, constitutions, judicial opinions, and certain classic scholarly treatises as if they were literary works';[8] this includes examination of 'how legal texts, like court decisions, utilize literary devices, as well as the study of legal hermeneutics'.[9] Robert Weisberg referred to law as literature as 'the 'more elusive part of the law-literature enterprise' and contended that it included 'legal writing in terms of style and rhetoric', as well as what he referred to as its 'hermeneutic subpart' – that is, 'the contemporary interest in the techniques of literary criticism being applied to judicial opinions and statutes in order to discern their meaning'.[10] The field can be interpreted very broadly indeed. As David S Caudill questioned, 'is every law school classroom discussion of the holding in a case as a judicial choice between two alternative narratives, one of which was more persuasive, an exercise in law as literature?'[11] For Mary Jane Schenck:

> Law 'as' literature has come to mean not mere reading to appreciate style, but reading legal documents or opinions, analyzing metaphors as socially constructed language, with the goal of deconstructing them. Reading law texts from a neo-Marxist or gender studies perspective, for instance, reveals the historical context of the law and hence a contingency that may justify social change.[12]

---

[6]   Robert Weisberg, 'The Law-Literature Enterprise' (1989) 1(1) *Yale Journal of Law & the Humanities* 1.

[7]   Norman P Ho, 'Literature as Law? The Confucian Classics as Ultimate Sources of Law in Traditional China' (2019) 31(2) *Law & Literature* 173.

[8]   Robert Weisberg, 'The Law-Literature Enterprise' (1989) 1(1) *Yale Journal of Law & the Humanities* 1.

[9]   Norman P Ho, 'Literature as Law? The Confucian Classics as Ultimate Sources of Law in Traditional China' (2019) 31(2) *Law & Literature* 173.

[10]   Robert Weisberg, 'The Law-Literature Enterprise' (1989) 1(1) *Yale Journal of Law & the Humanities* 1, 36, 2. Robin L West has noted that the law and literature movement comprises the 'literary' (reading literature for 'the value of its insights into the nature of law'), the 'jurisprudential' (exploring the 'literary narrative root' of law) and the 'hermeneutic' (using literature to 'glean meaning from legal texts'): Robin L West, 'Literature, Culture and Law at Duke University' in Austin Sarat, Cathrine O Frank and Matthew Anderson (eds) *Teaching Law and Literature* (Modern language Association, 2011) 98.

[11]   David S Caudill, *Stories about Science in Law: Literary and Historical Images of Acquired Expertise* (Ashgate, 2011) 13.

[12]   Mary Jane Schenck, 'Reading Law as Literature, Reading Literature as Law: A Pragmatist's Approach' (2013) 25 *Cahiers de Recherches Médiévales et Humanistes/ Journal of Medieval and Humanistic Studies* 9, 23–24.

However, despite the potential breadth of the conventional dichotomy employed in law and literature, the two terms 'law in literature' and 'law as literature' have actually tended to be interpreted narrowly. As a result, a number of other forms of law and literature have been identified. The study of law and literature has also been said to include the study of 'law of literature' – that is, the study of 'laws which impact the production and dissemination of literary texts, such as American laws on free speech.[13] This focuses on 'the regulation of literature by law (e.g., copyright, defamation, and obscenity) and its socio-ideological aspects'.[14] For Norman P Ho, another way of looking at the law and literature field is through the focus on 'literature and legal reform' – that is, 'how literature and literary movements have affected the development of law'.[15] Conversely, a number of scholars have maintained that 'literature in law' is the third category to have emerged, after 'law in literature' and 'law as literature'.[16] This involves the study of how legal sources use literature – in other words, how literature is used 'to attain various objectives – as means of persuasion, to make the facts understandable, to invoke empathy, to support legal reasoning, to foreshadow the ultimate decision, derive meanings to words, and sometimes just as a literary embellishment'.[17]

These various different labels all show the many different dimensions of law and literature as an interdisciplinary field. They can be contrasted with the dominant approaches within law and religion as a legal field in England and Wales, which mostly focuses on the equivalent of 'law of literature'. Indeed, for a time, the term 'law of religion was occasionally used as the label for the area of study – as shown by the original name of the undergraduate course at Cardiff, 'Comparative Law of Religion'.[18]

---

[13] Norman P Ho, 'Literature as Law? The Confucian Classics as Ultimate Sources of Law in Traditional China' (2019) 31(2) *Law & Literature* 173.

[14] Jeanne Gaakeer, 'Law and Literature' in Mortiner Sellers and Stephan Kirste (eds) *Encyclopaedia of the Philosophy of Law and Social Philosophy* (Springer, 2022).

[15] Norman P Ho, 'Literature as Law? The Confucian Classics as Ultimate Sources of Law in Traditional China' (2019) 31(2) *Law & Literature* 173.

[16] Apurval Mittal and Vishavjeet Chaudhary, 'Law and Literature: Interpretation of the Constitution' (2020) 1 *Bennett Journal of Legal Studies* 151, 154–55; Geraldine Gadbin-George, 'To Quote or Not to Quote: "Literature in Law" in European Court Decisions and Legal English Teaching' (2013) 64 *Asp La Revue du GERAS*, http://journals.openedition.org/asp/3842.

[17] Apurval Mittal and Vishavjeet Chaudhary, 'Law and Literature: Interpretation of the Constitution' (2020) 1 *Bennett Journal of Legal Studies* 151, 154–55.

[18] See Augur Pearce, 'England's Law of Religion – The History of a Discipline' in Norman Doe and Russell Sandberg (eds) *Law and Religion: New Horizons* (Peeters, 2010) 13.

It will be noted, however, that the label of 'literature as law' is missing from these schemas. Although the term is used by some scholars,[19] where it is defined, it is often interpreted narrowly as understanding the legal force of literature rather than the study of literature through a legal lens more broadly. Ho, for instance, defines 'literature as law' as the study of 'the use of what are considered literary texts as sources of law for judicial decision-making'.[20] Robin West has argued that while the term has been used narrowly to describe how cultural authorities such as Blackstone can be viewed as having legal authority,[21] it is echoed in the term 'culture as law', which can be understood as the analysis of 'culture of all descriptions, high, low, and mid-brow – *Law and Order, Perry Mason, LA Law, CSI, Ally McBeal* and so on – that constitute an irreducible if often ignored or unseen part of our law'.[22] Even this understanding, however, is a narrow interpretation that takes a very literal interpretation of the 'as'. West noted that examining literature as a form of law can shed light upon debates concerning legal pluralism by highlighting how a:

> firm distinction between positive law on the one hand and imaginative literature on the other is at best a (slightly overdrawn) contingent truth about the law, and the literature, of our times, and not a necessary truth about the essence of either.

Such an approach, he maintained, would underscore how 'the various distinctions that seem clear and intuitive to us between law and imaginative literature were likely not always so clear, and might not always be so in the future'.

However, the study of 'literature as law' can go further than this. Studying literature through a legal lens does not necessarily require studying literature as a legal authority. It follows from Weisberg's definition of 'law as literature' – as 'parsing of such legal texts as statutes, constitutions, judicial opinions, and certain classic scholarly treatises *as if* they were literary works'[23] – that the

---

[19]   Jarrell D Wright, 'Transcending Law and Literature: Literature as Law in Plato, Vico, and Shelley' (2017) 29(2) *Law & Literature* 291; Norman P Ho, 'Literature as Law? The Confucian Classics as Ultimate Sources of Law in Traditional China' (2019) 31(2) *Law & Literature* 173; Mary Jane Schenck, 'Reading Law as Literature, Reading Literature as Law: A Pragmatist's Approach' (2013) 25 *Cahiers de Recherches Médiévales et Humanistes/Journal of Medieval and Humanistic Studies* 9.

[20]   Norman P Ho, 'Literature as Law? The Confucian Classics as Ultimate Sources of Law in Traditional China' (2019) 31(2) *Law & Literature* 173, 174.

[21]   Robin L West, 'Literature, Culture and Law at Duke University' in Austin Sarat, Cathrine O Frank and Matthew Anderson (eds) *Teaching Law and Literature* (Modern Language Association, 2011) 98.

[22]   This has been developed and exemplified in William P MacNeil, *Lex Populi: The Jurisprudence of Popular Culture* (Stanford University Press, 2007).

[23]   Robert Weisberg, 'The Law-Literature Enterprise' (1989) 1(1) *Yale Journal of Law & the Humanities* 1 (emphasis added).

study of literature as law is the study of literary works *as if* they are legal texts. This involves studying literature not only as if it has legal authority, but also as if it were interpreted like a legal text. Studying literature through law can, therefore, highlight the commonalities of the two. As West noted:

> Law, like literature, is textual. Law, like all texts, literary and otherwise, therefore requires interpretation. And, for there to be interpretation, there must, in turn, be a community of to some degree like-minded interpreters. Positive law of all forms – statutory, common, and constitutional – and imaginative literature share enough of a 'to-be-interpreted' textual essence that it is fruitful to think of law and literature as forms of the same thing – texts requiring interpretation – at least with regards to how we distil meaning.[24]

As Jarrell D Wright put it, the study of literature as law, understood in this way, establishes 'equivalence between the poet and the legislator'.[25] Combining this with the established study of 'literature in law' allows 'law as literature' to be understood as the study of literature from a legal perspective. This allows law and literature to be conceptualised as including both the study of 'literature as law' (ie, the study of literature from a legal perspective) and the study of 'law as literature' (ie, the study of law from a literature perspective). This underscores the commonalities of both law and literature and the two modes of analysis. If the word 'as' is seen as requiring just the narrower study of literature as a source of law, then the word 'through' could be used instead. The field could be reconceptualised as the study of 'law through literature' and 'literature through law'. Regardless of the precise wording, such a distinction highlights the two modes of analysis and the two linked foci. Such an insistence that law and literature are linked allows scholars to 'experiment in reconstructing the aesthetic in legal terms or the legal in aesthetic terms'.[26]

As might be expected, outside the law and literature movement, the articulation, reliance and applicability of the 'X as law'/'law as X' distinction have varied from field to field.[27] In some conceptualisations, the word 'in' is used for both parts of the distinction. For instance, drawing upon the work of

---

[24]   Robin L West, 'Literature, Culture and Law at Duke University' in Austin Sarat, Cathrine O Frank and Matthew Anderson (eds) *Teaching Law and Literature* (Modern Language Association, 2011) 98.

[25]   Jarrell D Wright, 'Transcending Law and Literature: Literature as Law in Plato, Vico, and Shelley' (2017) 29(2) *Law & Literature* 291, 293.

[26]   Robin Weisberg, 'The Law-Literature Enterprise' (1989) 1(1) *Yale Journal of Law & the Humanities* 1, 4.

[27]   For discussion see the chapters in Daniel Newman and Russell Sandberg (eds), *Law and Humanities* (Anthem Press, 2024).

Edward W Soja,[28] Alexandre Kedar has distinguished between 'geography in law' – that is, 'how geography and social space affect law and legal development' – and 'law in geography': 'how law contributes to the social production of space, … [and] the role of law in constructing, organising and legitimating social spatiality.'[29] Similarly, David Delaney has made the distinction between 'law in space' – the way in which situated legal practices, such as 'legislation or formal legal judgment, contribute to the shaping and reshaping of the spacialities of social life' – and 'space in law': 'the analysis and / or critique of the work that spatial representations perform in legal discourse'.[30] The use of the word 'as', 'in' or 'though' seems to make little difference. The point of the distinction is to underscore the interdisciplinary nature of the study – or even the transdisciplinary character of the study. Applying the distinction highlights how the study of law and literature is the work of both academic lawyers and literature experts, and how the study of legal geography is similarly the product of both lawyers and geographers, for instance. The language may differ but the point remains the same: the study of 'law and X' involves the study of the legal dimensions of X as well as the examination of law from the perspective of X. This underscores that the 'law and …' analysis is a two-way process.

However, the 'X as law'/'law as X' distinction variously articulated may ironically perpetuate disciplinary distinctions that frustrate its inter- or transdisciplinary potential. In the context of law and literature, Wright suggested that the way in which law and literature 'is structured into two main branches that are based on relatively narrow understandings of the relationship between "law" and "literature"' has meant that the movement has 'tended more toward

---

[28]   Soja distinguished two ways of looking at the relationship between law and geography: the first 'focuses on how geography or more broadly social space, social spatiality, affects law and legal development', examining how 'the law has always involved itself with the location of things, with disputes over turf, territories, boundaries, borders, jurisdictions'; the second deals with the reverse – 'how law shapes geographies' – exploring how 'legal understandings and knowledge of law are applied to help in understanding the social production of space, how social spatiality is constructed and organized and expressed': Edward W Soja, 'Afterword' (1996) 48 *Stanford Law Review* 1421, 1425, 1426.
[29]   Alexandre Kedar, 'On the Legal Geography of Ethnographic Settler States: Notes Towards a Research Agenda' in Jane Holder and Carolyn Harrison (eds) *Law and Geography* (Oxford University Press, 2003) 402, 406–407. See also Russell Sandberg, *Subversive Legal History: A Manifesto for the Future of Legal Education* (Routledge, 2021), Chapter 7.
[30]   David Delaney, 'Beyond the Word: Law as a Thing of this World' in Jane Holder and Carolyn Harrison (eds) *Law and Geography* (Oxford University Press, 2003) 67, 68–69.

bidisciplinarity than interdisciplinarity'.[31] The use of the conjunction 'and' has also been singled out for blame on grounds of perpetuating a binary and instrumental approach.[32] And there is significant tension between 'those who see law and literature as distinct fields with their own ways of finding meaning, and those approaching all texts as performative and open to multiple interpretations'.[33] In the law and geography context, Nicholas Bromley has criticised similar distinctions on the basis that this approach 'not only impoverishes inquiry into what is a complex and profoundly subtle relation, but also implicitly constricts two self-contained categories of discrete objects'.[34] This criticism, however, does not mean that such distinctions should be rejected. Rather, it means that emphasis in terms of law and geography should be made of how, in the words of David Delaney, 'the legal and the spatial, the discursive and the material, are inextricable'.[35] And the same could apply to other fields, taking us back to the 'dialectical interaction' written about in the context of law and religion by Witte.[36]

It is notable that the 'X as law'/'law as X' distinction does not comfortably apply to all 'law and ...' fields. For instance, while it can be said that law and history involves the fusion of legal and historical analyses, it is difficult to follow the approach of other interactions to claim that law and history could include the study of history through the frame of law and the study of law through the frame of history.[37] In terms of law and culture, whether the 'X as law'/'law as X' distinction applies depends in part on how the interaction is conceptualised. The distinction could be applied to law and culture as a whole, in that this includes the study of popular culture from a legal perspective as well as the study of law as a form of popular culture. This second aspect could just about be applied to law and performing arts, including fields such as law

---

[31] Jarrell D Wright, 'Transcending Law and Literature: Literature as Law in Plato, Vico, and Shelley' (2017) 29(2) *Law & Literature* 291, 292.

[32] Jeanne Gaakeer, 'Law and Literature' in Mortiner Sellers and Stephan Kirste (eds) *Encyclopaedia of the Philosophy of Law and Social Philosophy* (Springer, 2022).

[33] This can be conceptualised as 'formalists vs. subjectivists or foundationalist vs. anti-foundationalists': Mary Jane Schenck, 'Reading Law as Literature, Reading Literature as Law: A Pragmatist's Approach' (2013) 25 *Cahiers de Recherches Médiévales et Humanistes/Journal of Medieval and Humanistic Studies* 9, 25.

[34] Nicholas Bromley, *Law, Space and Geographies of Power* (Guilford Press, 1994) xiii.

[35] David Delaney, 'Beyond the Word: Law as a Thing of this World' in Jane Holder and Carolyn Harrison (eds) *Law and Geography* (Oxford University Press, 2003) 67, 71.

[36] John Witte, Jr, 'The Study of Law and Religion in the United States: An Interim Report' (2012) 14 *Ecclesiastical Law Journal* 327, 328.

[37] Russell Sandberg, 'Law and History' in Daniel Newman and Russell Sandberg (eds) *Law and Humanities* (Anthem, 2024) 87.

and art or law and music. The study of law as a dramatic act and as a narrative could be examined through the study of the theatrical nature of the courtroom, for instance. However, this second aspect does not apply to some of the particular media that come under the law and culture umbrella. While television, film and graphic novels could be examined from a legal perspective, it would be difficult to see how law could be examined from any of these angles. The 'law as X' label will rarely apply – except, perhaps, in discussion of law as narrative where legal texts could be likened to these media in terms of style, format or authorship.

The 'X as law'/'law as X' distinction may be more relevant to the study of law and culture, where the field is divided not by discipline but instead by genre. The distinction would seem to apply to the study of law and drama or comedy. Such studies would include 'law as X' through the study of law as a dramatic or comedic discourse. Studying 'X as law' could be interpreted narrowly as the way in which dramatic or comedic sentiments are given legal effect (and perhaps also the legal regulation of the manifestations of these arts), but could more fruitfully be broadened to include the study of the dramatic or comedic works from a legal perspective. This includes how such works include or exclude discussion of law; how they frame legal ideas; and both how their study can both enriched by an appreciation of their legal dimension and how such texts can enrich understandings of law, justice and society. Similar conclusions can be reached in relation to the developing field of law and science fiction,[38] which has also emerged from the studies of law and literature and law and popular culture.[39] Although Kieran Tranter has argued that the 'general lawlessness' of much science fiction was a major reason why law and humanities scholars paid little attention to science fiction (given their preoccupation with 'law in literature'),[40] there is now ample evidence of the study of the legal aspects of science fiction texts – a study that can be referred to as the study of 'science fiction as law'.[41] 'Law as science fiction', by contrast, could be used to refer to the study of how science fiction concepts, tropes and framings can be used to understand, critique and reinterpret laws (in the form of legal texts and also as legal discourse). It is also possible to conceptualise two 'law and

---

[38]   Though this raises the question of how science fiction is to be defined and also risks downplaying the importance of different media.

[39]   For an account of its development, see, eg, Kieran Tranter, *Living in Technical Legality: Science Fiction and Law as Technology* (Edinburgh University Press, 2018) 4–9.

[40]   Ibid 7.

[41]   Even according to the narrowest interpretation of science fiction as law, there is room to study laws explored in science fiction texts such as Asimov's 'Three Laws of Robotics' or the 'Prime Directive' in *Star Trek*: ibid.

X' distinctions as overlapping with one another. Caudill has commented how, for instance:

> a fictional text about a scientists testifying in court is not only a literary representation of law (law *in* literature), as well as a literary representation of a scientist (science *in* literature) but the testimony of the scientist is both a legally significant event (law *as* literature) and a scientific text (science *as* literature) that can be analyzed using literary critical or rhetorical tools.[42]

Moreover, the study of law and science provides evidence of why the 'X as law'/'law as X' distinction is useful. Like other 'law and ...' fields, 'law and science' refers to the field of two distinct systems that nevertheless are forced to rely upon each other.[43] This is true of both legal practice – where science often provides or assists with evidence – and the academic study of law, where a debate exists as to how scientific law should be.[44] As Cedric Charles Gilson has noted:

> law increasingly depends on science for determination of legal truth, so that its conclusions can be drawn more securely ... Law has a high expectation of science and scientists in this regard owing to the objectivity, rigour and precision extolled in its methods. It is disappointed when its evidence is doubtful, experts disagree or prove unreliable.[45]

Yet despite (perhaps because of) this dependence, law and science are seen as being distinct in terms of scholarship and methodologies.[46] Michael Freeman noted that 'unlike scientific truth, law is created, not discovered', and that while 'natural scientists use data, ... legal scholarship, by contrast, works with events'.[47] As Gilson put it, 'one is concerned with fact (science) and the other with legality (law)'.[48]

---

[42] David S Caudill, *Stories about Science in Law: Literary and Historical Images of Acquired Expertise* (Ashgate, 2011) 6.

[43] Michael Freeman, 'Law and Science: Science and Law' in Michael Freeman and Helen Reece (eds) *Science in Court* (Ashgate, 1998) 1.

[44] Ibid 3. 'There is some irony that, long before the interrelationship between law and science was explored, legal scholarship purported to model itself on the model of natural science': ibid 1.

[45] Cedric Charles Gilson, *The Law–Science Chasm: Bridging Law's Disaffection with Science as Evidence* (Quid Pro Books, 2012) iii.

[46] Michael Freeman, 'Law and Science: Science and Law' in Michael Freeman and Helen Reece (eds) *Science in Court* (Ashgate, 1998) 1.

[47] Ibid 2.

[48] Cedric Charles Gilson, *The Law–Science Chasm: Bridging Law's Disaffection with Science as Evidence* (Quid Pro Books, 2012) iv.

Yet, as with other 'law and ...' fields, the different perspectives of science reveal much about themselves from one another. As Caudill has noted, 'law is rhetorical, social and institutional involving ethical dimensions, credibility, cultural authority, and unstable interpretations. But so is science'.[49] In particular, the interaction between Law and Science reveals the way in which both are constructs. As Gilson noted, 'that science is socially constructed is a matter of which law often is unaware of might find incredible'.[50] Grasping this is revelatory for law's understanding of science in that 'law should realise that science represents only a system of inquiry: it is not a privileged source of knowledge, however profound this appears from the outside'.[51] Moreover, this also underscores that the same is true of law. The 'X as law'/'law as X' distinction, then, not only highlights both the differences and the interdependencies between law and the other, but also underscores the transformation that can be achieved by seeing law through the lens of the other and by seeing the other from the lens of law.

***

This exploration of the various ways in which other 'law and ...' fields use the 'X as law'/'law as X' distinction highlights that, although there is some difference in the detail, generally interdisciplinary 'law and ...' fields possess a dual character: they include exploring X from the perspective of law and exploring law from the perspective of X. Witte's schema suggests that similarly, the interdisciplinary study of law and religion can be understood as involving the study of law as religion (the study of how laws and legal mechanisms can be understood religiously) and the study of religion as law (the study of how religious texts and practices can be understood legally). Understood as an interdisciplinary endeavour, law and religion involves both reading law religiously and understanding religion legally. In the words of Witte, this involves understanding the 'dialectical interaction' between law and religion:[52] the way in which the two co-constitute, challenge and complement one another and how an absolute line cannot be drawn between them.

It is unclear, however, how prevalent this approach is, even within US scholarship. A recent collection edited by David C Flatto and Benjamin Porat became the first such work to be predicated upon this distinction and notably

---

[49]   David S Caudill, *Stories about Science in Law: Literary and Historical Images of Acquired Expertise* (Ashgate, 2011) 140.

[50]   Cedric Charles Gilson, *The Law–Science Chasm: Bridging Law's Disaffection with Science as Evidence* (Quid Pro Books, 2012) v.

[51]   Ibid iv.

[52]   John Witte, Jr, 'The Study of Law and Religion in the United States: An Interim Report' 14 (2012) *Ecclesiastical Law Journal* 327, 327–28.

described this as 'a different perspective that has emerged in recent scholarship which regards law and religion as overlapping frameworks'.[53] For Flatto and Porat, this represented a move away from the dominant 'dichotomous paradigm' that has dominated law and religion studies to date. Reaching a similar conclusion to Witte, the editors opined that this newer focus reveals that 'law and religion arguably share similar properties, and may have a symbiotic relationship'.

The editors identified four main and, in their view, influential discourses to which the chapters in their volume contribute. First, there is the rise of political theology and the resulting problematisation of the category of religion and the nexus between law, politics and religion. Second, there is the discourse on secularism which has considered how secularism is itself a constructed category complicating the categories of law and religion. The questioning and modifications of traditional approaches to Church–State relations constitutes the third discourse; while the fourth comprises those works that have 'addressed the foundational theme of divine law'. It is striking that many of these discourses have developed in literature outside the law school, with the editors giving examples of works from religious studies, theology, philosophy, sociology and history which have formed part of these discourses. Their work underscores that an interdisciplinary approach to law and religion needs to include both the study of law as religion as well as the dominant and legalistic study of religion as law.

To date, however, the field of law and religion in the UK has rarely achieved this ambition. Though there are notable exceptions, the study of law and religion on this side of the Atlantic has not yet developed into an interdisciplinary endeavour. In England and Wales, law and religion has largely developed in law schools[54] and has focused on the 'legal dimensions on religion'; it has studied religion as law – how religious texts and practices can be understood legally. By contrast, little attention has been given to the 'religious dimensions of law': studying law as religion – how laws and legal mechanisms can be understood religiously.[55]

---

[53] David C Flatto and Benjamin Porat, 'Introduction' in David C Flatto and Benjamin Porat (eds) *Law as Religion, Religion as Law* (Cambridge University Press, 2023) 1.

[54] And there are important questions about the identity of the scholars who have done much of this work in terms of their religion, race, gender and geography, as well as their own religion or belief.

[55] This involves critically revisiting the concept of law, as noted by Anne Beutter, 'Concepts of "Law" as Both Tools and Objects in the Study of Religion: A Case From 1950s Ghana – Or When May A Christian Slaughter Sheep' (2023) *Method and Theory in the Study of Religion* (online).

In his 'interim report' of the study of law and religion in the US, Witte described how, 'in the vast new law and religion literature that has emerged in the American academy over the past three decades, ten themes stand out, some more prominent than others'.[56] The extent to which these trends are also identifiable in the English and Welsh literature is instructive in showing the extent to which law and religion studies in England and Wales lag behind the US experience.

Witte's first trend is that 'by far the largest body of law and religion scholarship is devoted to the American law of religious freedom'. This tendency can also be found in the English and Welsh literature. Questions concerning religious freedom as a constitutional and human right dominate the agenda in Europe as a whole, as shown by the traditional focus on Church–State relations or religion–State relations as it became known. However, as Witte noted, increasingly this requires the study of not only constitutional provisions but also a wide range of areas of law (including 'laws governing evidence, civil procedure, taxation, bankruptcy, labour, employment, workplace, military, immigration, prisons, hospitals, land use, zoning, education, charity, child care and more'),[57] as well as rules and norms created at sub-national levels. This shift has also occurred on this side of the Atlantic, as shown by criticism and revision by Norman Doe and myself of approaches of models of Church–State relations that focused mainly on constitutional provisions.[58] Yet even once the focus has shifted from the constitutional letter to the legal provisions that regulate religion, the approach remains State-centric. As Frank S Ravitch has noted, 'Law and religion is a vast field covering the many issues that arise when government and religion come into contact, as well as a number of issues entirely in the public sphere.'[59] It seems that law and religion studies in England and Wales are not that far behind the US model with regard to this first trend, though the focus here has been on the mainstream interactions.[60] As the work of Rebecca Riedel has highlighted, the dominant approach has been

---

[56]   John Witte, Jr, 'The Study of Law and Religion in the United States: An Interim Report' 14 (2012) *Ecclesiastical Law Journal* 327, 342.

[57]   Ibid 342–43.

[58]   Russell Sandberg and Norman Doe, 'Church–State Relations in Europe' (2007) 1(5) *Religion Compass* 561; Russell Sandberg, 'Church–State Relations in Europe: From Legal Models to an Interdisciplinary Approach' (2008) 1(3) *Journal of Religion in Europe* 329; and Norman Doe, *Law and Religion in Europe* (Oxford University Press, 2011).

[59]   Frank S Ravitch, *Advanced Introduction to Law and Religion* (Edward Elgar Publishing, 2023) 1.

[60]   As highlighted and in part corrected, however, by the case studies explored in Patrick S Nash, *British Islam and English Law: A Classical Pluralist Perspective* (Cambridge University Press, 2022).

on how religious freedom can be accommodated; less attention has been paid to the policing of religion as a harm, meaning that there has been little discussion of terrorism in the law and religion literature, for instance.[61]

Witte's second trend is related to the first: it consists of 'the study of comparative and international laws of religious freedom and of the religious sources and dimensions of human rights'.[62] This trend too is identifiable in Europe, not least due to the considerable attention given to the decisions of the European Court of Human Rights.[63] However, Witte is correct to assert that this study should not only focus on how law sees religion, but also include how religion sees law. He wrote that in the US, two 'small libraries of books' have developed: one has 'emerged analysing the wide range of human rights issues that confront religious persons and communities today'; while the other documents 'the contributions of the main world religions, especially Western Christianity, to modern understandings of human rights'.[64] While the central question of the first library of books 'is whether freedom of religion and belief is something distinctive or simply the sum of all the other rights that other parties can claim'; the second library focuses on 'whether human rights are a universal good of human nature or a distinctly Western (Christian) invention that has no easy resonance in other cultures with different founding beliefs and values'.[65] On this side of the Atlantic, although there are notable exceptions,[66] it would be fair to say that the first small library of books is getting increasingly fuller than the second.[67]

---

[61] Rebecca Riedel, 'A Critical Legal Study of the Prevent Duty: The Religious Dimension' (PhD thesis submitted to Cardiff University, 2023).

[62] John Witte, Jr, 'The Study of Law and Religion in the United States: An Interim Report' 14 (2012) *Ecclesiastical Law Journal* 327, 343.

[63] For discussion of the importance of the ECHR see Frank Cranmer, 'The European Convention on Human Rights: A Living Leading Work' in Russell Sandberg (ed) *Leading Works in Law and Religion* (Routledge, 2019) 55.

[64] John Witte, Jr, 'The Study of Law and Religion in the United States: An Interim Report' 14 (2012) 14 *Ecclesiastical Law Journal* 327, 344.

[65] Ibid 343. For an excellent example of this see Pauline Kollontai and Fredrich Lohamnn, *On the Significnace of Religion for Human Rights* (Routledge, 2023).

[66] See, e.g., Roger Rushton, *Human Rights and the Image of God* (SCM Press, 2004).

[67] The literature on the topic is vast, including several book-length accounts: Malcolm D Evans, *Religious Liberty and International Law in Europe* (Cambridge University Press, 1997); Caroline Evans, *Freedom of Religion and the European Convention on Human Rights* (Oxford University Press, 2002); and Paul M Taylor, *Freedom of Religion – UN and European Human Rights Law and Practice* (Cambridge University Press, 2005); Caroline K Roberts, *Freedom of Religion or Belief in the European Convention on Human Rights: A Reappraisal* (Cambridge University Press, 2023).

For Witte, the 'third large body of scholarship in American law schools has gathered around the perennially contested issues of law, religion and family life'.[68] Witte singles this out in particular due to the fact that 'historically in the West and in many religious communities still today, the marital household was viewed as both a spiritual and temporal institution, and sexual activity had both moral and corporeal dimensions'. He wrote that much scholarship has been dedicated to 'three new questions at the intersection of law, religion and family': the 'growing contests between religious liberty and sexual liberty'; issues arising from 'religiously based polygamy'; and 'the growing call by selected Muslims and other religious minorities to opt out of the State's family law system and into their own religious legal systems'.[69] Much ink has been dedicated to these issues in the UK too, especially in more recent years. While it may be questioned why the interaction with the family should be singled out as opposed to (say) the interaction with the education system, Witte's focus on 'law, religion and family life' is increasingly reflected in the literature in England and Wales, although much of the literature on Witte's third point tends to be categorised as family law rather than as law and religion here.[70] This is true of the significant literature on the interaction between religion and marriage law.[71] This is a sign perhaps that law and religion has become narrowly defined – or at least has not developed sufficiently.

Witte's fourth trend refers to work relating to the 'larger question about the overall place of religious legal systems in Western democracies and the forms and functions of law within organised religious bodies'.[72] This includes the study of what he refers to as 'internal legal systems' and what others have called 'the internal laws of religions'[73] or simply 'religious law'.[74] These are often seen as a topic discrete from the study of national and international laws

---

[68]　John Witte, Jr, 'The Study of Law and Religion in the United States: An Interim Report' (2012) 14 *Ecclesiastical Law Journal* 327, 344.

[69]　Ibid 345–46.

[70]　I have lost count of the number of people who have thought that I was a family law expert because I have written on this topic.

[71]　Such as Rajnaara C Akhtar, Patrick Nash and Rebecca Probert (eds), *Cohabitation and Religious Marriage* (Bristol University Press, 2020); and Rebecca Probert, Rajnaara C Akhtar and Sharon Blake, *Belief in Marriage: The Evidence for Reforming Weddings Law* (Bristol University Press, 2023).

[72]　John Witte, Jr, 'The Study of Law and Religion in the United States: An Interim Report' (2012) 14 *Ecclesiastical Law Journal* 327, 346.

[73]　Burkhard Josef Berkmann, *The Internal Law of Religions: Introduction to a Comparative Discipline* (Routledge, 2020). See also the articles in (2022) *Ancilla Iuris.*

[74]　Rossella Bottoni and Silvio Ferrari (eds), *Routledge Handbook of Religious Laws* (Routledge, 2019); Norman Doe, *Comparative Religious Law: Judaism, Christianity, Islam* (Cambridge University Press, 2018).

affecting religion. For instance, Ravitch begins his *Advanced Introduction to Law and Religion* by saying that: 'The field of law and religion also includes religious law, for example canon law, halacha, and shariah. While religious law is a fascinating – one worthy of many volumes – it is beyond the scope of this book.'[75]

The study of religious law is as pronounced on this side of the Atlantic, if not more pronounced as Witte conceded, and there is a growing move towards comparative study as scholars 'have seen clearly the need to deepen our legal, cultural and religious understandings across Muslim, Christian and Jewish lines and to develop a pan-Abrahamic jurisprudence of public, private, penal and procedural law'.[76] The work of Doe has been world-leading in this regard.[77] However, although there are some exceptions,[78] the focus is very much on Western religious systems and upon the most mainstream forms of the religion in question. And it invariably remains separated out from the general field of law and religion, similar to the approach of Ravitch's *Advanced Introduction*.

Witte identified his fifth trend as emerging from such works on religious law, writing that:

> the emerging new scholarship on religious legal systems has moved into a broader scholarly inquiry about the influence of world religions on the secular legal systems around them, both historically and currently. Part of this inquiry concerns the exportation, transplantation or accommodation of discrete internal religious rules or procedures into secular legal systems. But more of it concerns the influence of religious ideas and practices of each of these world religions on the public, private, penal and procedural law of the state.[79]

This study, of the influence of religion upon law, is neglected in the UK literature, with the exception of historical accounts of the legacy of the significant jurisdiction formerly enjoyed by the ecclesiastical courts. For Witte, however, such work falls under a sixth identifiable trend, since 'as a specialised form of this last topic, American jurists have long studied the historical influence of Christianity on the Western legal tradition'. This too has been a focus of UK

---

[75] Frank S Ravitch, *Advanced Introduction to Law and Religion* (Edward Elgar Publishing, 2023) 1.

[76] John Witte, Jr, 'The Study of Law and Religion in the United States: An Interim Report' (2012) 14 *Ecclesiastical Law Journal* 327, 348.

[77] John Witte Jr, 'Law at the Backbone: The Christian Legal Ecumenism of Norman Doe' (2022) 24(2) *Ecclesiastical Law Journal* 192.

[78] See, eg, Werner F Menski, *Hindu Law: Beyond Tradition and Modernity* (Oxford University Press, 2003); and Rebecca Redwood French and Mark A Nathan (eds), *Buddhism and Law: An Introduction* (Cambridge, 2015).

[79] John Witte, Jr, 'The Study of Law and Religion in the United States: An Interim Report' (2012) 14 *Ecclesiastical Law Journal* 327, 348.

scholarship. Indeed, as might be expected, it is in historical matters that there is greatest overlap between the UK and US literatures, with the work of Richard Helmholz being especially influential on both sides of the Atlantic.[80]

The seventh and eighth trends identified by Witte show a US focus on questions of legal philosophy. The seventh trend is that 'natural law theory is becoming a topic of growing interest in American law schools'; while the eighth is how 'natural law arguments often inform a related area of continued importance in law and religion study: the topic of legal ethics'.[81] Work along these lines has not been prevalent in the UK law and religion community, with the exception of an edited collection by Doe,[82] in which I called for a jurisprudence of Christian law.[83] There has been little focus on the question of religion and legal ethics, however – especially of the question Witte poses as the focus of this new area: 'What does it mean to be a Christian, Jewish, Muslim, Hindu or Buddhist lawyer at work in a secular legal system?'[84] Witte wrote that this is connected to the ninth trend, in that 'this last question – about the place of the religious believer in the legal profession – has raised the broader question of the place of overt religious arguments in legal discourse altogether'. This, too, has led to a small cluster of works in the UK literature.[85]

Witte's tenth and final trend is that 'questions of law and religious language have also raised broader questions about the overlaps between legal and theological interpretation, translation and hermeneutics'.[86] However, although it has been suggested that interdisciplinary work on law and religion in the UK should increasingly take this form,[87] to date there has been little interdisciplinary work under the law and religion banner that involves disciplines such as

---

[80]   As reflected in the essays in Troy Harris (ed), *Studies in Canon Law and Common Law in Honor of R H Helmholz* (Robbins Collection Publications, 2015).

[81]   John Witte, Jr, 'The Study of Law and Religion in the United States: An Interim Report' (2012) 14 *Ecclesiastical Law Journal* 327, 349, 350.

[82]   Norman Doe (ed) *Christianity and Natural Law: An Introduction* (Cambridge University Press, 2017).

[83]   Russell Sandberg, 'Towards a Jurisprudence of Christian Law' in Norman Doe (ed) *Christianity and Natural Law: An Introduction* (Cambridge University Press, 2017) 220. This is one of my law and religion publications of the last decade that I have not drawn on in this book.

[84]   John Witte, Jr, 'The Study of Law and Religion in the United States: An Interim Report' 14 (2012) *Ecclesiastical Law Journal* 327, 350.

[85]   Such as Jonathan Chaplin, 'Law, Religion and Public Reason' (2012) 1(2) *Oxford Journal of Law and Religion* 319.

[86]   John Witte, Jr, 'The Study of Law and Religion in the United States: An Interim Report' 14 (2012) *Ecclesiastical Law Journal* 327, 351.

[87]   Celia G Kenny, 'New Directions in the Confluence of Law and Religion' in Frank Cranmer, Celia Kenny, Mark Hill and Russell Sandberg (eds) *The Confluence of Law and Religion* (Cambridge University Press, 2016) 262.

linguistics, anthropology, media studies and the various forms of theology and religious studies.

It is notable that the US trends that are less evident in England and Wales are all outside the religion law/religious law distinction. In particular, the US experience seems more advanced in terms of exploring law religiously and developing interdisciplinary approaches. Indeed, even Witte's elucidation of law and religion does not and cannot capture the full possibilities of exploring all aspects of the interaction between religion and law. Yet Witte's conceptualisation of law and religion is preferable to that which has dominated in England and Wales – a conceptualisation that I have helped to create and which I have perpetuated.

7.   My confession

John Witte Jr's 'Interim Report' on law and religion in the US shows the potential of imagining law and religion as an interdisciplinary field which pays as much attention to law as religion as to religion as law.[1] This contrasts with how law and religion has developed in the first couple of decades of the twenty-first century in England and Wales as a legal sub-discipline. On this side of the Atlantic, the focus has been very much on religion as law and even there most work has concentrated on a very narrow understanding of the legal dimensions on religion. Attention has tended to be afforded to understanding how national and international laws regulate religion (which I have labelled as 'religion law') and the challenges that religious conviction (both individually and collectively held) pose for the State. There has been some growing focus upon how religious groups use law to regulate their own internal affairs (which I have referred to as 'religious law') but even there the focus in much of the literature has been very much upon debating the proper role of the State.

There are many reasons why this has been so. A lot of research on religion by legal scholars has been shaped by the legal controversies of the day. In the shadow of 9/11, moral panics about religious dress and symbols, whether religions can discriminate on grounds of sexual orientation and the operation of religious courts and tribunals commanded attention in both the headlines and the law journals. Moreover, the way in which law and religion quickly developed as a legal sub-discipline shaped its agenda. Although it lacks the shelves of textbooks that characterise most legal sub-disciplines, works in the field together with the organisation of papers at specialist conferences have nevertheless shaped what is included and what is excluded. The focus has been upon religious rights and the extent to which religious difference should be accommodated – in short, the 'problem' of religion in the public sphere.

This understanding of law and religion has been perpetuated in my work – not only in my publications, but also through my activities in creating LARSN, managing a law and religion book series, developing the undergraduate module on law and religion at Cardiff University and so on. The unintended effect of attempting to bolster law and religion as a mainstream legal sub-discipline has

---

[1]   John Witte, Jr., 'The Study of Law and Religion in the United States: An Interim Report' (2012) 14 *Ecclesiastical Law Journal* 327.

been to constrain the field in such a way that it became marginalised once its initial preoccupations became less newsworthy. In particular, blame can be attributed to the religion law/religious law distinction.

***

To recap, the religion law/religious law distinction was made to stress that the study of law and religion included the external study of how religion interacted with national and international legal authorities (called 'religion law') and the internal study of the rules, norms and laws developed by religious authorities themselves (called 'religious law'). Such a distinction was necessary, in my view, for a number of reasons. Although a number of terms have been used to describe the academic analysis of the way in which law interacts with religion, they have all been found to be insufficient and to focus solely on understanding religion legally, with an even narrower focus than the religion law/religious law distinction.

The term 'ecclesiastical law' is the label most prevalent historically in England and also popularly used by continental scholars: the sub-discipline is known as '*droit ecclésiastique*' in France; '*diritto ecclesiastico*' in Italy; and '*derecho eclesiástico*' in Spain.[2] However, there are at least three different (and contradictory) understandings of the term in English scholarship and practice.[3] Catholic scholars have used 'ecclesiastical law' to describe all the law created for the Church by God and by the Church. For example, Georg May has contended that the term 'ecclesiastical law' describes the 'entirety of the norms of the law laid down by God and by the Church', but does not include laws regulating Church affairs that are made by the State.[4] In contrast, continental scholars have used the term to describe exclusively to law created by the State for the Church.[5] For such scholars, 'ecclesiastical law' is synonymous with the phrase 'Church–State relations', now sometimes referred to as 'religion–State relations' – which itself is a problematic phrase since it gives the erroneous impression that religion is only affected by constitutional laws.[6]

---

[2]   There are some exceptions: in Germany, the sub-discipline is called *Staat kirchenrecht*. See Bridgette Basdevant-Gaudemet, 'Historie du Droit Ecclésiastique en Europe' in J Valle and A Hollerbach (eds) *The Teaching of Church–State Relations in European Universities* (Peeters, 2005) 1, 19.

[3]   Norman Doe, *The Legal Framework of the Church of England* (Clarendon Press, 1996) 12–15.

[4]   Georg May, 'Ecclesiastical Law' in K Rahner, *Encyclopaedia of Theology* (T &T Clark, 1981) 395.

[5]   See, for instance, the essays in J Valle and A Hollerbach (eds) *The Teaching of Church–State Relations in European Universities* (Peeters, 2005).

[6]   See, further, Russell Sandberg and Norman Doe, 'Church–State Relations in Europe' (2007) 1(5) *Religion Compass* 561; Russell Sandberg, 'Church–State

The first and second understandings of the term 'ecclesiastical law' are, therefore, completely contradictory. The third understanding of the term arises in the context of England, where the label has taken on a technical meaning being 'used to denote the law of the Church of England, howsoever created'.[7] This definition has been used by both the legislature[8] and the judiciary.[9] This third definition is both narrower and wider than the previous two. It is narrower in that it concerns exclusively the law pertaining to the Church of England. It is wider, however, in that – like the Catholic definition but unlike the continental definition – it includes laws made by the Church; and – like the continental definition but unlike the Catholic definition – it includes laws made for the Church by the State.

The term 'canon law' is also insufficient, since it too has been bestowed with several different, often contradictory meanings.[10] Even within the context of the Church of England, the term is sometimes used very narrowly simply to describe a particular source of law in the Church of England, the Canons;[11] while some commentators use the term to describe all law applicable to the Church of England.[12] It is questionable whether the term is useful to describe the norms of Christian groups other than the Church of England and the Catholic Church.[13] It is debatable whether the term can be used to describe the laws of Christian churches generally,[14] as shown by the increasing use of the

---

Relations in Europe: From Legal Models to an Interdisciplinary Approach' (2008) 1(3) *Journal of Religion in Europe* 329; and Norman Doe, *Law and Religion in Europe* (Oxford University Press, 2011).

[7]   Mark Hill, *Ecclesiastical Law* (3rd edition, Oxford University Press, 2007) 1.

[8]   See, for example, the Welsh Church Act 1914.

[9]   See, for example, *Aston Cantlow v Wallbank* [2001] EWCA Civ 713 para 8.

[10]   See Norman Doe, *The Legal Framework of the Church of England* (Clarendon Press, 1996) 12–13.

[11]   For example, 'the expression "canon law" is used restrictively to mean the Canons of the Church of England' (M Hill, *Ecclesiastical Law* (3rd edition, Oxford University Press, 2007) 2).

[12]   See, for instance, the assertion that canon law is 'so much of the law of England as is concerned with the regulation of the affairs of the Church of England'; its sources include theology (embracing divine law); the common law of England; and Acts of Parliament': Tim Briden and Brian Hanson, *Moore's Introduction to English Canon Law* (3rd edition, Mowbrays, 1992).

[13]   Gordon Arthur, *Law, Liberty and Church: Authority and Justice in the Major Churches in England* (Ashgate, 2006) 172.

[14]   Compare Silvio Ferrari, 'Canon Law as a Religious Legal System' in Andrew Huxley (ed) *Religion, Law and Tradition: Comparative Studies in Religious Law* (Routledge, 2002) 49, which focuses purely on the law of the Catholic Church.

term 'Christian law'.[15] The term 'canon law' is even more objectionable as a synonym for religious law generally, given its Christian connotations.

The religion law/religious law distinction grew out of the realisation that existing labels for the subject of study were inadequate. It also resulted from the realisation that law and religion needed to encompass the subjects of both the narrower and wider understandings of these existing phrases and the recognition that the study of the legal relationship between the Church of England and the State required the analysis of both these internal and external norms. The constitutional posture of the Church of England as being established by law means that several legal instruments and sources within the Church of England cannot be classified as being either internal or external in creation or application.[16] From the understanding that the law of the Church of England thus necessarily requires the study of both internally produced and externally produced laws came the insight that the same was likely true of other religious bodies, so this needed to be reflected in the study of law and religion. This was articulated in the religion law/religious law distinction, which was accompanied by the assertions that these were two complementary and overlapping entities, and that 'the study of Law and Religion is at least the study of Religion Law and Religious Law'.[17]

***

Comparing it with Witte's schema, the problem with my religion law/religious law distinction becomes clear. It focuses primarily, if not exclusively upon religion as law – on understanding religion legally. Religious law perhaps provides some focus on law as religion – reading religious norms and practices legally – but this has not been fully developed.[18] Other than that, attention is rarely paid to law as religion – reading legal practices through the lens of

---

[15]   Norman Doe, *Christian Law: Contemporary Principles* (Cambridge University Press, 2013).

[16]   Measures of the Church of England, for instance, are internally produced to the extent that they are created and developed by the General Synod of the Church of England; but are externally produced in that they are then considered by the Ecclesiastical Committee of the UK Parliament, require Royal Assent and, when enacted, have the same effect as an Act of Parliament. See Russell Sandberg, *Law and Religion* (Cambridge University Press, 2011), especially Chapter 4.

[17]   Russell Sandberg, *Law and Religion* (Cambridge University Press, 2011) 6.

[18]   Though there has been some work on the theology of law – on which see, eg, John Comaroff, 'Reflections on the Rise of Legal Theology' (2009) 53(1) *Social Analysis* 193; and, for a leading UK example, see David H McIlroy, *A Trinitarian Theology of Law* (Paternosters, 2009). See also Norman Doe, 'Law and Theology' in Daniel Newman and Russell Sandberg (eds) *Law and Humanities* (Anthem Press, 2024) 201.

religion. There is a need to study law and religion as two distinct spheres not only in how they interact with one another, but also in how they see and reconstruct one another on their own terms. The study of law and religion, therefore, needs to focus not only on the interactions between law and religion but also on understanding how religion is and can be understood legally and how law is and can be understood religiously – in other words, how law and religion regard, construct and reconstruct one another.

The development of law and religion as a legal sub-discipline has itself gone largely unquestioned. While literature in other 'law and ...' areas have developed with close interaction with people, literatures and methods from other disciplines, academic lawyers have dominated the study of law and religion in England and Wales, and the work in the field remains characterised by academic isolationism; references to work completed outside the law school is commonplace, but the synthesis of work and approaches from other parts of the academy within works of law and religion scholarship remains exceptional.

The legal nature of law and religion scholarship has narrowly construed and interpreted 'religion'. The work of Suhraiya Jivraj has criticised what she refers to as 'socio-legal law-and-religion scholarship' for 'conceptualizing religion in predominately theological terms such as belief /faith and practice', which 'tends to marginalize [the] racialization of non-Christianness' and understands religion 'as a contingent concept that can come to be produced within law'.[19] Jivraj argues that this is equally true of law and religion scholarship that accepts 'more complex notions of religious identity', in that these works perpetuate 'an onto-theological model of belief and ritual practice' that is 'so often left un-interrogated'.[20] She argues that a critical approach deriving from anthropology, religious studies and critical race studies is required that understands religion contextually and historically 'as contingent upon and as part of particular political, economic, and other circumstances' to 'challenge not only the onto-theological notion of religion through various methodological routes, but also the idea that there can be any fixed concept of religion at all'.[21]

Jivraj's critique underscores the problematic consequences of the isolated way in which law and religion scholarship has developed. The moral panics that provided its context have narrowed its focus and its ambition. They also highlight the question of the authorship of law and religion work. It is noticeable that much of the law and religion literature in England and Wales

---

[19]   Suhraiya Jivraj, *The Religion of Law: Race, Citizenship and Children's Belonging* (Palgrave, 2013) 82.
[20]   Ibid 28.
[21]   Ibid 6–7.

– particularly books with those two words or variations of those two words in the title – tend to be written or edited by white men who tend to be either Christian or agnostic (and even then are invariably culturally Christian). I include myself in this category. In writing about the various problems of law and religion over the years, I am writing about matters that are not problems for me. My assumptions, values and biases inform my work even in stating the legal position, let alone analysing it. Take, for instance, the religious rights claims made by Iftikhar Ahmad, Shabina Begum and Nadia Eweida. A number of compromises and accommodations were made for them prior to them bringing their cases. How can I – as someone who does not share their beliefs and background, and who has not faced any issues remotely similar – question, let alone determine, whether such accommodations were sufficient?

The problem of authorial bias is especially pronounced where such work explicitly and implicitly sets out to define the field. This could result in the conclusion that I should not be doing these things. I should not be writing this book. Yet it will not surprise you that I do not agree with that proposition. I think that academics can write as outsiders, but that we need to be conscious of that fact. This requires us to be not only reflective and critical of our own biases, but also committed to using our position to amplify the voices of those who lack our privilege. This is where we have been found wanting. There is a need to encourage, support and foster law and religion scholarship by authors who are not 'male, pale and stale', and who have not experienced a Christian-centric, Westernised upbringing. We also need to ensure that the voices of those we study and write about are heard and are not transmitted through, and thus constrained by, our framework. To date, this has been a failing of the field and a personal failure.

These concerns are rarely discussed in the law and religion literature. Aside from my navel gazing, little attention has been given to questioning how the field has developed and how it may develop in the future.[22] The near absence of textbook or student-friendly texts has meant that, unlike other legal areas, there have been only a few attempts to map the field as a whole – or even to formulate a conception (either explicitly or implicitly) of what is taught and researched under the banner of 'law and religion' in law schools. More significantly, perhaps, the reflections that have taken place have tended to describe and list research outputs. True, there have been some attempts to classify these and to predict trends for the future; but there has been little, if any attempt

---

[22] For notable exceptions, see Anthony Bradney, 'Politics and Sociology: New Research Agenda for the Study of Law and Religion' in Richard O'Dair and Andrew Lewis (eds) *Law and Religion* (Oxford University Press, 2001) 65; and the essays published as part of the 25th anniversary of the Ecclesiastical Law Society in (2012) 14 *Ecclesiastical Law Journal*.

to understand more broadly how law and religion has developed not just as a collection of outputs but as a community of scholars, and the values, biases, objectives and culture of that community (or indeed communities).

Law and religion has developed as a legal sub-discipline predicated upon the assumption that the presence of religion in the public sphere is problematic, and that this is something for the State and international bodies to solve. It focuses on religious rights. The juridification of religion – the rise of positive religious rights articulated in human rights and discrimination provisions – has undoubtedly stimulated the growth of law and religion. Yet the way in which the field has developed has been uneven. This may in part be because of the way in which these religious rights have become paper tigers; but it is also because of the way in which law and religion was fashioned as a legal sub-discipline, taking account of its topicality to institutionalise the field.

There are some signs that law and religion is as well established (if not more established) than some other newly formed legal sub-disciplines such as sports law or education law. This is evident in terms of the number of specialist journals, the establishment of bespoke book series and the thriving societies formed at both the national and international level. However, there are other signs that law and religion is less well established than other sub-disciplines. Law and religion lags behind other sub-disciplines in terms of the number of courses taught and the quantity of works aimed at a student readership, for instance. Law and religion has remained stuck in a state of adolescence.

There remains a lack of identity and a suspicion that law and religion may not be more than the sum of its parts – an undeveloped Frankenstein's monster of other 'proper' legal areas.[23] A suspicion remains that what we are dealing with is not the development of a new area of study but rather a number of separate areas of interaction between religion and discrete, well-established areas of law. Most of the time, the only connection that unites law and religion work is that its focuses on religion. Developments concerning religion in criminal law, discrimination law, human rights law, family law and so on can be understood solely in those terms. They are not interrelated to the degree that they ought to be understood as part of an overall body of law concerning religion. There is a question, therefore, as to whether the study of law and religion amounts to more than the sum of its parts. It needs to be asked whether recent years have simply seen questions concerning religion become of importance in discrimination law, human rights law, family law and so on;

---

[23]   Similar concerns have been raised in relation to family law, as discussed by Gillian Douglas, *An Introduction to Family Law* (2nd edition, Clarendon Press, 2004) 3–4. In relation to sports law, see, e.g., Mark James, *Sports Law* (Palgrave Macmillan, 2010) 19; and Simon Gardiner et al, *Sports Law* (3rd edition, Cavendish, 2006) 88–91.

or whether such developments are interrelated to the degree that they ought to be understood as part of an overall legal framework concerning religion. This is not simply a questioning of the boundaries between legal fields of study: dividing lines drawn in the name of convenience are always arbitrary and the product of their age. Rather, the question here is whether there exists an area of analysis and/or a body of law that justifies the existence of law and religion as a legal sub-discipline; or whether law and religion is better understood as an interaction between religion and a series of discrete legal topics. This requires contemplating the possibility that law and religion does not really exist.

Although law and religion has not to date become a fully formed legal sub-discipline, ironically, the structures set up in order to help grow the sub-discipline – such as specialist journals and associations – have ended up constraining it. Much law and religion work is being disseminated in ways and in places that limit its appeal to those already within the clique. There are, of course, exceptions – especially where the particular law and religion scholar is also an expert in the wider area of law, such as work on religious discrimination and international human rights law. However, generally law and religion scholars spend a lot of time talking to each other – at specialist conferences and in the pages of dedicated journals and book series.

There is a real risk of ghettoisation: a danger that law and religion scholars will be immune from and unable to shape wider debates within the discipline of law (not to mention the wider risks caused by the academic isolationism of law and religion scholarship that comes from such work being mainly situated in law schools). As Anthony Bradney has warned, the development of a common language may 'limit the possibilities or argument and conceal the realities of the subject-matter under discussion'.[24] Law and religion scholarship has not benefited as much as it could have done from wider expertise and insights (both in and outside of law schools). The commonly assumed context of the juridification of religion, which is seen as providing the catalyst for the expansion and development of law and religion scholarship, has also limited the focus and reach of law and religion scholarship. Indeed, it is striking that as the number of legal changes affecting religion has slowed down in recent years, the field has shown some signs of stagnation. The state of adolescence that law and religion finds itself in is very damaging, especially given how long it has now lasted for. The growth spurts of law and religion were now over a decade ago. Since then, the picture has been one of stagnation, if not decline. There are exceptions to the rule; but it is striking that much of the most impressive contributions in recent years have criticised the nature or assumptions of

---

[24]   Anthony Bradney, 'The Rise and Rise of Legal Education' (1997) 4 *Web Journal of Current Legal Issues*, http://webjcli.ncl.ac.uk/1997/issue4/bradney4.html.

law and religion scholarship[25] or have sought to position themselves outside the field, either explicitly or implicitly.[26]

The partial development of law and religion as a legal sub-discipline has, therefore, created the worst of both worlds. On the one hand, the fact that law and religion is not sufficiently advanced as a legal sub-discipline means that there is still a lingering perception that it is not stronger than the sum of its parts; that it is a Frankenstein's monster of discrete areas of law that happen to interact with religion but ultimately have little in common with each other and do not collectively constitute a legal framework. On the other hand, the attempt to formulate law and religion as a legal sub-discipline has meant that the field has become ghettoised, with law and religion scholars increasingly just talking to one another and with their work becoming isolated from developments and trends within the wider areas of law that they are writing about. Moreover, this has meant that law and religion has developed as an activity largely situated within law schools. Rather than developing as the interdisciplinary study envisaged by Witte,[27] the study of law and religion in England and Wales has largely been constrained to the study of the legal dimensions of religion – the extent to which the State can and should accommodate religious difference. The blossoming of interest in law and religion in England and Wales has been short-lived. The institutional developments that followed with improper haste have limited rather than facilitated the growth of the kind of interdisciplinary endeavour that Witte wrote about.

The very structures set up in order to help grow the sub-discipline have ended up constraining it. And I have played a role in that. The religion law/ religious law distinction, despite its good intentions, has narrowed rather than liberated the field. It should be abandoned. The various institutionalised man-ifestations of law and religion – the research groupings, book series, journals and so on – need not be scrapped but require reform; they need to be opened up as part of a wider interdisciplinary movement. This means that even the

---

[25]   This is particular true of work based on doctoral research: Patrick S Nash, *British Islam and English Law: A Classical Pluralist Perspective* (Cambridge University Press, 2022); Caroline K Roberts, *Freedom of Religion or Belief in the European Convention on Human Rights: A Reappraisal* (Cambridge University Press, 2023); Rebecca Riedel, 'A Critical Legal Study of the Prevent Duty: The Religious Dimension' (PhD thesis submitted to Cardiff University, 2023). See also the work of Méadhbh McIvor, who employs a social anthologist approach (Méadhbh McIvor, *Representing God: Christian Legal Activism in Contemporary England* (Princeton University Press, 2020)).

[26]   Such as Javier Garcia Oliva and Helen Hall, *Religion, Law and the Constitution: Balancing Beliefs in Britain* (Routledge, 2018), and the work on religion and marriage law.

[27]   John Witte, Jr, 'The Study of Law and Religion in the United States: An Interim Report' (2012) 14 *Ecclesiastical Law Journal* 327.

most foundational taken-for-granted principles and ideas need to be rethought. Having identified the problem, the question is now: what can be done about it? Before exploring a way forward, it is necessary to explore how other fields comparable to law and religion have developed and to examine what can be learned from the different ways in which they have grown. This will be the focus of the second part of this book.

Excursus I

Meanwhile, in an alternative timeline...

The victory of the Conservative Party in the UK's 1997 General Election was quite unexpected. The real shock, however, had occurred two years earlier, when John Redwood successfully challenged John Major in the leadership contest and became leader of the party and therefore Prime Minister. Redwood's government was Eurosceptic and populist and had won the 1997 election by demonising the Labour opposition – and in particular, its 'lefty lawyer' leader Tony Blair's enthusiasm for the European Union.

The Labour Party's manifesto commitment for a new Human Rights Act was particularly savaged by Redwood's Conservatives as a further means of giving up control to Brussels bureaucrats, ignoring the inconvenient fact that the human rights concerned came from the Council of Europe – an institution entirely separate from the European Union whose judicial bodies were based in Strasbourg. The Redwood government's hostility to the planned introduction of the euro in 1999 and a proposed European constitution led to debates about leaving the European Union in the right-wing media, encouraged by several cabinet ministers. In the end, the UK renegotiated its membership to ensure that the European Union was an economic union only: a trading bloc, but nothing else. While workers' rights increased in the rest of the European Union, Redwood's government instead reduced such rights, limiting laws on race and sex discrimination and declining to follow the other member states which outlawed discrimination on grounds of a host of protected characteristics including religion.

The events of 11 September 2001 led the Conservative government to tighten Anglo-American relations and anti-terror laws. They stood back as the press blamed and attacked Muslims, knowing that such minorities were unlikely to be among their voter base and believing that dog-whistle politics would strengthen their populist appeal. Much attention was also given to suppressing calls for Scottish self-government and making the public sector more efficient – by which the government meant making it much smaller.

In the universities, where the number of students continued to grow but at a gradual pace, academics continued to dream of reforms to enable social justice; but these increasingly proved to be pipedreams. Heightened regulation of the sector led to greater scrutiny of research activities, but a number of scholars continued to do their own thing. A small, disparate group of law academics published some works on religion, sometimes calling for modernisation of the law by such measures as the abolition of blasphemy laws, the prohibition of religious discrimination, the reform of the Christian basis of the law on religion in schools and the removal of Sunday trading laws. Compelling though their arguments often were, they got little attention. There were few, if any, legal developments for them to comment on and the chance of such reform seemed increasingly unlikely. Work prospered on the study of Church law under the auspices of the Ecclesiastical Law Society and the LLM course at Cardiff University, but these remained isolated developments which did little to elicit a wider academic interest in the subject. This was in part because publishing research on any aspect of law and religion was tricky. The mainstream legal journals were uninterested in what were often grossly hypothetical arguments and there were no specialist journals. A few brave publishers indulged the publication of a book or two but such works received little attention. When scholars from the continent or from the US visited, they observed that there was little to say about religion under English law, other than to observe upon the establishment of the Church of England. As they often commented, in England and Wales, law and religion as a field simply did not exist.

PART II

Reappraisal

In which alternative trajectories for law and religion are explored by looking at how other comparable fields have developed via a second life-changing moment.

8. The first comparator: law and inequalities

In the spring of 2016, it happened again: I experienced a second life-changing event that transformed the way I saw my work. And, like the earlier event that had introduced me to Norman Doe at my first public law lecture, this second life-changing event also took the form of an introduction. By this point, I was in charge of admissions for law at Cardiff University and was in attendance at one of our open afternoons. As usual, the event closed with an informal tea, coffee and Welsh cake session for those present to ask questions and to meet other members of staff. At this particular open afternoon, I met a new member of staff at the law school for the first time. Her name was Dr Sharon Thompson.

An initial conversation after the open afternoon attendees had left resulted in a realisation that we had common research interests around family law matters, given that I was continuing to work on questions that had been the focus of the Arts and Humanities Research Council/Economic and Social Research Council Religion and Society Programme on 'Social Cohesion and Civil Law: Marriage, Divorce and Religious Courts', which had taken place a few years previously. We arranged to meet for coffee to discuss this further. That later discussion over coffee was the most rigorous discussion and dissection of my work since my PhD viva. It was a very friendly grilling, but it was a grilling nonetheless! Thompson posed questions I had never been asked, raised issues I had not seen and caused me to question what I was trying to achieve and why. Discussion of Thompson's own work was similarly eye-opening and subsequently reading her work was a revelation.

Moreover, her phenomenal debut monograph opened my eyes to a more ambitious style of legal scholarship: one where doctrinal work was not only historicised and contextualised but also theorised using feminist perspectives. I read *Prenuptial Agreements and the Presumption of Free Choice: Issues of Power in Theory and Practice*[1] during a couple of long train rides and was buzzing in the same way I had been at that undergraduate lecture given by Doe. Each chapter took a different and bold approach to her research question.

---

[1] Sharon Thompson, *Prenuptial Agreements and the Presumption of Free Choice: Issues of Power in Theory and Practice* (Hart, 2015).

Reading Thompson's work, my initial reaction was that I needed either to quit or to up my game. I was also adamant that I wanted to work with her and learn from her. In particular, I was taken by the potential wider application of her feminist relational contract theory;[2] and in an article written in the summer of 2016 we applied and developed that theory to the context of religious tribunals.[3] While writing that piece, I experienced a thrill that I had not felt for years. I felt that my work was moving in new directions. The lens and focus had shifted from a top-down, institutionally based approach; and suddenly topics I had spent years writing about felt new, different and challenging.

In the same way as Doe's lecture on religion, law and society made sense of the two halves of my undergraduate degree, Thompson's work and discussions with her highlighted what my legalistic approach had been missing. It underscored the importance of exploring power dimensions and voices that had often been silenced or ignored. This fed into and galvanised my work on religious courts and tribunals, but also had a more far-reaching impact. Thompson was involved in setting up a law and gender research group at the law school, and this led me to contrast the law and gender movement – on which at this point I knew next to nothing – and the sub-discipline of law and religion. It prompted a great deal of reading, thinking and discussion of ideas, perspectives and literatures I was previously ignorant of.

In *Law and Religion*,[4] I had argued that the field should be seen as a legal sub-discipline like sports law or family law. However, now I began to question whether law and religion should instead be likened to law and gender and similar movements such as law and race. Indeed, comparisons could be drawn between the legal treatment of other areas of inequality: the protected characteristics found in the Equality Act 2010 included religion alongside other characteristics such as gender, race, age, disability and sexual orientation. This raised important questions about how religion was being framed by law. Yet law and religion as a sub-discipline seldom drew such connections. Some work on religious discrimination law did draw on other forms of discrimination. However, law and religion was not often put in the same context as law and

---

[2]   On which see also Sharon Thompson, 'Feminist Relational Contract Theory: A New Model for Family Property Agreements' (2018) 45(4) *Journal of Law and Society* 617. This was applied by the most senior Australian court in *Thorne v Kennedy* [2017] HCA 49; on which see Sharon Thompson, '*Thorne v Kennedy*: Why Australia's Decision on Prenups is Important for English Law' (2018) 48 *Family Law* 415.

[3]   Russell Sandberg and Sharon Thompson, 'Relational Autonomy and Religious Tribunals' (2017) 6(1) *Oxford Journal of Law and Religion* 137.

[4]   Russell Sandberg, *Law and Religion* (Cambridge University Press, 2011).

gender and law and race (or similarly named fields). The following two chapters begin to do precisely that.[5]

---

⁵ They will do so by focusing on the academics literatures relating to the two fields. There is, of course, a large but separate literature on religion generally that focuses on its interaction with race and gender. For discussion of this in the context of the sociology of religion, see Abby Day, *Sociology of Religion: Overview and Analysis of Contemporary Religion* (Routledge, 2020), especially Part III; and for an example of work that blends critical theory and feminist liberation theology, see Marsha A Hewitt, *Critical Theory of Religion: A Feminist Analysis* (Fortress Press, 1995).

9. Law and gender

In 2018, while I was editing two collections on the development of law and religion studies,[1] I was flicking through a new book edited by Rosemary Auchmuty published in the Great Debates in Laws series, entitled *Great Debates in Law and Gender*.[2] Auchmuty's book is structured around legal sub-disciplines, with each chapter 'identifying gender issues in traditional legal subject areas' such as property law, contract law, tort law and so on.[3] The idea was that law students would have recourse to it throughout their studies and that, having read the book, would:

> emerge from university recognising the importance of gender in everything they study, seeing it not as an optional add-on for a few people interested 'in that kind of thing' but integral to law-making and the legal process, as well as to their own lives.

Auchmuty's collection is an important and landmark publication. There is much more to be done in relation to emphasising gender in the law curriculum. However, it is telling that as gender is increasingly (and belatedly) being seen as important, it is not being set aside as a specialism (and as a result, being marginalised as something done only by specialists). Gender is rather seen as a factor that interacts with all areas of law and which provides a critique – an alternative way of looking at law that changes the outlook not just on the specific matter being examined, but generally. This reflects the work of Joanne Conaghan and, in particular, her brilliant monograph *Law and Gender*, in which she points out that gender is barely visible in conventional narratives and conceptualisations of law, questioning the assumptions of the 'official' position that the idea of law and legal fundamentals are at least meant to be independent of gender.[4] The conventional story told about gender by law presents gender as being what Conaghan has described as a historic trace; as

---

[1] Later published as: Russell Sandberg (ed), *Leading Works in Law and Religion* (Routledge, 2019); Russell Sandberg, Norman Doe, Bronach Kane and Caroline Roberts (eds), *Handbook of the Interdisciplinary Study of Law and Religion* (Edward Elgar Publishing, 2019).
[2] Rosemary Auchmuty (ed), *Great Debates in Law and Gender* (Palgrave, 2018).
[3] Rosemary Auchmuty, 'Introduction' in R Auchmuty (ed) *Great Debates in Law and Gender* (Palgrave, 2018) xi, xii.
[4] Joanne Conaghan, *Law and Gender* (Clarendon, 2013).

'remnants of a patriarchal legal past which law is gradually casting off'; as 'a mistake to be corrected within the conception of law as an essentially benign and progressive institution'.[5]

Conaghan's critique could be applied in relation to religion. The official legal narrative sees law as neutral and objective and independent of religion. Like gender inequalities, taints of religious privilege are presented as being in the past. However, to date, legal scholarship on religion has developed in a different way from legal scholarship on gender. A focus on religion in legal scholarship has emerged later and has developed much more as what Auchmuty called 'an optional add-on for a few people interested "in that kind of thing"'.

There is little work that looks at religious issues in traditional legal subject areas such as property law, contract law or tort law, either individually or in the way that Auchmuty's collection does.[6] Questions discussed by Conaghan about the theoretical relationship between law and gender have not been asked in relation to law and religion. Questions such as how religion has operated as a historical trace and as an ideology and how it is reflected in the law have seldom been raised – at least not in the law and religion literature in England and Wales.[7]

***

In her introduction to *Great Debates in Law and Gender*, Auchmuty suggested that scholarship relating to gender is called 'feminist scholarship' because 'the gender bias of law (and all social institutions) was first exposed by feminists'.[8] For Auchmuty, 'gender as a category of study emerged as a result of feminist struggles' and describes 'the relationship between men and women, which throughout Western history, has been one not simply of inequality but of power'.[9] She noted that although the term 'feminist scholarship' once 'seemed threatening' because 'it challenged received knowledge and traditional power

---

[5]   Ibid 77.

[6]   A series of edited collections resulting from the Center for the Study of Law and Religion at Emory University, first published as part of Cambridge University Press' Law and Christianity series and later published in Routledge's Law and Religion book series do move in that direction – but then only in relation to Christianity.

[7]   There is also, of course, the need for these questions to be raised about gender in the law and religion literature. See Marie A Failinger, Elizabeth R Schlitz and Susan J Stabile (eds), *Feminism, Law, and Religion* (Ashgate, 2013); and Sharon Thompson and Russell Sandberg, 'Multicultural Jurisdictions: The Need for a Feminist Approach to Law and Religion' in Russell Sandberg (ed) *Leading Works in Law and Religion* (Routledge, 2019) 179.

[8]   Rosemary Auchmuty (ed), *Great Debates in Law and Gender* (Palgrave, 2018) xi, xiv.

[9]   Ibid xiii.

structures', today such inequalities are 'well recognised' and so 'feminist scholarship has become a neutral term referring to a specialist field – the study of gender – not just the study of women, but the relation of women to men, in which the role of men is at least as important as that of women'.[10]

It is possible to discern a shift in feminist legal literature moving on from identifying a particular 'women's perspective' to instead regarding 'the framework of gender divisions as a general category for critical legal analysis' which has 'opened up the possibility that law's contribution to the gendering of its subjects might interact with other social forces'.[11] However, this does not mean that feminist research is synonymous with research about gender. Research about gender does not have to use feminist legal theory at all.[12] And feminist scholarship does not presume that gender is always relevant. Rather, as Conaghan points out, the proposition that it is a category of significance is the very hypothesis that such scholarship is seeking to explore. As she puts it, feminist method entails 'the application of gender as a category of analysis to a field of knowledge in order to generate new questions capable of informing and transforming research agendas'.[13] Feminist legal studies focuses on and highlights 'the ways in which law is implicated, in the twenty-first century, in all of these complicated, sometimes sophisticated, but always resolute structures of gender'.[14]

The field of feminist legal studies arose in the 1980s 'virtually simultaneously in Canada, the US, Britain, Australia and Scandinavia' as both 'an

---

[10]   Ibid xiv.

[11]   Earlier works tended to focus on women and the law, such as Albie Sachs and Joan Hoff Wilson, *Sexism and the Law* (Martin Robinson, 1978); Susan Atkins and Brenda Hoggett, *Women and the Law* (Blackwell, 1984); Julia Brophy and Carol Smart (eds), *Women in Law* (Routledge, 1985); and Sandra Fredman, *Women and the Law* (Claredon, 1997); Judith Bourne and Caroline Derry, *Women and Law* (Old Bailey Press, 2005). Compare: Joanne Conaghan, *Law and Gender* (Clarendon, 2013); and Judith Bourne and Caroline Derry, *Gender and the Law* (Routledge, 2018). Katherine O'Donovan's 1985 book *Sexual Divisions in Law* (Weidenfeld & Nicolson, 1985) is said to have 'represented a watershed in British feminist legal scholarship': Emily Jackson and Nicola Lacey, 'Introducing Feminist Legal Theory' in James Penner, David Schiff and Richard Nobles (eds) *Introduction to Jurisprudence and Legal Theory* (Butterworths, 2002) 779, 781.

[12]   Sharon Thompson, 'Are Methods in Law a Feminist Issue?' (Paper presented at the Gender Rules conference on 20 June 2016, available on the Law and Gender YouTube channel).

[13]   Joanne Conaghan, 'Labour Law and Feminist Method' (2017) 33(1) *International Journal of Comparative Labour Law* 93, 100.

[14]   Alison Diduck and Katherine O'Donovan, 'Feminism and Families' in Alison Diduck and Katherine O'Donovan (eds) *Feminist Perspectives on Family Law* (Routledge, 2006) 1, 6.

off-shoot of critical legal studies' and 'a development from the women's movement more generally'.[15] Its influence upon UK law schools was slowly felt but formed part of what Emily Jackson and Nicola Lacey have referred to as the 'gradual intellectualisation of law schools'.[16] This meant that by the dawn of the new millennium, feminist legal studies constituted 'a significant body of scholarship, competing with other jurisprudential theories for distinguished journals and texts'.[17] Feminism became one of, if not the, main critical approaches used in UK law schools.

There are a wide range of perspectives and traditions within feminist thought. A taxonomy of schools of feminist thought – such as the liberal, radical, cultural and postmodern – are often identified.[18] However, as Vanessa Munro has convincingly argued, talk of such classifications runs the risk that we 'lose sight of the basic and fundamental convictions that continue to animate and unite theorists across these divides'.[19] Although feminists are wary of attempts to identify essential or fundamental principles, this does not mean that identifying trends and general features of feminism is impossible.[20] Feminism in this context can be understood as a dynamic '*process* of engagement or interaction – a dynamic *movement* of ideas', which 'places distinctive substantive issues on the agenda of legal scholarship and legal theory'.[21] In particular, a feminist approach focuses on gender as a structural and ideological means of subordination and exclusion. For Conaghan, 'the application of

---

[15]   Joanne Conaghan, 'Labour Law and Feminist Method' (2017) 33(1) *International Journal of Comparative Labour Law* 93; MDA Freeman, *Lloyds Introduction to Jurisprudence* (9th edition, Sweet & Maxwell, 2014) 1079.

[16]   Emily Jackson and Nicola Lacey, 'Introducing Feminist Legal Theory' in James Penner, David Schiff and Richard Nobles (eds) *Introduction to Jurisprudence and Legal Theory* (Butterworths, 2002) 779, 780.

[17]   Joanne Conaghan, 'Reassessing the Feminist Theoretical Project in Law' (2000) 27(3) *Journal of Law and Society* 351, 352.

[18]   Patrica A Cain, 'Feminism and the Limits of Equality' (1990) 24 *Georgia Law Review* 803.

[19]   Vanessa Munro, *Law and Politics at the Perimeter: Re-evaluating Key Debates in Feminist Theory* (Hart, 2007) 11. Carole Pateman has suggested that such 'classification of feminists … suggests that feminism is always secondary, a supplement to other doctrines': Carole Pateman, *The Sexual Contract* (Polity Press, 1988) x.

[20]   Joanne Conaghan, 'The Making of a Field of the Building of a Wall? Feminist Legal Studies and Law, Gender and Sexuality' (2009) 17 *Feminist Legal Studies* 303, 304.

[21]   Joanne Conaghan, 'Reassessing the Feminist Theoretical Project in Law' (2000) 27(3) *Journal of Law and Society* 351, 356; Emily Jackson and Nicola Lacey, 'Introducing Feminist Legal Theory' in James Penner, David Schiff and Richard Nobles (eds) *Introduction to Jurisprudence and Legal Theory* (Butterworths, 2002) 779, 789.

a gender lens works to: (1) expose the operation of gender bias and neglect; (2) destabilise the normative and conceptual infrastructure; and (3) historicise and contextualise the field'.[22]

This entails asking what Auchmuty called the 'woman question': 'where are the women in this account?'[23] Moreover, this requires more than just rewriting legal stories in which women already appear. As Felice Batlan argued, engendering legal history is not only valuable in relation to areas such as domestic relations and family law where 'issues of women and gender readily appear'. It is also useful – possibly even more useful – when applied to 'those areas of law that on the surface appear to be ungendered'.[24] Paying attention to gender questions our basic assumptions and the explanations that have previously been given for legal and social change.[25] As Batlan put it:

> How does gender account for changes in law that historians have traditionally interpreted as the result of economic change? How does our understanding of the individuals' relationship to the state change when domestic relations law stands not at the periphery of law, but at its core?[26]

As Conaghan argues, this requires more than simply taking account of gender.[27] Gender is not seen as being 'external to law, carrying empirical and distributional, not conceptual or theoretical, significance'. Rather, gender is 'analytically central' and 'deeply constitutive' of law. Ideas about gender both are affected by and affect legal ideas. By choosing to explicitly recognise this – in other words, not to be silent on the gendered dimensions – issues of power are placed at the core of the discussions rather than on the margins.[28] The questioning of assumptions and explanations enables us to 'uncover the many mecha-

---

[22]   Joanne Conaghan, 'Labour Law and Feminist Method' (2017) 33(1) *International Journal of Comparative Labour Law* 93, 100.

[23]   Erika Rackley and Rosemary Auchmuty, 'Women's Legal Landmarks: An Introduction' in Erika Rackley and Rosemary Auchmuty (eds) *Women's Legal Landmarks: Celebrating the History of Women and Law in the UK and Ireland* (Hart, 2018) 1, 5.

[24]   Felice Batlan, 'Engendering Legal History' (2005) *Law & Society Inquiry* 823, 837.

[25]   Ibid 832, 824.

[26]   Ibid 824.

[27]   Joanne Conaghan, 'Labour Law and Feminist Method' (2017) 33(1) *International Journal of Comparative Labour Law* 93, 98.

[28]   Sharon Thompson and Russell Sandberg, 'Multicultural Jurisdictions: The Need for a Feminist Approach to Law and Religion' in Russell Sandberg (ed) *Leading Works in Law and Religion* (Routledge, 2019) 179, 184–85.

nisms by which men have retained power for themselves in law'.[29] Focusing on gender also shows how 'power becomes effectuated – that is, made real and material'.[30] This is what makes it an explicitly feminist project. As Thompson has put it, a feminist approach 'seeks to transform our understanding of the past by writing' stories 'back into legal history, while confronting the question of why [they have] been excluded from accounts'.[31] A feminist approach alters the lens through which we see law and the social world by shedding light on structural and entrenched gendered disadvantages that are perpetuated.[32] Employing a feminist perspective, then, means more than just focusing on gender; it requires a critical approach that highlights questions of power and demands a reappraisal of the status quo. Such a demand is often missing from law and religion literature.

***

At first glance, several of the older works that focused on 'women and the law' had contents pages that resembled those found in the law and religion literature. They tended to explore the position of women in the workplace and other areas of the public sphere. More recent work, however, by discussing and applying a feminist lens, differs considerably from the law and religion literature since it employs a particular perspective.[33] As I have argued elsewhere, five features of a feminist approach to law may be identified.[34] The following discussion recaps these five features while reflecting on whether they or similar features could apply to the law and religion literature. The diverse and dynamic nature of feminism means that care must be taken not to express these

---

[29] Rosemary Auchmuty, 'Recovering Lost Lives: Researching Women in Legal History' (2015) 42 *Journal of Law and Society* 34.

[30] Sandra Harding, *Whose Science, Whose Knowledge* (Cornell University Press, 2013) 150.

[31] Sharon Thompson, *Quiet Revolutionaries: The Married Women's Association and Family Law* (Hart, 2022) 13.

[32] By focusing on gender, feminist legal scholars seek to highlight and explore 'the gendered content of law and to probe characterizations positing themselves as neutral and, more specifically, ungendered': Joanne Conaghan, 'Reassessing the Feminist Theoretical Project in Law' (2000) 27(3) *Journal of Law and Society* 351, 359.

[33] Perhaps the nearest example is Rex Ahdar and Ian Leigh's work that explores the interaction of law and religion from a particular political philosophy: Rex Ahdar and Ian Leigh, *Religious Freedom in the Liberal State* (Oxford University Press, 2005). A second edition was published in 2013.

[34] Russell Sandberg, *Subversive Legal History: A Manifesto for the Future of Legal Education* (Routledge, 2021) 91 *et seq*. See also the 'six substantive and methodological characteristics of feminist legal history' identified by Erika Rackley and Rosemary Auchmuty, 'The Case for Feminist Legal History' (2020) 40(4) *Oxford Journal of Legal Studies* 878, 889–902.

five features in too dogmatic terms. Moreover, the feminist literature in the literature on intersectionality has stressed that people have a range of overlapping identities and are not defined solely by their gender. In this literature, the focus has 'shifted away from the concept of gender as an isolated category of analysis towards a concern with the way in which gender intersects with other categories of identity for purposes of understanding and combating inequality'.[35] It is worth noting that religion is less present in this literature than other forms of identity/inequality.

The first feature of feminism is that it is a grounded approach. A feminist lens dispenses with the usual 'top-down' analysis to focus instead on actual lived experiences.[36] As Conaghan puts it, feminist theory is built 'from the ground up, from the shared experience of women talking from personal testimonies, story-telling, consciousness-raising, and other revelatory techniques aimed at highlighting perspectives ignored by traditional narratives'.[37] This involves examining the everyday experiences of how women interact with the law. A focus on the concrete 'is one of the things that clearly demarcates feminist jurisprudence from mainstream legal theory'.[38] This is summed up by the conviction that 'the personal is the political'. This also requires a wider range of sources than is conventionally used in doctrinal legal scholarship, including the use of non-legal sources.[39] This approach can be contrasted with the 'top-down' approach found in much law and religion scholarship. Although there are some empirical studies, these are exceptional. And where non-academic voices are included, they tend to be those of religious leaders rather than adherents. The legal nature of much law and religion scholarship means that the religious perspectives are often forced to conform with the prevalent and often taken-for-granted traditional narratives that consider the existence of religion in the public sphere to be problematic.

Second, feminist scholarship exposes binary understandings about gender roles and social life. As Munro noted, 'women are identified with domestic

---

[35]   Joanne Conaghan, 'Intersectionality and the Feminist Project in Law' in Emily Grabham, Davina Cooper, Jane Krishnadas and Didi Herman (eds) *Intersectionality and Beyond: Law, Power and the Politics of Location* (Routledge, 2009) 21.

[36]   There is 'a rejection of abstraction and commitment to the importance of context': Vanessa Munro, 'The Master's Tools? A Feminist Approach to Legal and Lay Decision-Making' in Dawn Watkins and Mandy Burton (eds) *Research Methods in Law* (2nd edition, Routledge, 2018) 194, 196.

[37]   Joanne Conaghan, 'Reassessing the Feminist Theoretical Project in Law' (2000) 27(3) *Journal of Law and Society* 351, 364.

[38]   MDA Freeman, *Lloyds Introduction to Jurisprudence* (9th edition, Sweet & Maxwell, 2014) 1081.

[39]   Sharon Thompson, *Quiet Revolutionaries: The Married Women's Association and Family Law* (Hart, 2022) 9.

and family life, with reproduction and with passive but accessible (hetero) sexuality'.[40] A feminist legal approach shows how these gendered understandings are articulated in law – 'the myriad ways in which law constructs gender by invoking images of "woman" – and how this leads to and perpetuates structural disadvantage'.[41] As Thompson observed, 'feminist analyses can usefully break down the boundaries between public and private'.[42] A feminist perspective insists upon the connectedness and integrated nature of human existence, and highlights that lives 'are not splintered between private or public, personal or professional'.[43] This recasts not only the terrain but also the options that are available. A similar approach to law and religion could contest the dividing line often drawn between the two, reflecting John Witte Jr's vision of the field. A feminist approach within law and religion studies could also highlight the gendered experiences within religious groups and how these interact with the law, as well as contesting the public–private divide that is so influential in terms of how religion is seen in a legal context. An intersectional approach could take this further, correcting the artificial simplicity of just focusing on religion (or, indeed, just focusing on religion as defined by law).

Third, feminist approaches highlight how ideas are gendered. It is not just legal structures and institutions (and subjective understandings of such structures and institutions) that are gendered. A feminist approach can uncover the gendered nature of legal concepts and ideas themselves (and their application). As Conaghan observed, a feminist approach can show how 'legal concepts are gendered not just in their application, but also in their meaning and scope'.[44] This can include taking 'a sceptical approach towards claims of law's rationality and neutrality'.[45] A feminist approach emphasises that law is not a 'neutral arbiter'.[46] This questions the very foundations of the legal system

---

[40] Vanessa Munro, *Law and Politics at the Perimeter: Re-evaluating Key Debates in Feminist Theory* (Hart, 2007) 12.

[41] Joanne Conaghan, 'Reassessing the Feminist Theoretical Project in Law' (2000) 27(3) *Journal of Law and Society* 351, 361.

[42] Sharon Thompson, *Quiet Revolutionaries: The Married Women's Association and Family Law* (Hart, 2022) 14.

[43] Marie A Failinger, Elizabeth R Schlitz and Susan J Stabile, 'Foreword' in Marie A Failinger, Elizabeth R Schlitz and Susan J Stabile (eds) *Feminism, Law, and Religion* (Ashgate, 2013) xiii, xv.

[44] Joanne Conaghan, 'Reassessing the Feminist Theoretical Project in Law' (2000) 27(3) *Journal of Law and Society* 351, 360–61.

[45] Vanessa Munro, 'The Master's Tools? A Feminist Approach to Legal and Lay Decision-Making' in Dawn Watkins and Mandy Burton (eds) *Research Methods in Law* (2nd edition, Routledge, 2018) 194, 196.

[46] Sharon Thompson, *Quiet Revolutionaries: The Married Women's Association and Family Law* (Hart, 2022) 15.

since as Thompson observed, 'the notion of law's neutrality is a powerful force which helps maintain public confidence in the legal system and reinforces the assumption that the law will be applied equally to everyone'.[47] A feminist approach is critical in that it 'invites the application of a gender lens to a seemingly genderless space or operation' and 'helps to flush out any hidden norms lurking unacknowledged behind a gender-neutral façade'.[48] It shows how gender is actually 'analytically central' to and 'deeply constitutive' of law. As with any field of study, a similar approach to law and religion would expose the 'conceptual and normative architecture supporting the field of knowledge, thereby inviting its (critical) scrutiny'.[49] Such an approach could be used to highlight and critique processes of inclusion and exclusion; assumptions made; the authority given to certain voices; and the importance afforded to particular topics and arguments. Indeed, such a critique is likely to require the deconstruction and reconstruction of the field.

Fourth, feminist approaches emphasise the agency of those experiencing disadvantage, subordination and exclusion. A feminist perspective brings to the fore the experiences and achievements of women. This is overlooked in traditional legal scholarship, where women are 'portrayed as the passive recipients of legal and social change, as subjects rather than initiators of legal reform'.[50] This requires paying attention only to voices which are heard less often. A feminist approach also reveals the nature of legal change, recognising the agency of women. This is in contrast to conventional accounts that present 'hard-fought-for legal change, for example, as a simple response to shifts in "social attitudes"'.[51] A grounded feminist approach can reveal the importance of the role of activism not only where such activism was successful, but also where it was seemingly unsuccessful.[52] As Thompson asserted, 'investigating why change did *not* happen can be as important as exploring why it did'.[53]

---

[47] Ibid 16.

[48] Joanne Conaghan, 'Labour Law and Feminist Method' (2017) 33(1) *International Journal of Comparative Labour Law* 93, 101.

[49] Ibid 107.

[50] Though this needs to be careful not to promote a 'heroine' myth: Erika Rackley and Rosemary Auchmuty, 'The Case for Feminist Legal History' (2020) 40(4) *Oxford Journal of Legal Studies* 878, 884, 881.

[51] Ibid.

[52] Sharon Thompson, *Quiet Revolutionaries: The Married Women's Association and Family Law* (Hart, 2022) 14.

[53] Ibid 155. See also ibid 145–49. Thompson's account of the Married Women's Association highlights the importance of their supposed failures. She noted not only that failures can be precursors to successes, but also that the Association saw its results differently than orthodox accounts have assumed. She cited one Executive Committee report that 'described their work as being more notable for its "ricochets" than its

A feminist approach can understand why change is slowly achieved and how it is often the result of compromise, and can point to the importance of piecemeal achievements.[54]

Crucially, a feminist approach focuses on the power dynamics at play in particular situations. In Thompson's words, it 'directs critical fire at how social and legal structures create and reinforce power imbalances'.[55] A feminist approach does not assume that men necessarily have an oppressive role but 'it recognises that there is a power dimension between men and women'.[56] This involves paying attention 'to the tacit understandings affecting intimate relationships'.[57] In the context of law and religion, this is likely to entail a deeper awareness of the ways in which the parties involved and implicated in religious relationships (adherents, group officials, State officials, those outside the group – not to mention the family and cultural bonds that these people are involved in negotiating and renegotiating) interact, interpret and use (and are represented in) law.

Fifth, a feminist approach seeks to bring about social change. As Conaghan put it, feminism is concerned 'not just with describing or interpreting social arrangements but also with changing them, that is, with prescribing and effecting transformation, informed by a range of normative ideals including sexual equality, social justice, and individual self-development'.[58] This means that feminist scholarship can, and often does, have a political dimension. However, academic feminism has a different 'validatory framework' from feminism as a political movement: while 'as a scholarly engagement, feminism (seeks to) acquire(s) respectability and legitimacy through its explanatory and interpretative power; as a political movement ... it gains its legitimacy through its ability visibly to bring about political change'.[59] This means that feminist legal studies both expresses and interrogates feminism as a political movement.[60] Again, this highlights the difference between law and gender and law

---

"bulls-eyes": 'The "bulls-eyes" are marked clearly by a new statute or precedent. The ricochets are the ostensible failures, that did in fact leave their mark.' The report concluded that: 'Experience has taught us not to expect the bulls-eyes, but to view with satisfaction such ricochets as have furthered our cause': ibid 227.

[54] See ibid 178 *et seq.*

[55] Ibid 14.

[56] Sharon Thompson, *Prenuptial Agreements and the Presumption of Free Choice: Issues of Power in Theory and Practice* (Hart, 2015) 9.

[57] Sharon Thompson, 'Feminist Relational Contract Theory: A New Model for Family Property Agreements' (2018) 45(4) *Journal of Law and Society* 617, 629.

[58] Joanne Conaghan, 'Reassessing the Feminist Theoretical Project in Law' (2000) 27(3) *Journal of Law and Society* 351, 375.

[59] Ibid 355.

[60] Ibid 356.

and religion scholarship. Law and religion scholarship often has an emphasis upon reform but the normative ideals on which it is based are less clear and more varied. Some law and religion work is clearly written from a religious perspective; other work takes a secular stance; other work again either is not clear in terms of its standpoint or simply seeks to achieve legal clarity. It is clear that the political motivation and assumptions of much law and religion literature should be questioned more than it is. The way in which feminism in the academy has interacted with feminism as a political movement could be emulated in law and religion by consideration of role and difference between academic commentator and activist.

This sketch of some of the main characteristics of feminist legal studies underscores some of the differences between law and gender and law and religion scholarship, and also suggests that a feminist or perhaps otherwise critical approach to law and religion could enhance the field in several respects. Indeed, it is noticeable that feminist scholarship has become much more prevalent in law schools than law and religion work, but has achieved this success without becoming a separate sub-discipline. As Conaghan noted:

> Feminists, in keeping with other dissonant traditions, have not been generally receptive to efforts to impose upon them conceptual, classificatory and/or other normative orderings. The inclination rather has been to resist such efforts and to voice concerns about their disciplinary and normalising effects.[61]

Perhaps this highlights where law and religion has gone wrong: the institutional trappings that have ironically constrained the field. Law and religion work has found itself at the margins of legal studies because the lure of mainstream legal status has led to the erection of institutional structures that have promoted law and religion studies as a specialism. It might have been better for law and religion to operate as a dissonant tradition. However, operating as such brings new pressures and dilemmas. Feminists have paid attention to and debated the issue of where feminist legal studies should position itself to perform its critique. Work of a critical persuasion often has the problem of finding itself part of the very thing that it is seeking to criticise. Not only is removal from the context impossible, but also a retreat away from the mainstream blunts the critique by relegating it to the margins. Conaghan wrote of:

> The recurrent anxiety—evident within feminist legal studies in particular—about whether and where to locate feminist scholarship within broader fields of the

---

[61]   Joanne Conaghan, 'The Making of a Field of the Building of a Wall? Feminist Legal Studies and Law, Gender and Sexuality' (2009) 17 *Feminist Legal Studies* 303, 304.

discipline. For example, is feminist legal studies best positioned at the margins of law (where, arguably, it can more easily retain its critical edge) or should feminist scholars strive towards the absorption and incorporation of feminist perspectives within the legal academic mainstream?[62]

Such concerns and dilemmas are, for, Conaghan 'an inevitable and necessary feature of critical scholarship'. These concerns would come to the fore, therefore, if law and religion developed a critical approach. The next chapter, which examines the field of law and race, will focus on this by exploring what law and religion scholarship could learn from one aspect of law and race scholarship in particular: the politically controversial critical race theory.

---

[62] Ibid.

10. Law and race

The adjective 'critical' has kept popping up in the context of the approach to which law and religion scholarship should aspire. Yet the word 'critical' is so often employed that it risks becoming meaningless. A 'critical' approach often just means analysing or evaluating; at best, this can be an act of deconstruction. Yet this is not the sense in which the word 'critical' is being used when reference is made to feminism as a 'critical' movement. Rather, the word 'critical' here relates to what is sometimes referred to as 'the critical turn'.

In *Religion, Law and Society*, I highlighted the importance of the 'swinging Sixties' as ushering in a cultural revolution that saw the death of deference.[1] The focus there was on its effect upon religion, drawing on the work of Callum Brown,[2] to suggest that a second wave of secularisation occurred as people lost their faith in institutions. However, my subsequent work has highlighted the importance of this period in terms of its transformation in academia. The death of deference which began in the 1960s resulted in the critical turn. This saw the questioning of metanarratives and certainties, and a movement to reorientate scholarship to reject 'top-down' analyses and attempt to give voice to those who were marginalised. This coincided with what is often styled 'the postmodern turn'. Although the term 'postmodern' is sufficiently ubiquitous to appear in secondary school syllabuses, it remains controversial. There are various different understandings of the term 'postmodernity', originating from a range of disciplines.[3] As Jean-François Lyotard wrote, 'simplifying to the extreme', the term 'postmodern' can be defined as 'incredulity towards metanarratives'; and the term 'postmodern age' can be used to describe a 'transition [that] has been under way since at least the end of the 1950s'.[4] The concept of postmodernity may be understood as the rejection of the metanarratives of modernity. Postmodernism is characterised by the 'breaking up of grand narratives',

---

[1]   Russell Sandberg, *Religion, Law and Society* (Cambridge University Press, 2014) 167.

[2]   Callum G Brown, *Religion and Society in Twentieth-Century Britain* (Pearson, 2006) and Callum G Brown, *The Death of Christian Britain* (2nd edition, Routledge, 2009).

[3]   For an entertaining introduction to several postmodernist theorists, see Arthur A Berger, *Postmortem for a Postmodernist* (Sage, 1997).

[4]   Jean-François Lyotard, *The Postmodern Condition* (Manchester University Press, 1984) xxiv, 3, 15.

a rejection of positivism and the rise of pluralism and cultural relativism. As Zygmunt Bauman put it, postmodernity is a rejection of 'the typically modern view of the world' as 'one of an essentially ordered totality'.[5]

A postmodern or critical approach can be and has been applied to law. It questions law's autonomy, objectivity and certainty.[6] It delivers a critique of the idea of law as an autonomous, objective and legitimate normative mechanism.[7] It questions the dominant assumption that law provides an objective means to resolve the conflict between individual and social interests. As Alan Hunt noted, a critical approach stresses that law is actually a mere pragmatic response 'which reflects the unequal distribution of power and resources whilst claiming to act in the name of a set of universal social values'.[8] This underlines how every judge is 'a political actor effecting a particular political agenda'.[9] Robert W Gordon wrote that the critical approach is based on two main ideas: 'false legitimation' – that is, 'the complacent idea that the legal system in force is about as efficient, just and rational a system that it could be'; and 'false necessity' – that is, the idea that the legal system 'could not be reformed except in minor ways without risking economic and political catastrophe'.[10]

In the context of law, these ideas are often linked with the critical legal studies movement. This had a significant presence in US law schools in the late twentieth century but had less of an impact in England and Wales.[11] It has been described as 'the *enfant terrible* of contemporary legal studies', on the basis that it 'delights in shocking what it takes to be the legal establishment'.[12] It is often considered that the heyday of the critical movement has now passed. Mariana Valverde has written that critical legal studies is now 'a mature, if not frankly elderly, literature'.[13] However, 'the echoes of its intervention are still

---

[5] Zygmunt Bauman, *Legislators and Interpreters* (Polity, 1987) 3. See further Zygmunt Bauman, *Intimations of Postmodernity* (Routledge, 1992), Chapter 9.

[6] See, e.g., Roberto Mangabeira Unger, *The Critical Legal Studies Movement: Another Time, A Greater Task* (Verso, 2015).

[7] Alan Hunt, 'The Theory of Critical Legal Studies' (1986) 6 *Oxford Journal of Legal Studies* 1, 4.

[8] Ibid 5.

[9] Ian Ward, *Introduction to Critical Legal Theory* (2nd edition, Cavendish, 2004) 144.

[10] Robert W Gordon, *Taming the Past: Essays on Law in History and History in Law* (Cambridge University Press, 2017) 220.

[11] Roger Cotterrell, 'Power, Property and the Law of Trusts: A Partial Agenda for Critical Legal Scholarship' (1987) 14(1) *Journal of Law and Society* 77.

[12] Alan Hunt, 'The Critique of Law: What is "Critical" about Critical Legal Theory?' (1987) 14(1) *Journal of Law and Society* 5.

[13] Mariana Valverde, *Chronotopes of Law: Jurisdiction, Scale and Governance* (Routledge, 2015) 47, 31.

audible in legal scholarship'.[14] Although the critical legal studies movement has often been associated with Marxism,[15] as Peter Fitzpatrick and Alan Hunt noted, 'in Britain critical legal studies has been eclectic: the key traditions informing debate have been Marxism, feminism and critical social theory of the Frankfurt variety'.[16] Indeed, the decline in interest in Marxism has meant that the 'critical legal studies' banner has largely been replaced by particular focuses on critical race, feminist and sexualities studies.[17] As Robert Gordon noted, these intellectual movements have prospered because they had the advantage 'of being allied with active movements for social and legal change outside the academy'.[18] Much of the discussion in the previous chapter falls under this camp and the same is true of much of the literature on race and decolonisation.

This is epitomised by the landmark work of Fọlúkẹ́ Adébísí, who has convincingly argued that decolonisation requires us to think differently about how we teach, talk about and study law.[19] For understandable and very astute reasons, increased attention has been paid to decolonisation in recent years. However, the ubiquity of the term poses the risk that it might become a managerial buzzword, reduced to an item on a well-meaning but often performative checklist. There is a danger that paying lip service to the need to combat racial inequality – whether it be focusing on Black History Month or having one lecture on a module address the matter – might do more harm than good, suggesting that the issue can be boxed off as a topic and dealt with in isolation. Adébísí's work, however, goes beyond this. It upsets and challenges such thinking (or non-thinking). Taking decolonisation seriously requires rethinking, deconstructing and reconstructing the very foundations upon which legal education is built upon.

For Adébísí, the law school and law as a discipline are fields of 'promise and disappointment': 'we teach our students a particular vision of a particular

---

[14]   Christopher Tomlins, 'What is Left of the Law and Society Paradigm after Critique? Revisiting Gordon's "Critical Legal Histories"' (2012) 37 *Law & Social Inquiry* 155, 156.

[15]   On which see Maurice J Holland, 'A Hurried Perspective on the Critical Legal Studies Movement: The Marx Brothers Assault the Citadel' (1985) 8 *Harvard Journal of Law and Public Policy* 239.

[16]   Peter Fitzpatrick and Alan Hunt, 'Critical Legal Studies: Introduction' (1987) 14(1) *Journal of Law and Society* 1, 2.

[17]   However, see Samuel Moyn, 'Reconstructing Critical Legal Studies' (2023) *Yale Law School, Public Law Research Paper* (online).

[18]   Robert W Gordon, '"Critical Legal Histories Revisited": A Response' (2012) 37 *Law & Social Inquiry* 200, 204.

[19]   Fọlúkẹ́ Adébísí, *Decolonisation and Legal Knowledge: Reflections on Power and Possibility* (Bristol University Press, 2023).

world' that 'has been derived from a limited way of thinking' which she identi-fies as being 'Euro-modern'.[20] Although clinical and socio-legal studies allows some 'room to break these seals', overall 'as a discipline and as a profession, the field retains immense untapped potential to contemplate the transformation of the current world, marked as it is by massive inequality, political instabil-ity, large scale poverty, and impending environmental collapse'. Instead, the curriculums and research agendas of law schools tend to be 'quite narrowly defined by supposed national needs'.[21] The nature of doctrinal legal education has suppressed critical reasoning and dissent. This has meant that the truth claims of legal knowledge are rarely raised at all, let alone treated as problem-atic.[22] The dominance of private law renders legal education into a study of 'rich people's law'. Their location within universities means that 'structural inequalities produced by long-standing universities' processes also compound the hierarchisation of knowledge' in law schools. In short, Adébísí illustrated how:

> claims to objectivity deny the enfolded truth of the world in which its legal knowl-edge has been and is being produced and transmitted. A claim to all-seeing objec-tivity, neutrality and universality refuses to engage with the workings of power, the restriction of possibility in legal meanings, as well as the universalised 'particular' that is Western masculinist law.[23]

Legal knowledge then 'fundamentally denies its own ontology'.[24]

As Adébísí recognised, these points are well established in 'critical legal studies and its offshoots', which seek 'to trouble the presumed objectivity, pos-itivist, neutrality, and transparency of Euro-modern law'.[25] Yet she maintains that this literature 'does not go far enough in those ambitions', in that it often takes 'an atomised approach to confronting power, either conceptually (law and economic theory; law and gender; law and race) or jurisdictionally'. She therefore calls for critical legal studies to be read together with decolonising theories 'to offer us an after-world, beyond this apocalypse, rather than mere evaluation'. While many works in the critical legal studies tradition pivot towards nihilism, Adébísí's focus is on reconstruction: equipping the reader

---

[20]   Ibid 1, 2.
[21]   Ibid 4. Although she notes that the law school 'is home to many universes – a pluriversal space', this is undermined by the 'untranslatability of these universes' and the way that they are 'inherently woven into Euro-modern law means that only one of these universes is made dominant and universal'.
[22]   Ibid 5.
[23]   Ibid 6.
[24]   Ibid 7.
[25]   Ibid 8.

'to radically redesign the world'.[26] Her vision is optimistic, empowering, inspirational and emancipatory. As she put it, 'it is up to us all to collectively discern the very nature of the law, its history, and use, so that we may together determine where we want it to take us'.[27]

Adébísí distinguished between decolonisation 'that merely *acknowledges* the colonial nature of the discipline and decolonisation that seeks to *disrupt* and *dismantle* the colonial nature of the world'.[28] Decolonisation, for Adébísí, necessarily involves this latter form. Noting how existing structural limitations 'should not lead us to an abandonment of decolonisation as praxis but, may help us not to over-exaggerate the impact of our activity within it', she argued that 'we can, within these structures, reimagine the world we want our epistemologies to produce'.[29] Decolonisation, therefore, does not relate simply to curriculum or research redesign or innovation; rather, serves it 'as an immediate, continuing, and stubborn refusal of colonial conditions of domination, dispossession, and dehumanisation as well as of the epistemologies that keep coloniality eternally reemergent'.

Decolonisation and Legal Knowledge: Reflections on Power and Possibility is underpinned by the conviction that 'for the discipline to embrace decolonisation as praxis, academics must very deliberately acknowledge and oppose the problematic premises upon which the discipline has been advanced'.[30] This epitomises what a critical approach entails: such an approach requires academics to confront these questions as part of their reappraisal of the whole edifice of what we call 'society'. Centering on race, like focusing on gender, provides an exemplar of how a critical approach within law and religion could develop.[31] Despite the obvious and often legally significant overlaps between the categories of religion and race, much of the law and religion literature (especially that which developed in England and Wales in the early twenty-first century) distinguishes and excludes discussion of race.[32] In *Law and Religion*, I noted that 'one result of current understandings of what religion law includes is that much of the literature on ethnic minority rights and legal pluralism is often

---

[26]   Ibid 12.

[27]   Ibid 13.

[28]   Ibid 11 (original emphasis).

[29]   Ibid 12.

[30]   Ibid 10.

[31]   The critical turn has had little effect upon law and religion scholarship as the lone cry of Suhraiya Jivraj highlights: Suhraiya Jivraj, *The Religion of Law: Race, Citizenship and Children's Belonging* (Palgrave, 2013), discussed above in Chapter 7.

[32]   Indeed, there has been litigation as to whether a belief that the critical theory approach to racism is misconceived is itself protected as a religion or belief for the purposes of the Equality Act: *Corby v Advisory, Conciliation and Arbitration Service* [2023] ET Case No 1805305/2022.

excluded'.[33] Although the subsequent literature on religious courts and tribunals has sometimes been understood under the umbrella of legal pluralism,[34] generally it remains the case that the literatures on law and religion and law and race are still separate.

This chapter seeks to make connections between the two and does so by drawing upon a particular aspect of the study of law and race: critical race theory. Although this is just one school of thought,[35] critical race theory has been chosen since it highlights the activist dimension that is also present in the feminist approach surveyed in the previous chapter.[36] It underscores how race (like gender – and, by extension, like religion) is not a mere problem for law to solve but rather a means of questioning, critiquing and reconstituting law. Critical race theory is a politically controversial and often misunderstood movement. In 2020, to close a House of Commons debate on Black History Month, the then Minister for Equalities Kemi Badenoch declared that the UK government stood 'unequivocally against critical race theory':

> Lots of pernicious stuff is being pushed, and we stand against that. We do not want teachers to teach their white pupils about white privilege and inherited racial guilt. Let me be clear that any school that reaches those elements of critical race theory as fact, or that promotes partisan political views such as defunding the police without offering a balanced treatment of opposing views, is breaking the law.[37]

The Minister was not clear as to what the government objected to. Presenting any theory as fact and/or not providing a balanced treatment of opposing views is always problematic in an educational setting. The government's objection to critical race theory seems to be that it is political. Yet, depending on how the word 'political' can be defined, this is true of most theories and approaches that seek to analyse and improve our understandings of and the actual nature of

---

[33] Russell Sandberg, *Law and Religion* (Cambridge University Press, 2011) 11.

[34] See, e.g., the essays in Russell Sandberg (ed) *Religion and Legal Pluralism* (Ashgate, 2015).

[35] For a discussion of its placing within theories of decolonisation, see Folúkẹ́ Adébísí, *Decolonisation and Legal Knowledge: Reflections on Power and Possibility* (Bristol University Press, 2023), Chapter 1.

[36] Critical race theory has generally been less influential in Europe than in the US: Mathias Moschel, *Law, Lawyers and Race: Critical Race Theory from the US to Europe* (Routledge, 2016). Critical race theory has had most influence in England in the field of education: Paul Warmington, 'Critical Race Theory in England: Impact and Opposition' (2020) 27(1) *Global Studies in Culture and Power* 20. See also Namita Chakrabarty, Lorna Roberts and John Preston, 'Critical Race Theory in England' (2012) 15(1) *Race, Ethnicity and Education* 1.

[37] House of Commons Hansard, 12 October 2000, Vol 682.

the world around us. Given that it seems that critical race theory is too radical for the minister's liking, then the approach merits further investigation.

***

Critical race theory can be dated back to a particular workshop held on 8 July 1989 in Madison, Wisconsin.[38] Although this workshop was entitled 'New Developments in Critical Race Theory', which suggested that the movement already existed, the term 'critical race theory' was actually created for this event.[39] Critical race theory became a movement of activists and scholars who were 'engaged in studying and transforming the relationship among race, racism and power'.[40] It was at first a movement in American law schools, focusing on how racism was institutionalised in and by law.[41] It sprang from a realisation that the advances of the civil rights era of the 1960s in America had stalled and were being rolled back.[42] A generation of scholars – including Derrick Bell, Richard Delgado, Alan Freeman, Charles Lawrence, Mari Matsuda, Patricia Williams and Kimberlé Williams Crenshaw – realised that 'new theories and strategies were needed to combat the subtler forms of racism that were gaining ground'.

The critical race theory movement considered many of the same issues that were being explored in work on civil rights and ethnic studies but placed them in a broader setting.[43] Moreover, as Richard Delgado and Jean Stefancic pointed out, critical race theory rejected the focus on incremental step-by-step progress as advocated by traditional civil rights discourse. Rather, it questioned the very foundations of society: it explored the biases within and the effect of supposedly neutral provisions, including the law. It was designed 'not only to name, but to be a tool for rooting out inequality and injustice'.[44] This 'critical' approach scrutinised the 'unseen, largely invisible collection of patterns and

---

[38] There were also pre-workshop formations that often gathered in hotel rooms and in other spaces often before, during and after professional conferences: Kimberlé Williams Crenshaw, 'Twenty Years of Critical Race Theory: Looking Back to Move Forward' (2011) 43(5) *Connecticut Law Review* 1253, 1298.

[39] Ibid 1263.

[40] Richard Delgado and Jean Stefancic, *Critical Race Theory: An Introduction* (3rd edition, New York University Press, 2017) 3.

[41] Derrick A Bell, 'Who's Afraid of Critical Race Theory?' (1995) *University of Illinois Law Review* 893, 898.

[42] Richard Delgado and Jean Stefancic, *Critical Race Theory: An Introduction* (3rd edition, New York University Press, 2017) 4.

[43] Ibid 3.

[44] A Javier Treviño, Michelle A Harris and Derron Wallace, 'What's so Critical about Critical Race Theory?' (2008) 11(1) *Contemporary Justice Review* 7, 8.

habits' that allows domination to occur.[45] As Adébísí noted, the foundational tenets of critical race theory 'implicate law in the (re)production, entrenchment and normalisation of socially constructed race':[46] a process that 'essentialises and naturalises the materiality of hierarchised categories' so that '"whiteness" is identified as a system of both material and psychological advantage, yet its invisibility allows the quotidian functioning of structural racism to remain uninterrogated'.[47] Like other radical approaches, there are many different strands of critical race theory and significant tension about whether it has any central propositions and, if so, how these can be articulated. However, Richard Delgado and Jean Stefancic suggested that many critical race scholars would agree on the following six propositions.[48]

The first proposition is that 'racism is ordinary, not aberrational', in that racism is perpetuated in 'the usual way society does business, the common, everyday experience of most people'.[49] This means that racism is difficult to address and cannot be addressed by liberal approaches which seek a 'colourblind' approach and formal equality in the sense of treating everyone the same, because such policies can 'remedy only the most blatant forms of discrimination'. As Adébísí noted, 'societal focus is only captured by the most blatant and often violent isolated instances of individual racism'.[50] Applying a similarly critical approach to the context of religion could highlight the way in which religious illiteracy, if not discrimination, is the norm in liberal, secular societies; and the way in which attempting to treat everyone equally actually entrenches more subtle but still problematic forms of discrimination. Such discrimination might not only demonstrate a secular bias but also might be weighted towards Christianity, or at least a cultural form of Christianity that has persisted despite secularisation.[51] This is shown in an article by sociologist

---

[45]   Richard Delgado and Jean Stefancic, *Critical Race Theory: An Introduction* (3rd edition, New York University Press, 2017) 5.

[46]   Folúkẹ́ Adébísí, *Decolonisation and Legal Knowledge: Reflections on Power and Possibility* (Bristol University Press, 2023) 30–31.

[47]   Ibid 31.

[48]   Richard Delgado and Jean Stefancic, *Critical Race Theory: An Introduction* (3rd edition, New York University Press, 2017) 8–11.

[49]   Ibid 8. This proposition is expressed in Charles R Lawrence, 'The Id, the Ego, and Equal Protection. Reckoning with Unconscious Racism' (1987) 39 *Stanford Law Review* 317; and Derrick Bell, *Faces at the Bottom of the Well: The Permanence of Racism* (Basic Books, 2018 [1992]).

[50]   Folúkẹ́ Adébísí, *Decolonisation and Legal Knowledge: Reflections on Power and Possibility* (Bristol University Press, 2023) 31.

[51]   See the work of Grace Davie on this.

of religion James Beckford on what he called 'banal discrimination'.[52] This developed the work of Michael Billig[53] to contend that English law is characterised by the existence of 'low-level, unthinking, but sometimes institutional discrimination' in favour of 'mainstream Christian churches and against the more marginal' religious communities and organisations.

The second proposition of critical race theory identified by Delgado and Stefancic is known as 'interest convergence' or 'material determination': the idea that racism serves important purposes for the dominant group, who therefore have little reason to eradicate it.[54] This means that the changes that do occur which seem to be a triumph of civil rights are often nothing of the sort and actually result from the self-interest of the white elite.[55] As Adébísí noted: 'what is often considered progress towards racial equality only happens because of "interest convergence", when the interests of those racialised white converge with the interests of those racialised as non-white.'[56] Racism not only is the result of 'matters of thinking, mental categorization, attitude and discourse', but also is the means by 'which society allocates privilege and status'.[57] This has been cemented into law.[58] In the religion context, such an approach could highlight the Christian and/or secular bias that is similarly cemented into law. This is shown by the way in which the existence of religion in the public sphere is seen as a problem and the way in which religion itself is understood in a Christian way.

The 'social construction' thesis is Delgado and Stefancic's third proposition. This holds that, rather than being biological and objective, inherent or fixed, race is actually the product of social thoughts and relations: 'races are categories that society invents, manipulates, or retires when convenient.'[59] The articulation of race as a social construct has become 'a mantra' in critical race

---

[52]   James A Beckford, 'Banal Discrimination: Equality of Respect for Beliefs and Worldviews in the UK', in D Davis and G Besier (eds) *International Perspectives on Freedom and Equality of Religious Belief.* (J.M. Dawson Institute of Church-State Studies, 2002) 25.

[53]   Michael Billig, *Banal Nationalism* (Sage, 1995).

[54]   Richard Delgado and Jean Stefancic, *Critical Race Theory: An Introduction* (3rd edition, New York University Press, 2017) 9.

[55]   See Derrick Bell, *Silent Covenants: Brown v Board of Education and the Unfulfilled Hopes for Racial Reform* (Oxford University Press, 2005).

[56]   Folúkẹ́ Adébísí, *Decolonisation and Legal Knowledge: Reflections on Power and Possibility* (Bristol University Press, 2023) 31.

[57]   Richard Delgado and Jean Stefancic, *Critical Race Theory: An Introduction* (3rd edition, New York University Press, 2017) 21.

[58]   See Cheryl I Harris, 'Whiteness as Property' (1993) 106 *Harvard Law Review* 1709.

[59]   Richard Delgado and Jean Stefancic, *Critical Race Theory: An Introduction* (3rd edition, New York University Press, 2017) 9.

theory.[60] This does not deny the fact of biology and genetics, but stresses the importance of nurture over nature. The idea of religion as a social construct is particularly interesting and important in this regard. The question of whether religious identity is ascribed or achieved is pivotal but often overlooked. There is also the need to explore and contrast how religion is constructed differently by various societal groupings: the 'official' construction of religion by the State may well differ from that developed by believers; and indeed there will be variations between adherents to different belief systems and crucially also within belief systems. Seeing religion as a social construct also underscores that religious doctrines and ideas will be interpreted and followed differently by individuals. This is a point that the courts have struggled with when interpreting Article 9 of the European Convention on Human Rights, especially when considering domestic indirect discrimination laws that require proof of group disadvantage.

Delgado and Stefancic's fourth proposition is 'differential racialization': 'the idea that each race has its own origins and ever-revolving history.'[61] This means that race was never simply 'out there' to be discovered but was invented 'in a quite literal sense'.[62] Differential racialisation highlights 'the ways the dominant society racializes different minority groups at different times, in response to shifting needs'.[63] This means that popular images and stereotypes of various minority groups also shift over time. As Adébísí noted, 'whiteness operates as material properly in its capacity, not only to adduce material benefit, but also to exclude and include'.[64] Applied to the religious context, this again stresses heterogeneity and the way in which religious convictions develop over time and in response to changing stimulus. This underlines Lord Nicholls' point in *Williamson*[65] that 'freedom of religion protects the

---

60   Robert S Chang, 'Critiquing "Race" and Its Uses: Critical Race Theory's Uncompleted Argument' in Francisco Valdes, Jerome McCristal Culp and Angela P Harris (eds) *Crossroads, Directions, and a New Critical Race Theory* (Temple University Press, 2002) 87.

61   Richard Delgado and Jean Stefancic, *Critical Race Theory: An Introduction* (3rd edition, New York University Press, 2017) 10.

62   Robert L Hayman, Jr and Nancy Levit, 'Un-natural Things: Constructions of Race, Gender, and Disability' in Francisco Valdes, Jerome McCristal Culp and Angela P Harris (eds) *Crossroads, Directions, and a New Critical Race Theory* (Temple University Press, 2002) 159.

63   Richard Delgado and Jean Stefancic, *Critical Race Theory: An Introduction* (3rd edition, New York University Press, 2017) 10.

64   Folúkẹ́ Adébísí, *Decolonisation and Legal Knowledge: Reflections on Power and Possibility* (Bristol University Press, 2023) 31.

65   *R v Secretary of State for Education and Employment and others ex parte Williamson* [2005] UKHL 15 at para 22.

subjective belief of an individual' and requires us to take this to its logical conclusion. This has lessons for the courtroom in terms of questioning the merits of expert testimony, and also has lessons for the academy in terms of not grouping religious claims and accepting the need to revisit issues that seemed to be resolved. It also reminds us that the 'official' State understanding of religion develops over time and serves as a means of inclusion and exclusion; where the line is drawn is a matter of political choice.

Adherence to 'intersectionality and anti-essentialism' represents the fifth proposition highlighted by Delgado and Stefancic. As discussed in the previous chapter, this means that no one is defined by one 'single, easily stated, unitary identity' such as their race. Rather, everyone has 'potentially conflicting, overlapping identities, loyalties and allegiances'.[66] For Adébísí, intersectionality is of particular importance to critical race theory because 'it highlights how the essentialisation of identity renders the legal system unable to attend to the combination of vulnerabilities (race, gender, sexuality, class, ability, and so on) that are themselves often a product of social forces'.[67] Although religion is absent from Adébísí's list, it is clear that 'religion' too is a concept that has become legally essentialised in a way that often has little in common with how religious identities are developed by adherents. Moreover, there is a need to consider what Adébísí terms 'the combination of vulnerabilities' and what equality law dubs 'protected characteristics' in light of each other. A holistic approach is needed so that we do not fall at the first hurdle by narrowing interpreting religion, race, sexuality and so on as separate identities, raising distinct issues and capable of being understood in isolation. For law and religion scholars, this underscores the folly of erecting distinctions between religion and other forms of identity such as race and gender. It underscores that the institutional ghettoisation of law and religion scholarship is inherently problematic. By exclusively focusing on religion (and in some, but not enough, cases on non-religious belief), the academic and legal analyses are artificially separating and exploring one dimension of the lived lives of those involved. This might suggest that the focus should be on law and intersecting inequalities rather than upon religion, race or gender in isolation.

---

[66]   Richard Delgado and Jean Stefancic, *Critical Race Theory: An Introduction* (3rd edition, New York University Press, 2017) 11. For a classic statement see Kimberlé Williams Crenshaw, 'Demarginalizing the Intersection of Race and Sex: A Black Feminist Critique of Antidiscrimination Doctrine, Feminist Theory and Antiracist Politics' (1989) *University of Chicago Legal Forum* 139.

[67]   Folúkẹ́ Adébísí, *Decolonisation and Legal Knowledge: Reflections on Power and Possibility* (Bristol University Press, 2023) 31. Different approaches exist such as critical race feminism. On which see, for example, Adrien K Wing (ed), *Critical Race Feminism: A Reader* (2nd edition, New York University Press, 2003).

The sixth proposition put forward by Delgado and Stefancic is the 'voice of colour' thesis. This holds that 'because of their different histories and experiences with oppression', minority races can communicate to majority matters that the majority are unlikely to know.[68] This seems to sit uncomfortably with the fifth proposition in that it privileges racial identities. Yet this proposition usefully highlights the distinct nature of racial identities and the unique perspective lived experience brings. As Delgado and Stefancic put it, minority status 'brings with it a presumed competence, to speak out about race and racism'. This raises the debate as to whether outsiders can comment on such issues, or at least highlights that outsiders need to recognise their limitations and support the need for greater representation. These limitations apply not only to the substance of what is said but also to how it is said. And such considerations apply as much to religion as they do to race. There is a need to attempt to capture the lived experiences of adherents, and this also requires academic bystanders to explicitly recognise shortcomings in achieving this and their own biases and privilege. Greater attention needs to be afforded to recognising and combating the influence of the 'official' State-informed social construct of religion upon academic analysis. We need to be alert to the extent to which even seemingly technical academic analyses perpetuate endemic narratives about religion that are divorced from the lived experiences of those affected by the regulation.

A corrective can be provided by the 'legal storytelling' movement, which urges minority racial groups 'to recount their experiences with racism and the legal system and to apply their own unique perspectives to assess law's master narratives'. This use of allegorical stories – as found in the work of Derrick Bell and Patricia Williams – draws 'on a long history with roots doing back to the slave narratives, tales written by black captives to describe their condition and unmask the gentility that white plantation society pretended to'.[69] As with feminism, this is a grounded approach that reveals everyday experiences and cultures. It opens a window onto ignored or alternative realities because 'members of this country's dominant racial group cannot easily grasp what it is like to be nonwhite'.[70] It therefore provides a cure for silence: 'Stories can give them a voice and reveal that other people have similar experiences.'[71] It can often have a 'destructive function', whereby counterstories are used 'to challenge, displace, or mock these pernicious narratives and beliefs'.[72]

---

[68] Richard Delgado and Jean Stefancic, *Critical Race Theory: An Introduction* (3rd edition, New York University Press, 2017) 11.
[69] Ibid 45.
[70] Ibid 46.
[71] Ibid 51.
[72] Ibid 49, 50.

It serves 'as a way of countering the metanarratives – the images, precon-
ceptions, and myths – that have been propagated by the dominant culture
of hegemonic Whiteness as a way of maintaining racial inequality'.[73] This
informs the methodological approach taken by critical race theory: 'writing
and lecturing is characterized by frequent use of the first person, storytelling,
narrative, allegory, interdisciplinary treatment of law, and the unapologetic use
of creativity'.[74]

This is not to say that all critical race theory work is characterised by the use
of 'literary models as a more helpful vehicle than legal precedent'.[75] Derrick
Bell, who pioneered such work,[76] also wrote an influential textbook on the
topic.[77] However, as Delgado and Stefancic point out, revisionist history was
one of the hallmarks of the movement: such work 're-examines America's historical record, replacing comforting majoritarian interpretations of events with
ones that square more accurately with minorities' experience'.[78] Such accounts
achieve this by providing the evidence that has sometimes been suppressed to
support those new interpretations. As with feminist approaches to legal history,
this requires exploring a wider range of sources. The work of Kendall Thomas,
for instance, sought to explore a legal history of a US Supreme Court decision
'from the bottom up' by allowing the people involved to speak for themselves.[79]
Such work also questions the autonomy of the law and linear ideas of progress.
Delgado and Stefancic noted that revisionism holds 'that to understand the zigs
and zags of black, Latino and Asian fortunes, one must look to matters like
profit, labor supply, international relations and the interest of elite whites'.[80]
Law and religion scholarship has much to learn from such approaches. Critical
race theory, like the critical movement generally, highlights the need for

---

[73]   A Javier Treviño, Michelle A Harris and Derron Wallace, 'What's so Critical
about Critical Race Theory?' (2008) 11(1) *Contemporary Justice Review* 7, 8.

[74]   Derrick A Bell, 'Who's Afraid of Critical Race Theory?' (1995) *University of
Illinois Law Review* 893, 899.

[75]   Derrick Bell, *Faces at the Bottom of the Well: The Permanence of Racism* (Basic
Books, 2018 [1992]) xxi.

[76]   See ibid and Derrick Bell, *And We are Not Saved: The Elusive Quest for Racial
Justice* (Basic Books, 1989).

[77]   Derrick Bell, *Race, Racism and American Law* (6th edition, Aspen, 2008); the
first edition was published in 1980.

[78]   Richard Delgado and Jean Stefancic, *Critical Race Theory: An Introduction* (3rd
edition, New York University Press, 2017) 25.

[79]   Kendall Thomas, '*Rouge et Noir* Reread: A Popular Constitutional History of the
Angelo Herndon Case' (1992) 65 *Southern Californian Law Review* 2599.

[80]   Richard Delgado and Jean Stefancic, *Critical Race Theory: An Introduction* (3rd
edition, New York University Press, 2017) 25.

a historical approach.[81] Where law and religion scholarship has a historical dimension, it tends to be used in a top-down manner, documenting the trajectory of the State and its rulers. It tends to adopt a narrative of progress, praising the move towards what is conceptualised as religious toleration and the respect of religious freedom. It is very much a 'winner's history' which, as Rebecca Riedel has noted, pays little attention to religious radicalism.[82] This needs to change. Whether this includes literary models or not, there is a need to reconstruct the stories we tell about law and religion to focus on lived experiences. The histories constructed need to reflect the stories of those involved rather than linear expectations that come from wider histories. Once again, we need to stop forcing religion into a State-centric, legalistic and Western straitjacket.

This is what a critical approach can achieve. It can highlight and question the often implicit power dimensions that exist, showing that what is often presented as being universal, natural and objective is nothing of the sort. A critical approach can lead to deconstruction and ideally also reconstruction. The last two chapters have shown how the literatures on law and gender and law and race have embraced this challenge. They have not provided an illustrative – let alone exhaustive – literature review, but have rather highlighted some of the main characteristics of this critical approach, comparing this to the development of law and religion as an academic field. This has underscored how a critical approach is needed to combat the way in which law and religion has developed institutionally and how this has entrenched its Christian and/or secular biases. There is a need to uncover the way in which law has understood religion in its own terms and to explore the ramifications of this. Critical perspectives applied in relation to law and gender and law and race highlight how underdeveloped law and religion is.

---

[81] H Timothy Lovelace Jr commented that in America, 'critical race theory had become embedded in legal history', at least in relation to the history of civil rights: H Timothy Lovelace Jr, 'Critical Race Theory and the Political Uses of Legal History' in Markus D Dubber and Christopher Tomlins (eds) *The Oxford Handbook of Legal History* (Oxford University Press, 2018) 621, 625.

[82] Rebecca Riedel, 'A Critical Legal Study of the Prevent Duty: The Religious Dimension' (PhD thesis submitted to Cardiff University, 2023).

11. The second comparator: law and humanities

Over the last decade since the publication of *Religion, Law and Society*,[1] my teaching and research interests have shifted towards legal history. The origins of this focus can be found in the last chapter of *Religion, Law and Society* itself. There, in exploring Norman Doe's call for a 'Sociology of Law on Religion',[2] I examined his suggestion that the sociology of law could play a significant role in expanding the study of religion, law and society. I rejected, however, Doe's call for a new discipline and tangentially reflected on how the sociology of law has itself been limited by its treatment as a legal specialism. In a further tangent, I further speculated that the same was true of legal history. Remembering how pivotal the module on legal history had been during my undergraduate studies,[3] I argued that the sociology and history of law should not be limited to the fringe of legal studies but should rather be part of the methodological toolkit for all lawyers. My publications in the decade since have elaborated and refined this argument in relation to legal history.[4]

There was no grand plan to shift my specialism from law and religion to legal history. As ever, this came about simply as a result of following questions and developing arguments that I found interesting. It also occurred as a result of reintroducing the legal history module and teaching on it alongside Doe at first and then with Sharon Thompson. Again, their influences had a huge and incalculable effect upon me. Doe's doctoral study had been in the field of legal

---

[1]   Russell Sandberg, *Religion, Law and Society* (Cambridge University Press, 2014).

[2]   Norman Doe, 'A Sociology of Law on Religion – Towards a New Discipline: Legal Responses to Religious Pluralism in Europe' (2004) 152 *Law and Justice* 68.

[3]   That module, taught by Professor Thomas Watkin, had a different transformative effect upon me than Doe's module on the comparative law of religion. The latter helped me make sense of my law degree; the former module helped me bring together the law component of the degree with the sociology subjects I was also studying. Yet both, in their own ways, would go on to set an agenda that became something of an adventure.

[4]   Chiefly, Russell Sandberg, *Subversive Legal History: A Manifesto for the Future of Legal Education* (Routledge, 2021); and Russell Sandberg, *A Historical Introduction to English Law: Genesis of the Common Law* (Cambridge University Press, 2023).

history and his work in the last few years has moved back in that direction.[5] Thompson's work has increasingly taken a historical approach, culminating (at time of writing) in a critically acclaimed monograph that has raised the bar for feminist legal history in particular and legal history in general.[6]

Initially I gave no thought to how to describe the shift in my own research and how to now describe my research interests. However, the need to complete bureaucratic forms and Internet profiles prompted further thought. I saw the two areas as complementing each other.[7] Seeking to conjoin or at least link together what to some seemingly appeared disparate aspects of my research profile, I ended up typing the words: 'my research interrogates the interaction between Law and Humanities.' In the conclusion to *Subversive Legal History: A Manifesto for the Future of Legal Education* I went off on a now customary tangent to briefly reflect upon placing legal history under the law and humanities umbrella – a thought I developed further in shaping and contributing to an edited collection on law and humanities.[8]

***

Grouping law and religion under the umbrella of law and humanities scholarship is complicated by the fact that defining precisely what is meant by 'the humanities' is difficult.[9] Austin Sarat, Matthew Anderson and Cathrine O Frank, referring to the humanities, have noted that:

> neither institutional attempts to define it (merely as a group of disciplines not found in the social and natural sciences), nor efforts to identify a common methodological foundation (for example, in interpretation) could succeed because they were either too restrictive or too broad.[10]

---

5   Norman Doe, *Fundamental Authority in Late Medieval Law* (Cambridge University Press, 1990).

6   Sharon Thompson, *Quiet Revolutionaries: The Married Women's Association and Family Law* (Hart, 2022).

7   Indeed, in recent years I have been delighted to be asked to contribute chapters and the like that blend my two interests.

8   Daniel Newman and Russell Sandberg (eds), *Law and Humanities* (Anthem Press, 2024).

9   Costa Douzinas noted that the humanities 'are a consummately modern and decidedly American invention': Costa Douzinas, 'A Humanities of Resistance: Fragments for a Legal History of Humanity' in Austin Sarat, Matthew Anderson and Cathrine O Frank (eds) *Law and Humanities: An Introduction* (Cambridge University Press, 2010) 49.

10   Austin Sarat, Matthew Anderson and Cathrine O Frank, 'Introduction: On the Origins and Prospects of the Humanistic Study of Law' in Austin Sarat, Matthew Anderson and Cathrine O Frank (eds) *Law and Humanities: An Introduction* (Cambridge University Press, 2010) 1, 9.

This leaves us with the kind of understanding offered by Rens Bod ('the humanities have generally been defined as the disciplines that investigate the expressions of the human mind')[11] or Steven Cammiss and Dawn Watkins ('the branch of learning concerned with human culture' and which reflects the 'cultural turn').[12] Perhaps the defining point is simply that the subjects are not scientific (or perhaps wholly scientific) in outlook. Yet that raises questions as to how to define 'scientific'.

Although law and humanities continues to defy categorisation, it has certainly grown as a field – not only in the US, where the *Yale Journal of Law and the Humanities* was the first scholarly journal devoted exclusively to the field, but also subsequently on this side of the Atlantic.[13] Although socio-legal studies have become ubiquitous in terms of legal research, particularly in the UK,[14] there has also been an increase in interdisciplinary scholarship on law that draws upon the humanities.[15] While socio-legal approaches tend to understand law as a social system, approaches from humanities subjects can provide a richer understanding of the nature of law. David Nelken has written of the need to develop 'a much more complex picture of law' where 'analogies are more likely to be drawn between law and theology or law and literary theory than between law and the social and policy sciences'.[16] Sionaidh Douglas-Scott has written that 'law is as much a matter of culture as it is a system of rules',

---

[11]   Rens Bod, *A New History of the Humanities* (Oxford University Press, 2013) 1.

[12]   Steven Cammiss and Dawn Watkins, 'Legal Research in the Humanities' in Dawn Watkins and Mandy Burton (eds) *Research Methods in Law* (2nd edition, Routledge, 2018) 86, 87.

[13]   Research centres or clusters titled as 'Law and Humanities' exist at Birkbeck, Warwick and Northumbria Universities, being parts of law schools and including experts in legal history. Journals include *Law and Humanities* and *Law, Culture and the Humanities*.

[14]   A decade ago, Mathias Siems and Daithí Mac Síthigh argued that legal scholars in the UK were faced with a choice as to 'whether to "go American" in moving closer to social sciences, or "go German" in remaining closer to the humanities': Mathias M Siems and Daithí Mac Síthigh, 'Mapping Legal Research' [2012] *Cambridge Law Journal* 651, 673. See also the essays in Caroline Hunter (ed) *Integrating Socio-Legal Studies into the Law Curriculum* (Palgrave, 2012); Dermot Feenan (ed), *Exploring the 'Socio' of Socio-Legal Studies* (Palgrave, 2013); and as means of response, David Cowan and Daniel Wincott (eds), *Exploring the 'Legal' in Socio-Legal Studies* (Palgrave, 2016).

[15]   The continued existence of these two options is reflected by the way in which funding for legal research projects is available from both the AHRC and the ESRC.

[16]   David Nelken, 'Can Law Learn from Social Science?' (2001) 35 *Israel Law Review* 205, 211.

and has maintained that law 'has its own aesthetic and may be envisioned as a creative art form as much as a science'.[17]

Regarding law as a cultural art form enables the uncovering of its nature and construction. As the introduction to the first issue of the *Yale Journal of Law and the Humanities* put it, the general aim is 'to restore to legal studies a proper place for the question of values'.[18] For Austin Sarat et al, in the law and humanities:

> critical impulses abound, not looking to save or humanize law or lawyers, but to expose their hidden assumptions that structure their work, the values that privilege some views and silence others, the identities that law privileges and those it pushes to the margins and, in doing so, to call law and lawyers to account.[19]

This seems suspiciously similar to socio-legal analyses of law as a social construct with a hint of critical legal studies.

In their exploration of how law and humanities has developed, Sarat et al posit the origins of law and humanities in the US in the law and literature movement – in particular, James Boyd White's seminal book *The Legal Imagination*.[20] This led to a focus on the language of law and on law as a language. As Sarat et al put it:

> If this point of view could be reduced to a maxim, it might be this: Law is a language and language matters. Another way to put it would be to say that the education of lawyers should include the cultivation of a meaningful appreciation of law as rhetoric practice – not just in the sense of an art of persuasion, but of a disciplined, textual self-directed habit of reading, speaking, and above all, writing, that has at its root critical understanding of the links among language, consciousness, and power.[21]

The strong literary focus in the law and humanities movement has been countered, however – most notably by Robin L West[22] – on the grounds that such

---

[17] Sionaidh Douglas-Scott, *Law after Modernity* (Hart, 2013) 253.

[18] Owen M Fiss, 'The Challenge Ahead' (1988) 1 *Yale Journal of Law and Humanities* viii, x.

[19] Austin Sarat, Matthew Anderson and Cathrine O Frank, 'Introduction: On the Origins and Prospects of the Humanistic Study of Law' in Austin Sarat, Matthew Anderson and Cathrine O Frank (eds) *Law and Humanities: An Introduction* (Cambridge University Press, 2010) 1, 11.

[20] James Boyd White, *The Legal Imagination* (University of Chicago Press, 1973).

[21] Austin Sarat, Matthew Anderson and Cathrine O Frank, 'Introduction: On the Origins and Prospects of the Humanistic Study of Law' in Austin Sarat, Matthew Anderson and Cathrine O Frank (eds) *Law and Humanities: An Introduction* (Cambridge University Press, 2010) 1, 4.

[22] Robin L West, 'Communities, Texts and Law: Reflections on the Law and Literature Movement' (1988) 1 *Yale Journal of Law and Humanities* 154.

an approach would 'leave out much that is nontextual in our interaction with actual people'.[23] There has been a call for perspectives which 'pushes beyond the literary' and raises the question: 'how would a study of the way in which law constitutes persons proceed'?[24] This invariably takes us back to talk of culture.[25] This, then, poses its own problems: the word 'cultural' can become as generic and meaningless as the word 'social' often becomes in socio-legal studies.

Simon Stern et al have argued that:

> to practice the humanities is to approach, with certain attitudes and sensitivities, a multitude of practices of making (of making things, making meaning, making senses) including relations between those practices of making and the values that may be at stake in such practices and their relations to each other.[26]

Crucially, they note that these 'attitudes and sensitivities' include 'sensitivity not so much (and certainly not only) to the regular and patterned, but instead to the irregular and unpatterned' paying attention to 'the unpredictability of human behavior'; 'sensitivity to the blind spots in our abilities to sense who is in anger, suffering or vulnerable'; and 'sensitivity to the apparently superficial, superfluous, unnecessary, insufficient, marginal, or-by-the-by'.[27] As Stern et al note, while conventionally a law and humanities approach has 'associated law with legal doctrines and rhetoric, in particular, and have looked to the humanities for representations of legal actors and dilemmas, and for ethical resources that can shed light on legal problems', humanities needs to be more widely drawn to 'encompass not only history, literature, art, and philosophy but the whole range of fields that use interpretative methods to study creativity, expression, and the imagination'.[28] They noted:

> These include many fields – such as architecture, geography, book history, cognitive studies, science and technology studies, and performance studies – that influence,

---

[23]   Austin Sarat, Matthew Anderson and Cathrine O Frank, 'Introduction: On the Origins and Prospects of the Humanistic Study of Law' in Austin Sarat, Matthew Anderson and Cathrine O Frank (eds) *Law and Humanities: An Introduction* (Cambridge University Press, 2010) 1, 7.

[24]   Ibid 7–8.

[25]   Steven Cammiss and Dawn Watkins, 'Legal Research in the Humanities' in Dawn Watkins and Mandy Burton (eds) *Research Methods in Law* (2nd edition, Routledge, 2018) 86, 87.

[26]   Simon Stern, Maksymillan Del Mar and Bernadette Meyler, 'Introduction' in Simon Stern, Maksymillan Del Mar and Bernadette Meyler (eds) *The Oxford Handbook of Law and Humanities* (Oxford University Press, 2020) xxi, xxii.

[27]   Ibid xxiii.

[28]   Ibid xxiv.

and are influenced by legal concepts and methods, but that appear only sporadically, if at all, in law journals.

This heterogeneous list underscores the lack of a clear definition. Yet this looseness is apt given that this also reflects the nature of the grouping itself. Sara Ramshaw has argued that law and humanities exists 'not as a "canon" per se, but as a "field without a canon" or a canon that resists canonization'.[29] For Ramshaw, by its very nature, law and humanities needs to 'leap ahead fearlessly to properly defy disciplinary boundaries and move the field beyond siloed thinking'; this 'is one of the preliminary aims of law and humanities scholarship and pedagogy'. This requires using the rigour found within humanities disciplines,[30] without insisting upon disciplinary distinctions. As Hyo Yoon Kang has noted, in law and humanities scholarship, the 'literal adhesive is the "and"'.[31] The 'and' holds 'together the field as an un-disciplined montage of different disciplinary insights'.[32] This can be reflected in the 'X as law'/'law as X' distinction, which shows how the interaction between the two operates in both directions. Situating law as part of the humanities, then, encourages subversive thinking about boundaries, disciplines and methods. A humanities understanding of law emphasises that a rich methodological toolkit is needed to understand the various dimensions of law, and that this extends beyond seeing law as a social science.

***

This digression into the nature of law and humanities as a field prompts the follow-up question: should the study of law and religion be placed under this umbrella? Law and religion is not a branch of law like contract law, tort law or trusts law because it does not correspond with a certain legal action. Rather, as I argued in *Law and Religion*[33] and subsequent publications, law and religion can be said to be a sub-discipline like family law, educational law, media law

---

[29]   Sara E Ramshaw, 'Law and Humanities: A Field without a Canon' (2019) 19(1) *Law, Culture and the Humanities* 77, 79.

[30]   The risk is otherwise that 'Law and Humanities courses end up entertaining and lightening the heavy load of law students as well as giving them a useful cultural gloss': Costas Douzinas, 'A Humanities of Resistance: Fragments for a Legal History of Humanity' in Austin Sarat, Matthew Anderson and Cathrine O Frank (eds) *Law and Humanities: An Introduction* (Cambridge University Press, 2010) 49, 56.

[31]   H Yoon Kang, 'Is There (Should There Be) a Law and Humanities Canon?' (2023) 19(1) *Law, Culture and Humanities* 60, 63.

[32]   Ibid 66. See also Sara Ramshaw, 'Conclusion: Subverting the Law and Humanities Canon' in Daniel Newman and Russell Sandberg (eds) *Law and Humanities* (Anthem Press, 2024) 225.

[33]   Russell Sandberg, *Law and Religion* (Cambridge University Press, 2011).

and sports law because it is the study of a body of law that relates to a 'an entity ... which has meaning ... outside the legal domain', to quote Gillian Douglas' definition of family law.[34] For Douglas, 'the essence of family law is that part of the law which is concerned with the recognition and regulation of certain family relationships and the implications of such recognition', as well as the ramifications of non-recognition. Family law might be an unhappy comparison since there is now a Family Court that deals with some family law matters. Yet the general point stands. Religion – like the family, education, media and sports – are social entities. They are, to use sociological language, agencies of socialisation: places where we learn how to behave in society. They are all separate but overlapping social systems.

Douglas' definition of 'family law' can be applied to all of these fields. For instance, it can be said that education law is that part of the law that is concerned with the recognition and regulation of educational establishments and the rights of citizens to such establishments (Douglas noted that the goal of family policy – a 'stable family life' – is recognised by both domestic and international law and that the right to family life is protected as a human right).[35] The same can be said of media law and sports law. However, law and religion does not fit this template so neatly. It does fit if we rely upon the religion law/religious law distinction. Media law and sports law are both clearly are concerned not only with the effect of 'external' national and international laws but are also concerned with the 'internal' laws or rules made as a means of self-regulation.[36] That second dimension of the subject is analogous with religious law.

Yet while this framework supports the idea that law and religion includes the study of religion law and religious law, it does not go further than this. To return to Witte's terminology:[37] comparing law and religion to the laws affecting and developed by other agencies of socialisation (eg, the family, education, media, sport) focuses solely on seeing these things legally; it does not extend to seeing the law through their lens. Indeed, such talk does not seem to fit naturally. While it is meaningful to talk about studying the 'religious dimensions of law', such language does not naturally fit with the other social systems. This is

---

[34]   Gillian Douglas, *An Introduction to Family Law* (2nd edition, Clarendon Press, 2004) 3.

[35]   Ibid 4.

[36]   The same could be said of family law if the study of regulation within the family is included. The move towards private ordering of family law disputes and the rollback of the State poses questions here as to where the line is drawn between the external and internal and how the external can be defined.

[37]   John Witte, Jr, 'The Study of Law and Religion in the United States: An Interim Report' (2012) 14 *Ecclesiastical Law Journal* 327.

perhaps why they tend not to be referred to as 'education and the law', 'media and the law', 'family and the law' and so on.

However, there is more to it than this. Religion is not simply a social system. It is both a social system and a form of identity. It is both a collective and individual endeavour. And, crucially, although it can be said that religion is an aspect of identity, it is not always the product of choice. Of course, religious identity can be changed though conversion or through adopting a new religion or belief. However, it is an identity that is often initially ascribed rather than achieved. Indeed, it is something that can be both ascribed and achieved – and delineating the two is often far from straightforward. Religious identity is often a complex mixture of ascribed and achieved statuses and can often be a complex mix of individual and collective identities. This is why census results on religion are so unreliable: the forms require people to fit in a box where the reality is not so straightforward. For instance, how do you state in a word a reality where you were born and raised in a particular faith, believe in some of the moral tenets – which, incidentally, are common to most world religions and humanistic standpoints – and attend a place of worship on very special occasions to appreciate its cultural value more than anything else? Perhaps, for many, the only accurate summary is 'it's complicated'.

The way in which religion can be both ascribed and achieved and can have individual and collective dimensions is reflected in how laws do not only see religious freedom as a human right (in the same way as the goals of family, media, education and sports policy are articulated as typically individualised human rights), but also regard religion as a protected characteristic – a basis upon which people are discriminated against. The list of 'protected character-istics' in Section 4 of the Equality Act 2010 – 'age; disability; gender reassign-ment; marriage and civil partnership; pregnancy and maternity; race; religion or belief; sex; [and] sexual orientation' – shows that the mixture of achieved and ascribed status is not unique to religion. This raises the question of whether law and religion ought to be compared not against family law, education law and the like, but rather against other forms of inequality and discrimination. That has been the focus of the previous chapters, taking gender and race as exemplars.

Religion also relates to an area of study; the study of religion (in various different ways) is long established. This is also true of the other social systems with courses and departments dedicated to family studies, education, media studies and sports studies. Yet religion is taught throughout the education system. Indeed, in England, the study of religion is compulsory for as long as a pupil remains in school.[38] Religion is often regarded as part of the humanities, together with history and geography.[39] However, unlike these other fields (and, indeed, law), the study of religion is multidisciplinary. 'Religious studies' is an umbrella term for a number of disciplinary approaches to studying religion.[40] By contrast, although there are a number of disciplinary approaches that can be applied to law, geography and history, each of these subjects has a clear and distinct methodological approach often linked to the 'internal' study of the subject in question. Situating religious studies within the humanities is less straightforward. The same is true of positioning law and religion under the law and humanities umbrella. Sara Ramshaw has noted that religion and theology are 'disciplines often missing from law and humanities collections or handbooks'.[41]

The next two chapters, however, attempt to do just that by comparing law and religion to the development of two studies that can be placed under the law and humanities umbrella. Again, our choice is selective. The focus is on the other two humanities subjects commonly taught within the school system: history and geography.[42] These are perhaps not obvious choices within the law and humanities literature.[43] But they have been chosen since their development

---

[38]   In Wales, religion, values and ethics is now only compulsory until the mandatory school leaving age: see Russell Sandberg, *Religion in Schools: Learning Lessons from Wales* (Anthem Press, 2022).

[39]   In the curriculum for Wales, humanities is one of the six Areas of Learning and Experience (AoLEs) that underpin the curriculum. The humanities AoLE is understood as encompassing geography; history; religion, values and ethics; business studies; and social studies.

[40]   Grace Davie has referred to religious studies as 'hovering, at times uneasily, in between' theology and sociology: Grace Davie, *The Sociology of Religion* (2nd edition, Sage, 2013) 6. For a discussion of the interplay between law and theology, see Norman Doe, 'Law and Theology' in Daniel Newman and Russell Sandberg (eds) *Law and Humanities* (Anthem Press, 2024) 201.

[41]   Sara Ramshaw, 'Conclusion: Subverting the Law and Humanities Canon' in Daniel Newman and Russell Sandberg (eds) *Law and Humanities* (Anthem Press, 2024) 225, 226.

[42]   As with the last two chapters, we will be looking at how the fields have developed in order to compare the development of law and religion. As before, there is also work that calls for the application of these disciplinary perspectives to law and religion. For instance, calls have been made for law and religion to take a more historical approach. See Meadhbh McIvor, 'Histories of Law and Religion' (2020) 46(1) *Religious Studies Review* 29 and Peter W Edge, 'History, Sacred History and Law at the Intersections of Law, Religion and History' in T Grass et al (eds) *The Church and the Law* (Cambridge University Press, 2020) 508.

[43]   It is curious that the three humanities subjects most widely taught throughout the education system are not those that we think about when we think of law and humanities; we often begin with law and literature instead. Indeed, the study of how the three

in England and Wales contrasts with that of law and religion. One of them provides inspiration on the path that law and religion should follow; the other a warning of a future that law and religion should avoid. And the difference between the two comes down to their respective relationship with the critical turn.

---

humanities disciplines interact with law does not fall neatly into the 'law and ...' movements that could be said to characterise the law and humanities movement. We tend to speak of 'legal history' rather than 'law and history' and 'legal geography' rather than 'law and geography'.

12. Law and history

Legal history in English and Welsh law schools is a clearly recognised legal sub-discipline. It is a specialism within law schools, often taught as an optional module. It has developed the institutional trappings of a legal sub-discipline, perhaps more than most: there are specialist conferences, book series and journals – though some work does appear in general law journals, particularly the *Cambridge Law Journal* that is linked to the law faculty at Cambridge, which has a particular reputation for legal history. It is a well-known and respected field. Legal history, therefore, provides an example of what law and religion could have developed into had it continued down the road of becoming a legal sub-discipline and becoming more established.

Yet an examination of the development of legal history provides a warning for law and religion. The development of legal history as a legal specialism has constrained it. The way in which papers are presented and works are written, to be accessible only to fellow specialists, has led to its decline. Legal history is less visible in law schools today than it once was: history appears less in the textbooks of the core legal subjects; the topic is taught less; and, although it is often assumed that law students and scholars have somehow picked up an understanding of the history of English law, it is likely that the reverse is true and that there is a lack of historical literacy. The story of legal history, therefore, provides a salutary lesson for law and religion; although recent years have seen attempts to restore legal history to the beating heart of the law curriculum.[1]

***

Although there have been legal historians of note before and since, Frederic William Maitland (1850–1906) is often seen as the founder of the modern study of legal history in England and Wales.[2] The modern study of English

---

[1]   This chapter summarises arguments developed in full in Russell Sandberg, *Subversive Legal History: A Manifesto for the Future of Legal Education* (Routledge, 2021). Like that book, it focuses entirely on the experience in England and Wales. As with law and religion, the picture is radically different in the US, where legal history – including the history of the English common law – is much more firmly established, with a variety of methodological approaches taken.

[2]   Ian Ward, *English Legal Histories* (Hart, 2019) 11.

legal history can be traced back to the second half of the nineteenth century and to Maitland's body of 'seemingly miraculous writing' – much of which was published posthumously,[3] which has resulted in a 'superhuman myth engulfing him'.[4] Maitland has been hailed as a 'patron saint' and 'the master' of English legal history,[5] with revisions to his views regarded as 'heresies'.[6] As SFC Milsom eulogised, Maitland's work 'established both the subject and the assumptions on which historians have worked ever since' – so much so that those interested in the history of English law still invariably begin with Maitland: 'Their questions still take the form: was Maitland right?'[7]

Maitland's reputation rests upon his method: he pioneered the use of primary legal materials. He was renowned for his introductions to numerous editions of primary materials prepared for the Selden Society and other organisations. The Selden Society, formed in 1886 with Maitland serving as its literary director until the end of his life, has been referred to as 'the living memorial which perpetuates not only the work but also the spirit of Maitland'.[8] Maitland is acclaimed as 'the legal historian's historian'.[9] His work has been renowned not only by lawyers but also by historians. For Michael Lobban, Maitland 'was

---

[3] Perhaps his best-known work of legal history published in his lifetime was Frederick Pollock and Frederic W Maitland, *The History of English Law* (2nd edition, Cambridge University Press, 1968 [1898]). The first edition was published in 1895 with a second edition in 1898. His major posthumous publications notably include Frederic W Maitland, *The Constitutional History of England* (Cambridge University Press, 1941 [1908]); and Frederic W Maitland, *Equity, Also the Form of Action at Common Law* (Cambridge University Press, 1909). See also HAL Fisher (ed), *Collected Papers of Frederic William Maitland, Downing Professor of the Laws of England* (3 volumes, Cambridge University Press, 1911). Maitland also authored works on political philosophy and biography.

[4] SFC Milsom, 'Maitland' (2001) 60(2) *Cambridge Law Journal* 265.

[5] Thomas G Watkin, 'Feudal Theory, Social Needs and the Rise of the Heritable Fee' 10 *Cambrian Law Review* 39, 41.

[6] SFC Milsom, 'Introduction' in Frederick Pollock and Frederic W Maitland, *The History of English Law* (2nd edition, Volume 1, Cambridge University Press, 1968 [1898]) xxiii, xxv.

[7] SFC Milsom, 'Introduction' in Frederick Pollock and Frederic W Maitland, *The History of English Law* (2nd edition, Volume 1, Cambridge University Press, 1968 [1898]) xxiii, ix, xi, xxiv; SFC Milsom, *A Natural History of the Common Law* (Columbia University Press, 2003) xiv. Though some accounts now begin with Milsom's heretical criticisms of Maitland: Ralph V Turner, 'Henry II's Aims in Reforming England's Land Law: Feudal or Royalist' in EB King and SJ Ridyard (eds) *Law in Medieval Life and Thought* (Sewanee Medieval Studies, 1990) 121, 122.

[8] Theodore FT Plucknett, 'Frederic William Maitland' (1951) 26 *New York University Law Review* 10.

[9] KJM Smith and JPS McLaren, 'History's Living Legacy: An Outline of "Modern" Historiography of the Common Law' (2001) 21 *Legal Studies* 251, 261.

one of the central figures who helped to turn the study of history into a professional pursuit, in which the scholar was encouraged to spend long hours in the archives reading primary sources'.[10] Maitland's work also emphasised to historians the importance of looking at law. He regarded legal documents as being 'the best, often the only evidence that we have for social and economic history, for the history of morality, for the history of practical religion'.[11]

As Ian Ward pointed out, legal history 'was born of the same positivist impulse that drove forward modern historiography and historical writing'.[12] Maitland subjected the law of the past to the same, if not more scrutiny as academics were applying in analysing the law of the present. In so doing, Maitland inspired a legalistic doctrinal approach. As Sarah E Hamill noted, historians have dismissed 'some legal history as bad history or at least not useful history with utility being work that historians will use themselves'.[13] David Sugarman observed that belittling law and legal history has become 'fair sport among historians', who have often 'stigmatized law and legal historians (with some notable exceptions) as intrinsically unhistorical, given their preoccupation with reading the past in the light of modern legal doctrine'.[14] Legal history also became increasingly neglected. William Holdsworth noted that legal history was the 'one great exception' to the general renaissance in historical studies, and that 'the absence of general legal history from the list of subjects in which the law student must satisfy his examiners' would be seen as 'a very curious phenomenon' were we all not so familiar with these oddities.[15] Even within law schools, legal history declined. Legal history has been described as 'slowly and inevitably dying—or ... [as having] been in a coma for the last 30 years, at least'.[16]

---

[10] Michael Lobban, 'The Varieties of Legal History' (2012) 5 *Clio@Themis* 1, 4.

[11] Frederic W Maitland, 'Why the History of English Law has not been Written' in HAL Fisher (ed) *Collected Papers of Frederic William Maitland, Downing Professor of the Laws of England* (Cambridge University Press, 1911) Vol 1, 480, 486.

[12] Ian Ward, *English Legal Histories* (Hart, 2019) 11.

[13] Sarah E Hamill, 'Review of Legal History' (2019) 28(4) *Social & Legal Studies* 538, 541–42.

[14] He also noted a key reason for this: 'Divorcing history from law and legal history spoke to the self-identity of modern professional historians': David Sugarman, 'Promoting Dialogue between History and Socio-Legal Studies: The Contribution of Christopher W Brooks and the "Legal Turn" in Early Modern English History' (2017) 44(S1) *Journal of Law and Society* S37, S39.

[15] William S Holdsworth, 'The Place of English Legal History in the Education of English Lawyers: A Pleas for its Further Recognition' in AL Goodhart and HG Hanbury (eds) *Sir William S Holdsworth: Essays in Law and History* (Clarendon Press, 1946) 20, 21.

[16] Daniel Siemens, 'Towards a New Cultural History of Law' (2012) 2 *InterDisciplines* 18, 19.

Maitland himself recognised that even in his day, legal history was 'not flourishing quite as it ought to flourish'.[17] In his 1888 inaugural lecture at Cambridge, he bemoaned how legal history was not being constrained 'by any lack of evidence'; rather, this was due to 'the limits of our leisure, our strength, our studiousness, our curiosity'.[18] He regretted how the English legal historian was 'overburdened by our materials' and so 'has but flitted over the surface'.[19] Maitland's reason for this was that the very people who could competently carry out legal historical research were legal practitioners – because 'a thorough training in modern law is almost indispensable for any one who wishes to do good work on legal history'[20] – and such persons were 'as a rule very unlikely to attempt it' because even 'if they have the taste they have not the time, the ample leisure, that is necessary for historical research'.[21]

Maitland's conclusion was based on the idea that legal and historical approaches were distinct. He suggested that the lawyer and the historian used 'two different logics, the logic of authority, and the logic of evidence': 'what the lawyer wants is authority and the newer the better; what the historian wants is evidence and older the better.'[22] It followed that legal history work could only be completed by lawyers – and this meant practitioners, since 'the object of a law school must be to teach law, and this is not quite the same thing as teaching the history of law'.[23] Maitland insisted that 'we should not wish to see a professor of law breaking and entering the close of the professor of history'.[24]

Yet this is exactly what Maitland did. As Theodore Plucknett put it, Maitland's inaugural lecture reflects his then undeveloped and 'imperfect view of the place of legal history' and 'his later career must be read as the gradual abandonment of the propositions laid down in 1888'.[25] Maitland's subsequent career shows how the historical study of law can prosper as an academic

---

[17]   Frederic W Maitland, 'Why the History of English Law has not been Written' in HAL Fisher (ed) *Collected Papers of Frederic William Maitland, Downing Professor of the Laws of England* (Cambridge University Press, 1911) Vol 1 480, 497.

[18]   Ibid 481.

[19]   Ibid 483.

[20]   Ibid 493.

[21]   Ibid 494.

[22]   Ibid 491.

[23]   Ibid 494.

[24]   Maitland's conclusion was reached at a time when legal education in the universities was at its infancy. As Baker noted, in Maitland's day, 'there were few academic lawyers of any kind, ... the only legal history taught at Oxford or Cambridge was Roman, and ... the only expertise in ancient legal records was to be found among practising barristers in the inns of court': John H Baker, 'Why the History of English Law has not been Finished' (2000) *Cambridge Law Journal* 62, 63.

[25]   Theodore FT Plucknett, *Early English Legal Literature* (Cambridge University Press, 1958) 13.

rather than as a practitioner pursuit. Maitland as a professor of law did break and enter into the close of the historian by writing and contributing works of general history. However, despite his own work, Maitland's designation of legal history as a lawyer's pursuit stuck. A separation developed between legal history as largely carried out in law schools and the study of law historically which occurred in history departments. This more or less corresponded with a second distinction: that between internal and external approaches.

As Sarah E Hamill has noted, legal history became a 'disparate and often jurisdictionally divided field'.[26] The basic distinction, to put it crudely, is between what may broadly be styled doctrinal and socio-legal approaches to law generally.[27] A distinction can be drawn between the 'old' or 'internal' legal history on the one hand, which is largely doctrinal, and the 'new' or 'external' legal history on the other hand, which is largely socio-legal.[28] In the first camp, work explores the doctrinal development of legal ideas, concepts and institutions.

Internal legal history is associated with the Cambridge legal historians who followed Maitland. It is preoccupied with the genealogy of legal doctrine'.[29] Its approach is 'internal to the extent that it is based on primary sources that are legal' – that is, sources such as reported cases, actions in the plea rolls

---

[26]   Sarah E Hamill, 'Review of Legal History' (2019) 28(4) *Social & Legal Studies* 538. For a detailed account of the development of legal history, see KJM Smith and JPS McLaren, 'History's Living Legacy: An Outline of "Modern" Historiography of the Common Law' (2001) 21 *Legal Studies* 251; and Michael Lobban, 'The Varieties of Legal History' (2012) 5 *Clio@Themis* 1.

[27]   A number of areas of legal history scholarship are difficult to place within the internal–external distinction. This includes institutional legal history and the literatures on legal archaeology and legal biography. On legal archaeology, see AW Brian Simpson, *Leading Cases in the Common Law* (Oxford University Press, 1995); and Emma Nottingham, 'Digging into Legal Archaeology: A Methodology for Case Study Research' (2022) 49(S1) *Journal of Law and Society* S16. On legal biography, see William Cornish, *Life Stories and Legal Histories* (Selden Society, 2015); David Sugarman, 'From Legal Biography to Legal Life Writing: Broadening Conceptions of Legal History and Socio-Legal Scholarship' (2015) 42(1) *Journal of Law and Society* 7 and the other essays published in that special issue; Victoria Barnes, Catharine MacMillan and Stefan Vogenauer, 'On Legal Biography' (2020) 41(2) *Journal of Legal History* 115 and the other essays published in that special issue; and the discussion in Sharon Thompson, *Quiet Revolutionaries: The Married Women's Association and Family Law* (Hart, 2022) 49 *et seq.*

[28]   The difference between the internal and external approaches was articulated in Robert W Gordon, 'J. Willard Hurst and the Common Law Tradition in American Legal Historiography' (1975) 10 *Law & Society Review* 9, 11.

[29]   David Sugarman, 'Promoting Dialogue between History and Socio-Legal Studies: The Contribution of Christopher W Brooks and the "Legal Turn" in Early Modern English History (2017) 44(S1) *Journal of Law and Society* S37.

and yearbooks, statutes and early legal literature.[30] It examines 'law on its own terms', exploring 'the law that would have been recognized by lawyers in its times'.[31] Although this is most commonly referred to as the 'internal' or 'old' legal history,[32] a number of other labels are used, such as 'orthodox'[33] or 'classical'[34] legal history.[35]

In the second camp, work explores how law exists as one of many social institutions and how law is shaped by (and shapes) other social institutions and society as a whole. This is the 'external' or 'new'[36] legal history, also sometimes called 'socio-legal history'[37] or 'the social history of law'.[38] Generally speaking, these two types of legal history are carried out by different groups of people. The 'old' internal doctrinal legal history tends to be carried out in law schools by those who call themselves legal historians and is associated with all the institutional trappings (such as journals, conferences and associations) that have developed within legal history.[39] By contrast, the 'new' external socio-legal history tends to be done elsewhere: in history departments, where law plays a significant role despite the focus shifting from constitutional history to social history; but also in law schools, where many scholars are engaged in research that includes, to a greater or lesser extent, the historical development of their area of study. However, neither of these groups tend to

---

[30]   Jonathan Rose, 'Studying the Past: The Nature and Development of Legal History as an Academic Discipline' (2010) 31(2) *The Journal of Legal History* 101, 118–19.

[31]   David Ibbetson, 'What is Legal History a History of?' in Andrew Lewis and Michael Lobban (eds) *Law and History* (Oxford University Press, 2004) 33, 34.

[32]   E.g., David Ibbetson, 'What is Legal History a History of' in Andrew Lewis and Michael Lobban (eds) *Law and History* (Oxford University Press, 2004) 33.

[33]   Alan Hunt, 'The New Legal History: Prospects and Perspectives' (1986) 10 *Contemporary Crises* 201, 202.

[34]   Jonathan Rose, 'Studying the Past: The Nature and Development of Legal History as an Academic Discipline' (2010) 31(2) *The Journal of Legal History* 101, 117.

[35]   See also the work of Rosemary Hunter, distinguishing *legal* history – which 'focuses on primarily on statutes, cases and judges (and legal practice)' – and legal *history*, which 'explores the legal dimension of historical problems': Rosemary Hunter, 'Australian Legal History in Context' (2003) 21 *Law and History Review* 607, 613.

[36]   Alan Hunt, 'The New Legal History: Prospects and Perspectives' (1986) 10 *Contemporary Crises* 201.

[37]   Christopher W Brooks, *Lawyers, Litigation and English Society Since 1450* (Hambledon Press, 1998) 179.

[38]   Michael Lobban, 'The Varieties of Legal History' (2012) 5 *Clio@Themis* 1, 20.

[39]   Indeed, this is often the focus of critique by historians: Laura Cahillane, 'The Use of History in Law: Avoiding the Pitfalls' in Laura Cahillane and Jennifer Schweppe (eds) *Legal Research Methods: Principles and Practicalities* (Clarus Press, 2016) 57, 61.

refer to themselves as 'legal historians' or attach themselves to the institutional trappings. The entrenchment of the differences between these two approaches to legal history has led to its neglect.

External legal history has its roots in the critical turn. Ian Ward has noted that since the 1970s,[40] 'a broader inter-disciplinary and contextual approach began to gain a foothold in the academy' and 'people started to matter'.[41] In history departments, this 'critical turn' was manifest in the new social history that paid attention to the lived lives of ordinary people in the past and took a much more grounded approach. Law became a facet of this social history. As Smith and McLaren observed, the work of EP Thompson and his protégés at Warwick:

> opened up interest in the legal history of the eighteenth and nineteenth centuries, encouraged scholars to consider how law was experienced within society and espe-cially by the poor and unenfranchised, raising a host of awkward questions about the claimed objectivity and rationality of law in history.[42]

In law schools, this same critical turn manifested itself in socio-legal studies; but for most socio-legal scholars, legal history (in its prevalent 'internal' guise) became regarded and attacked as an exemplar of the purely doctrinal approach. As David Sugarman pointed out, legal history 'attracted the suspicion of socio-legal scholars in that it underpinned and legitimated a preoccupation with the narrow technicalities of the law and the treatment of law as largely divorced from the society, politics, and economy in which it operated'.[43] This meant that for many advocating a socio-legal approach, 'the moral was clear: the less history the better'. However, for the minority of socio-legal scholars who turned to history in their work (usually as a result of their quest to answer their research questions), the history to which they turned was not legal history but the new social history that 'brought the relationships between law and

---

[40]   Smith and McLaren observed that it was possible to identify both internal and external approaches in legal history long before the 1970s, but also noted that before that 'arguably the only out and out attempt at an "external" narrative account of the full span of English legal history was Alan Harding's *A Social History of English Law* (Penguin, 1966)': KJM Smith and JPS McLaren, 'History's Living Legacy: An Outline of "Modern" Historiography of the Common Law' (2001) 21 *Legal Studies* 251, 272.

[41]   Ian Ward, *English Legal Histories* (Hart, 2019) 11.

[42]   KJM Smith and JPS McLaren, 'History's Living Legacy: An Outline of "Modern" Historiography of the Common Law' (2001) 21 *Legal Studies* 251, 308.

[43]   David Sugarman, 'Promoting Dialogue between History and Socio-Legal Studies: The Contribution of Christopher W Brooks and the "Legal Turn" in Early Modern English History' (2017) 44(S1) *Journal of Law and Society* S37, S38.

class, race and gender to the fore'.[44] Socio-legal scholars interested in history embraced the methodologies of social historians.[45] Such history also became important to the critical legal studies movement as a whole, with critical legal history developing alongside this, particularly in the US.

The heterogonous nature of those who can be grouped under the external approach, their differing backgrounds and perspectives as well as their frequent unwillingness to be regarded as legal historians meant that this new external approach became neither a key component of legal history, the legal sub-discipline, nor a body of scholarship in its own right.[46] External legal history engaged with periods and areas of law that were previously neglected in the internal legal history literature. External legal history focused on modern history,[47] and particularly upon criminal justice.[48] It explored the political, social, economic and cultural causes and effects of changes, including a number of works that focus on gender,[49] as well as the importance of other

---

[44] Jim Phillips, 'Why Legal History Matters' (2010) 41 *Victoria University of Wellington Law Review* 293, 298.

[45] Laura Cahillane, 'The Use of History in Law: Avoiding the Pitfalls' in Laura Cahillane and Jennifer Schweppe (eds) *Legal Research Methods: Principles and Practicalities* (Clarus Press, 2016) 57, 61.

[46] As Sugarman has noted, law and history 'were competitors for academic legitimacy, cultural authority, student numbers, and material support, making boundary maintenance part of their raison d'être' (David Sugarman, 'Promoting Dialogue between History and Socio-Legal Studies: The Contribution of Christopher W Brooks and the "Legal Turn" in Early Modern English History' (2017) 44(S1) *Journal of Law and Society* S37, S38). And history and socio-legal studies have different methods and assumptions: 'Socio-legal scholars may treat history as largely a repository of examples and data that they can draw upon for their own purposes. But historians may regard this as ransacking secondary sources in order to "theorize the facts", an exercise whose potential pitfalls include over-simplification': ibid s39–40.

[47] See, e.g., AH Manchester, *Modern Legal History* (Butterworths, 1980); William R Cornish and Geoffrey de N Clark, *Law and Society in England 1750–1950* (Sweet & Maxwell, 1989) (a new edition of this was published as William R Cornish et al, *Law and Society in England 1750–1950* (2nd edition, Hart, 2019)); and the work cited by David Sugarman and GR Rubin, 'Towards a New History of Law and Material Society in England 1750–1914' in GR Rubin and David Sugarman (eds) *Law, Economy & Society* (Professional Books, 1984) 1.

[48] There has also been a notable 'turn to history' in constitutional and international law, as well as in the development of law and literature and legal biographies: David Sugarman, 'Promoting Dialogue between History and Socio-Legal Studies: The Contribution of Christopher W Brooks and the "Legal Turn" in Early Modern English History' (2017) 44(S1) *Journal of Law and Society* S37, S41.

[49] See, for instance, Laura Gowing, *Domestic Dangers: Women, Words and Sex in Early Modern London* (Oxford University Press, 1996); and Garthine Walker, *Crime, Gender and Social Order in Early Modern British History* (Cambridge University Press, 2009).

non-legal developments.[50] Moreover, the new external legal history often presented itself as being in opposition to the prevalent internal legal history. As Sarah E Hamill put it: '"Good" legal history is no longer an endless "and then" of judicial decisions but a "why this at this time" approach. Legal historians are expected to read around the law and capture the contexts which shaped it.'[51] External legal history was regarded as a necessary corrective to the internal approach.[52] As Alan Harding provocatively put it, the external approach 'does at least try to be real history; to relate the development of law as a whole, and forwards, to the development of English society not to race backwards as a bundle of legal doctrines'.[53]

These criticisms and the caricaturing of the internal legal history mainstream have led to a hesitation on their part to engage in with the external approach. The result has been that the internal legal historical approach – and legal history as a sub-discipline – retreated from the mainstream of legal scholarship. As Lorie Charlesworth has noted, the domination of 'a close-knit group of mostly (male) academics who took their law degrees from the Universities of Cambridge, Oxford and London where they occupy prestigious law chairs, some of which have always been designated for legal historians', has led to the area being unattractive to outsiders.[54] A vicious circle has been created: the denigration of internal doctrinal legal history has resulted in the retreat and

---

[50] Leading works include EP Thompson, *Whigs and Hunters* (Allen Lane, 1975) and Douglas Hay et al, *Albion's Fatal Tree* (Allen Lane, 1975). There has also been a focus on the history of the legal professions, though Brookes was critical of the lack of the literatures on the history of crime and the history of the legal profession 'either to communicate much with each other or to make a significant impact on the social and political history of the England between 1500 and 1800': Christopher W Brooks, *Lawyers, Litigation and English Society Since 1450* (Hambledon Press, 1998) 179.

[51] Sarah E Hamill, 'Review of Legal History' (2019) 28(4) *Social & Legal Studies* 538, 540.

[52] Sarah Wilson has distinguished 'conventional *legal history*'s interest in the value of understanding law's own history for the present with *modern history*'s commentaries on the value of history for understanding society today': Sarah Wilson, 'Value and Values in Higher Education: Some Reflections from the UK on the Subversive Dimensions of Historical Approaches in the Study of Law' in Helen Gibbon et al (eds) *Critical Legal Education as a Subversive Activity* (Routledge, 2023) 149, 154.

[53] Alan Harding, *A Social History of English Law* (Penguin, 1966) 9. Christopher Brookes stated that 'thanks to the general interest over the past half century in so many aspects of social history, including questions about the political awareness and "agency" of the people outside the landed elite, any study of law that concentrates only on high politics is bound to seem unsatisfactory and myopic': Christopher W Brooks, *Law, Politics and Society in Early Modern England* (Cambridge University Press, 2008) 9.

[54] Lorie Charlesworth, 'On Historical Contextualisation: Some Critical Socio-Legal Reflections' (2007) 1 *Crimes and Misdemeanours* 1, 27.

ghettoisation of such work; and this decrease in the appetite to produce doctrinal internal legal history in a way that is accessible enough for non-specialists in legal history has fuelled the criticisms of externalists, who see legal history as being not for them. The prevalent perception of legal history as taught and researched in law schools remains predominantly internal and doctrinal. The external approach, though fashionable, neither has replaced nor co-exists with the internal approach as representing – let alone epitomising – how legal history is seen as an academic field. The internal–external division has had a significant detrimental effect upon the stagnation of the historical study of law in English law schools.

***

This sketch of the development of legal history in England and Wales poses a warning about the future of law and religion. Although legal history remains much more well established than law and religion, it too demonstrates a state of decline. The development of legal history as a legal specialism has limited its impact and led to divisions. The field has become exclusive and has shielded itself from the critical turn. The main areas of growth are kept at a distance from the mainstream of the sub-discipline. Legal history shows the risk of institutionalisation: what happens when a field becomes increasingly inward looking. The ghettoisation of law and religion is likely to have a similar if not more disastrous effect, given that it has never been as well developed as legal history has been. The premature institutionalisation of law and religion scholarship has meant that the field has become an inward-facing clique showing signs of wear and fatigue. In the same way that many religious rights cases are now being argued without reference to Article 9, exceptional scholarship that could be placed under the law and religion umbrella is rejecting such a classification.

However, legal history also helps point to the way forward for law and religion studies. Recent years has seen a revival of interest in the historical study of law, often by those outside the internal legal history world.[55] Central to this has been the growth of interest in areas such as law and gender and law and race that have an important historical dimension. There have also been steps towards overcoming the impasse between internal and external approaches. My own work on *Subversive Legal History*[56] has suggested that internal and

---

[55]   A number of new law and history-related networks have been set up which are characterised by their inclusivity such as the Law and History Network in the Southwest, the Northern Legal History Group and Selden's Sisters, which champions the work of women in legal history.

[56]   Russell Sandberg, *Subversive Legal History: A Manifesto for the Future of Legal Education* (Routledge, 2021).

external responses should not be placed in opposition to one another; they are necessarily complementary.[57] Drawing upon a remark by John Baker that 'Law flits uncomfortably between intellectual and social history',[58] I recast the internal–external division as instead highlighting the existence of two major traditions within legal history scholarship: one that examines law from an intellectual history dimension (exploring the development of legal ideas) and the other that looks at law from a social history dimension (exploring the development of interface between law and society). As with my earlier work on law and religion, I stressed that legal history included 'at least' these two dimensions; that there was no clear dividing line between the two; and that the two dimensions were 'raised in order to underscore that they are both valid and complementary to each other'.[59] I also stressed that this articulation should not be taken as requiring both of the two approaches to be present at all times.[60]

However, despite these qualifications, the use of new labels risks repeating the mistake I made in formulating the religion law/religious law distinction. In the same way that law and religion was understood as being the study of religion law and religious law, legal history might fall into the trap of being seen as just the study of intellectual legal history and social legal history. The answer, I suggest, is to understand legal history as an inherently interdisciplinary study. The changing wording and focuses of the labels is less important than the move towards inclusion. The problem inhibiting legal history is the way in which it has developed as a legal specialism.

Ironically, the answer to this can be found in revisiting and reclaiming the work of the person seen as the founder of modern legal history: Maitland. While Maitland's legacy of subjecting historical primary sources of law to

---

[57] This no doubt reflected my concerns about the effects of my own distinction between religion law and religious law in the context of law and religion scholarship. I regretted how the internal–external distinction tended to caricature the nature and scope of internal work and depicted a binary watertight distinction between two forms of history and two types of historian that is reductionist, trite and incorrect. In the legal history context, I suggested that the particular, technical and grounded evidence unearthed by internal legal history complements would be complemented by the contextual, wider and interdisciplinary insights gleamed through external legal history.

[58] John H Baker, 'Criminal Courts and Procedure, 1550–1800' in JS Cockbourn (ed) *Crime in England 1500–1800* (Methuen, 1977) 15.

[59] Russell Sandberg, *Subversive Legal History: A Manifesto for the Future of Legal Education* (Routledge, 2021) 50.

[60] The *Oxford Handbook of Legal History* takes a slightly different approach from what I proposed. It has a section dedicated to approaches to legal history which includes chapters on legal history as legal scholarship, social history, political history, intellectual history, doctrinal history, cultural history and economic history, as well as a number of related chapters: Markus D Dubber and Christopher Tomlins (eds) *The Oxford Handbook of Legal History* (Oxford University Press, 2018).

the same doctrinal study rigour as modern law has been influential in terms of developing the internal approach to legal history, it is often overlooked that elements of the external approach can also be found in Maitland's scholarship.[61] As Jonathan Rose pointed out, even Maitland's most doctrinal work 'focuses on institutional and doctrinal development': 'it is not purely legal, as he understands the relationship of law to a broader social and political context'.[62] Much of it involved 'political, social, and economic contexts'; and this is even more true of his work as a whole, which is 'extensive, varied, and eclectic, abounding in ideas, insights, and concepts'. As Bell has noted, Maitland's work 'was never channelled in a single groove or pointed to a single end; he has a lively, flexible mind that was always ready to follow a hint from the data that it happened to be processing'.[63] This included the questioning of received wisdoms and a 'spirit which causes one to go around looking for skeletons in closets which might be exposed'.[64] Moreover, although Maitland's work pre-dated the critical turn, it is possible to identify a critical or subversive approach in his scholarship. As Elton has noted, for Maitland, 'historical enquiry demanded the subversion of what had been said before'.[65] Moreover, Maitland saw the function of legal history as being emancipatory. In a letter he wrote that:

> The only direct utility of legal history ... lies in the lesson that each generation has an enormous power of shaping its own law. I don't think that the study of legal history would make men fatalists; I doubt that it would make them conservatives. I am sure that it would free them from superstitions and teach them that they have free hands.[66]

The lessons that revisiting the work and spirit of Maitland have for the development of legal history can and should also apply in relation to law and

---

[61] It is fitting that, as Michael Lobban has pointed out, the proponents of both internal and external legal history 'would probably trace their professional genealogy to one man, F.W. Maitland': Michael Lobban, 'The Varieties of Legal History' (2012) 5 *Clio@Themis* 1, 4.

[62] Jonathan Rose, 'Studying the Past: The Nature and Development of Legal History as an Academic Discipline' (2010) 31(2) *The Journal of Legal History* 101, 114.

[63] HE Bell, *Maitland: A Critical Examination and Assessment* (Adams & Charles Black, 1965) 108.

[64] He added that, 'Perhaps it is putting it too strongly to imply that Maitland had a polemic spirit, but there is no doubt that when he thought he saw a historical truth, he hewed to the line and let the chips fall where they might': James R Cameron, *Frederick Maitland and the History of English Law* (University of Oklahoma Press, 1961) 65.

[65] GR Elton, *F W Maitland* (George Weidenfeld and Nicolson, 1985) 21.

[66] FW Maitland, 'Letter from Maitland to AV Dicey, c. July 1896', quoted in CHS Fifoot, *Frederic William Maitland* (Harvard University Press, 1971) 143.

religion. There is a need to move away from institutional trappings that tend towards exclusivity. Conventional distinctions that limit the development of the field of enquiry need to be rethought. Inclusivity and interdisciplinarity provide the direction of travel and – as suggested in previous chapters looking at scholarship on gender and race – a critical approach needs to be taken. This is challenging and might sound unachievable. But the good news for both legal history and law and religion is that this is a path already trodden. Legal geography (variously labelled) provides an exemplar of the inclusive, interdisciplinary and critical future that is needed.

13. Law and geography

In their valuable agenda-setting introduction to an edited book, Irus Braverman, Nicholas Bromley, David Delaney and Alexandre Kedar suggested that there have been 'three modes of legal geography research':

> The first mode of legal geography includes disciplinary work in law or in geography that is modelled on the conventional image of import and export. The second is an interdisciplinary pursuit in which scholars in law and geography draw on the work of another and seek to contribute to the development of a common project. The third mode moves beyond the interdisciplinary to transdisciplinary, or perhaps postdisciplinary, modes of scholarship. Although these three modes exist concurrently, the general trajectory over time has been from disciplinary to interdisciplinary and, finally, to postdisciplinary orientations.[1]

As Braverman et al concede, this classification is contestable in two respects. First, their 1980s starting point is contentious, given that explorations of the relationship between law and geography pre-dated this. Indeed, the term 'legal geography' was first used by German scholars in the 1920s and work on intertwining of the spatial and the legal has existed for generations,[2] albeit typically taking other forms and labels such as 'comparative law'.[3] Second, the three modes should not be understood in a linear manner. There is a further weakness in their articulation: their schema suggests that legal geography is a homogenous body of scholarship when it is not. Much work on what we might call legal geography is not 'conducted self-consciously' under such a banner.[4] And even where a label is applied to such work, a number of different banners are

---

[1]   Irus Braverman, Nicholas Bromley, David Delaney and Alexandre Kedar, 'Introduction: Expanding the Spaces of Law' in Irus Braverman, Nicholas Bromley, David Delaney and Alexandre Kedar (eds) *The Expanding Spaces of Law: A Timely Legal Geography* (Stanford University Press, 2014) 1, 2.

[2]   Alexandre Kedar, 'On the Legal Geography of Ethnographic Settler States: Notes Towards a Research Agenda' in Jane Holder and Carolyn Harrison (eds) *Law and Geography* (Oxford University Press, 2003) 402, 405.

[3]   See Nicholas Bromley, *Law, Space and Geographies of Power* (Guilford Press, 1994) 28–29.

[4]   Jane Holder and Carolyn Harrison, 'Connecting Law and Geography' in Jane Holder and Carolyn Harrison (eds) *Law and Geography* (Oxford University Press, 2003) 3.

used, including 'law and geography' and 'law and space'. Braverman et al's modes should, therefore, be treated as ideal types. Their three modes need to be understood as showing not a linear story of progression but three forms of legal geography work: academic isolationism, critical legal geography and the post-disciplinary project. These three forms of work provide a contrast to the disciplinary development of legal history and law and religion, and can serve as an inspiration for writers in these fields. In particular, it shows what can be achieved where a critical inclusive approach is taken that does not develop as a disciplinary specialism in law schools with its own institutional apparatus.[5]

***

The first type of law and geography research was characterised by academic isolationism. The relationship was 'both poorly documented and inadequately theorized'.[6] Space was frequently taken as a given by legal writers;[7] precious few 'consciously concerned themselves with the geographies of social and political life'.[8] This was reciprocated: geographers appeared blasé about law and very few afforded it attention. For Bromley, before the late 1980s, any conversation between the two 'tended not only to be muted, but to replicate a view of the world that treats time and space as analytically quite distinct, related in circumscribed ways'.[9] This has similarities with much of the law and religion literature to date, which has focused on exploring religion legally.

Powerful institutional and intellectual barriers perpetuated this academic silence in relation to law and geography.[10] Although both socio-legal scholarship and human geography had strong interdisciplinary traditions,[11] their

---

[5]   This chapter summarises arguments developed in full in Russell Sandberg, *Subversive Legal History: A Manifesto for the Future of Legal Education* (Routledge, 2021), Chapter 7.

[6]   Nicholas Bromley, *Law, Space and Geographies of Power* (Guilford Press, 1994) vii.

[7]   David Delaney, Richard T Ford and Nicholas Bromley, 'Preface: Where is Law?' in Nicholas Bromley, David Delaney and Richard T Ford (eds) *The Legal Geographies Reader* (Blackwell, 2001) xiii, xvi.

[8]   Nicholas Bromley, *Law, Space and Geographies of Power* (Guilford Press, 1994) viii, 27.

[9]   Nicholas Bromley, 'From "What?" to "So What?": Law and Geography in Retrospect' in Jane Holder and Carolyn Harrison (eds) *Law and Geography* (Oxford University Press, 2003) 13, 22.

[10]   Nicholas Bromley, *Law, Space and Geographies of Power* (Guilford Press, 1994) vii.

[11]   David Delaney, *The Spatial, the Legal and the Pragmatics of World-Making: Nomospheric Investigations* (Routledge, 2010) 9.

institutional and disciplinary nature seemed 'antithetical to mutual exchange'.[12] As Bromley put it, 'geography – as a formal social science – and law – as a professionalized vocation – seem to lack a common theoretical and analytic vocabulary'. There are echoes here of Maitland's discussion of the different roles of the historian and the lawyer. The difference is that the development of legal geography came much later than legal history and developed from both disciplines.

The first steps were extremely tentative. Lawyers studying geographical topics did not problematise geography, while geographers studying legal topics did not problematise law. Occasional articles in legal journals by the likes of Gerald Neuman,[13] John Calmore[14] and Gerald Frug[15] explored geographical topics but only from the perspective of law. Similarly, on the geography side, the few human geographers who began writing about legal topics did so exclusively from the perspective of their home discipline. They took 'law as a given and were not concerned with debates about law within legal scholarship'.[16] The development of legal geography was 'sparse and unsystematized'.[17] However, this was to be to its advantage.

The reason why legal geography developed further than this and took on an interdisciplinary bent is because its undeveloped state meant that it was significantly shaped by the critical turn. Unlike in legal history, where the result of the critical turn was the development of a new form of analysis outside the canon of legal history, in legal geography the critical turn animated the very core of the scholarship. The undeveloped state of legal geography meant that it responded to the critical turn differently than established fields like legal history did. Legal geography arose afterwards and was infused by the critical movements that were developing in both disciplines: the critical legal studies movement and the critical geography movement. These movements saw scholars in both disciplines holding for 'scrutiny the central, organizing apparatus

---

[12] Nicholas Bromley, *Law, Space and Geographies of Power* (Guilford Press, 1994) 4.
[13] Gerald Neuman, 'Territorial Discrimination, Equal Protection and Self-Determination' (1987) 135 *University of Pennsylvania Law Review* 261.
[14] John Calmore, 'Radicalized Space and the Culture of Segregation: Hewing a Stone of Hope from a Mountain of Despair' (1995) 143 *University of Pennsylvania Law Review* 1233.
[15] Gerald Frug, 'The Geography of Community' (1996) 48 *Stanford Law Review* 1047.
[16] Nicholas Bromley, *Law, Space and Geographies of Power* (Guilford Press, 1994) 4.
[17] Ibid 28.

of their disciplines – the rule of law, and space'.[18] The relationship between the two movements and their convergence into the legal geography project is a matter of debate. Braverman et al suggested that the shift towards a 'strong and explicit commitment to interdisciplinary research and programmatic bridge building' was 'triggered' by the critical legal studies movement.[19] However, Nicholas Bromley suggested that, although both drew on wider theoretical debates, critical geographical inquiry ran parallel to but independent from critical legal studies.[20] He saw a 'critical legal geography' as developing 'as part of a much broader shift in theoretical human geography'.[21] Indeed, Franz von Benda-Beckmann, Keebet von Benda-Beckmann and Anne Griffiths suggested that the 'spatialization of social theory has been prompted by a critical social geography and a heightened interest in the effects of globalization'.[22] There are parallels here again with the contested and complex relationship between socio-legal studies and social history. The important thing is not who influenced whom but rather that, as Braverman et al noted, 'legal scholars and human geographers were suddenly reading the same theorists, asking similar questions, and taking account of one another's scholarship'.[23] This did not happen – or at least not to the same extent – in legal history or law and religion.

The result of this critical turn was that legal geography now problematised orthodox notions of both law and space. It also examined both space from the perspective of law and – crucially – law from the perspective of space. Edward W Soja distinguished two ways of looking at the relationship between law

---

[18]   Jane Holder and Carolyn Harrison, 'Connecting Law and Geography' in Jane Holder and Carolyn Harrison (eds) *Law and Geography* (Oxford University Press, 2003) 3, 4.

[19]   Irus Braverman, Nicholas Bromley, David Delaney and Alexandre Kedar, 'Introduction: Expanding the Spaces of Law' in Irus Braverman, Nicholas Bromley, David Delaney and Alexandre Kedar (eds) *The Expanding Spaces of Law: A Timely Legal Geography* (Stanford University Press, 2014) 1, 4.

[20]   Nicholas Bromley, *Law, Space and Geographies of Power* (Guilford Press, 1994) 44–45.

[21]   Ibid 28. Edward Soja regarded this as the postmodern turn which 'led to an exploration of a multiplicity of alternatives to the more rigid structures that have tended to evolve within': Edward Soja, 'Afterword' (1996) 48 *Stanford Law Review* 1421, 1422.

[22]   Franz von Benda-Beckmann, Keebet von Benda-Beckmann and Anne Griffiths, 'Space and Legal Pluralism: An Introduction' in Franz von Benda-Beckmann, Keebet von Benda-Beckmann and Anne Griffiths (eds) *Spatializing Law: An Anthropological Geography of Law in Society* (Routledge, 2009) 1.

[23]   Irus Braverman, Nicholas Bromley, David Delaney and Alexandre Kedar, 'Introduction: Expanding the Spaces of Law' in Irus Braverman, Nicholas Bromley, David Delaney and Alexandre Kedar (eds) *The Expanding Spaces of Law: A Timely Legal Geography* (Stanford University Press, 2014) 1, 4.

and geography: the first 'focuses on how geography or more broadly social space, social spatiality, affects law and legal development', examining how 'the law has always involved itself with the location of things, with disputes over turf, territories, boundaries, borders, jurisdictions'; while the second deals with the reverse – 'how law shapes geographies' – exploring how 'legal understandings and knowledge of law are applied to help in understanding the social production of space, how social spatiality is constructed and organized and expressed'.[24] This 'geography in law'/'law in geography' distinction – to use the labels offered by Alexandre Kedar[25] – stressed how 'the legal and the spatial, the discursive and the material, are inextricable'.[26] This should have been the aim of the religion law/religious law distinction in law and religion scholarship and the intellectual history/social history distinction in legal history. However, what is notable is that, unlike those distinctions, the 'geography in law'/'law in geography' distinction reflects both sides of the 'X as law'/'law as X' distinction. It is therefore more in line with John Witte Jr's categorisation of law and religion, including the 'religious dimensions of law' and the 'legal dimensions of religion' as well as 'the interaction of legal and religious ideas and institutions, norms and practices'.[27] It underscores how legal geography provides more than an external critique of law, understanding its place and relationship to other social systems; it also provides a new way to explore and challenge the internal workings of law.

Legal geography has achieved this by going beyond the 'X as law'/'law as X' distinction. As Nicholas Bromley has noted, such a dichotomous distinction 'implicitly constricts two self-contained categories of discrete objects'.[28] One of the hallmarks of the law and geography movement is that it has included

---

[24]   Edward W Soja, 'Afterword' (1996) 48 *Stanford Law Review* 1421, 1425, 1426.

[25]   Alexandre Kedar, 'On the Legal Geography of Ethnographic Settler States: Notes Towards a Research Agenda' in Jane Holder and Carolyn Harrison (eds) *Law and Geography* (Oxford University Press, 2003) 402, 406–07. See also the similar distinction between 'law in space' and 'space in law' drawn by David Delaney: David Delaney, 'Beyond the Word: Law as a Thing of this World' in Jane Holder and Carolyn Harrison (eds) *Law and Geography* (Oxford University Press, 2003) 67, 68–69.

[26]   David Delaney, 'Beyond the Word: Law as a Thing of this World' in Jane Holder and Carolyn Harrison (eds) *Law and Geography* (Oxford University Press, 2003) 67, 71.

[27]   John Witte, Jr, 'The Study of Law and Religion in the United States: An Interim Report' (2012) 14 *Ecclesiastical Law Journal* 327.

[28]   Nicholas Bromley, *Law, Space and Geographies of Power* (Guilford Press, 1994) xiii.

but also transcended the two disciplines of law and geography. As Jane Holder and Carolyn Harrison put it, many contributors to the legal geography project:

> offer not just a geographical dimension to law – or a view of law in its geographical context. Instead, an attempt is made to identify how law and geography bear upon each other, and draw out the points of contrast, support, complicity, especially with respect of taken-for-granted distinctions between the social and the material, the human and non-human, and what constitute people and things.[29]

This is what Witte meant by 'the interaction of legal and religious ideas and institutions, norms and practices'. This focus of legal geography has come about because, although the legal geography project is sometimes seen as arising from the intersection of the disciplines of law and geography, noticing and filling the gap between the two,[30] it is not commonly understood to be a distinct sub-discipline of either.[31] This is in stark contrast to legal history and law and religion, which are both largely seen as sub-disciplines of law (with similarly focused work in history and religious studies departments not commonly being included within the canon). The difference, then, is that the legal geography project is interdisciplinary and not institutionalised.[32] It is not a sub-discipline found within law schools, with its own specialist journals, book series and professional associations; and it is rarely taught. This has meant that legal geography is not yoked to one discipline and rather can become, in the words of Braverman et al, 'a truly interdisciplinary intellectual

---

[29]   Jane Holder and Carolyn Harrison, 'Connecting Law and Geography' in Jane Holder and Carolyn Harrison (eds) *Law and Geography* (Oxford University Press, 2003) 3.

[30]   David Delaney, 'Beyond the Word: Law as a Thing of this World' in Jane Holder and Carolyn Harrison (eds) *Law and Geography* (Oxford University Press, 2003) 67; Luke Bennett and Antonia Layard, 'Legal Geography: Becoming Spatial Detectives' (2015) 9(7) *Geography Compass* 406, 407.

[31]   'Legal geography is not a subdiscipline of human geography, nor does it name an area of specialized legal scholarship': Irus Braverman, Nicholas Bromley, David Delaney and Alexandre Kedar, 'Introduction: Expanding the Spaces of Law' in Irus Braverman, Nicholas Bromley, David Delaney and Alexandre Kedar (eds) *The Expanding Spaces of Law: A Timely Legal Geography* (Stanford University Press, 2014) 1.

[32]   Braverman et al note that although legal geography 'shares important conceptual similarities with other interdisciplinary and subdisciplinary endeavours' such as law and society and legal history, in that it foregrounds space rather than the social or time, the difference that allows it to be interdisciplinary is that law and geography 'occupies little institutional presence': Irus Braverman, Nicholas Bromley, David Delaney and Alexandre Kedar, 'Introduction: Expanding the Spaces of Law' in Irus Braverman, Nicholas Bromley, David Delaney and Alexandre Kedar (eds) *The Expanding Spaces of Law: A Timely Legal Geography* (Stanford University Press, 2014) 1, 1–2.

project': 'It is less a "field" than braided lines of inquiry that have emerged out of the confluence of various intellectual interests.'[33] As Luke Bennett and Antonia Layard point out, a 'co-constitutive approach became a leitmotif of Legal Geography';[34] such work became categorised as being a co-production of scholars which was not characterised by disciplinary attachments.

***

The fact that it developed in the heat of the critical turn meant that 'the law and geography project became not merely contextual, but profoundly critical'.[35] Legal geography developed as 'a "critical" geographic scholarship that professes a sensitivity to power and politics'.[36] Although a range of lawyers[37] and geographers[38] contributed to this project, this inherently critical approach was epitomised by Nicholas Bromley's 1994 monograph *Law, Space and Geographies of Power*.[39] As Gareth A Jones pointed out, paying attention to the spatiality of law can 'show up important influences on the positivism of law, including informal social institutions and practices such as community,

---

[33] Ibid 1.

[34] Luke Bennett and Antonia Layard, 'Legal Geography: Becoming Spatial Detectives' (2015) 9(7) *Geography Compass* 406, 408.

[35] Jane Holder and Carolyn Harrison, 'Connecting Law and Geography' in Jane Holder and Carolyn Harrison (eds) *Law and Geography* (Oxford University Press, 2003) 3, 4.

[36] Nicholas Bromley, *Law, Space and Geographies of Power* (Guilford Press, 1994) 27.

[37] Braverman et al mention the work of Davina Cooper (Davina Cooper, *Governing Out of Order: Space, Law and the Politics of Belonging* (Rivers Oram Press, 1998)) and Eve Darian Smith (Eve Darian Smith, *Bridging Divides: The Channel Tunnel and English Legal Identity in the New Europe* (University of California Press, 1999)), as well as special issues of journals such as the 'Surveying Law and Border' issue of *Stanford Law Review* in 1996 which included an afterword from Edward Soja: Irus Braverman, Nicholas Bromley, David Delaney and Alexandre Kedar, 'Introduction: Expanding the Spaces of Law' in Irus Braverman, Nicholas Bromley, David Delaney and Alexandre Kedar (eds) *The Expanding Spaces of Law: A Timely Legal Geography* (Stanford University Press, 2014) 1, 6.

[38] Commentators often hail Gordon L Clark, *Judges and the Cities: Interpreting Local Autonomy* (University of Chicago Press, 1985) as one of the two pivotal texts alongside Bromley's 1994 book. See ibid 4–5 and David Delaney, *The Spatial, the Legal and the Pragmatics of World-Making: Nomospheric Investigations* (Routledge, 2010) 11. Clark as a geographer drew upon sophisticated legal philosophical resources to argue how 'our institutions make and remake society through their interpretative and determinant actions': Gordon Clark, *Judges and the Cities: Interpreting Local Autonomy* (University of Chicago Press, 1985) xi.

[39] Nicholas Bromley, *Law, Space and Geographies of Power* (Guilford Press, 1994).

custom, and citizenship'.[40] This has the effect of 'destabilising the normatively and objectivity of law'. This raises the question of what is needed to animate law and religion scholarship in a similar manner. It might mean destroying law and religion as a legal subdiscipline. Bromley noted how:

> Both critical lawyers and critical geographers have rejected legal science and spatial science, respectively, concentrating on the political significance of law and space, both within their disciplines and within wider social life. As a result, the gap between law and geography becomes less tenable.[41]

Bromley noted that this 'would seem a self-destructive, even suicidal, act'.[42] However, he argued that it is actually a reconstructive act that may 'provide the basis for a fuller and richer account of both law and space'. He was not arguing for the dominance of political science; rather that the focus should be on the way in which the fusion of the legal and the spatial is political. For Bromley, the entanglement of law and space means that legal geography cannot be seen as the bridge between law and space because 'the argument here is that there is no gap to bridge'.[43] Rather the 'perceived divide is merely a function of an institutional categorization' which needs itself to be supplanted. A critical approach highlights questions of power and how they are perpetuated through discourse.[44] Crucially, it also reveals the power relations between disciplines.[45] The solution for Bromley is not to reject disciplinary specialisms but to

---

[40]   Gareth A Jones, 'Camels, Chameleons and Coyotes: Problematizing the "Histories" of Land Law Reform' in Jane Holder and Carolyn Harrison (eds) *Law and Geography* (Oxford University Press, 2003) 169, 186.

[41]   Nicholas Bromley, 'From "What?" to "So What?": Law and Geography in Retrospect' in Jane Holder and Carolyn Harrison (eds) *Law and Geography* (Oxford University Press, 2003) 13, 22.

[42]   Nicholas Bromley, *Law, Space and Geographies of Power* (Guilford Press, 1994) 5.

[43]   Ibid 37.

[44]   Delaney, Ford and Bromley wryly note that 'critical social theory in the last generation has highlighted – perhaps to the point of obsession – the connections between discourse and power': David Delaney, Richard T Ford and Nicholas Bromley, 'Preface: Where is Law?' in Nicholas Bromley, David Delaney and Richard T Ford (eds) *The Legal Geographies Reader* (Blackwell, 2001) xiii, xix.

[45]   Bromley identifies a hierarchy at work whereby 'law vigorously places knowledge, with a suspicion of that deemed to lie outside its boundaries. External influences, such as geography, are thus admitted – if they are admitted at all on law's terms': Nicholas Bromley, 'From "What?" to "So What?": Law and Geography in Retrospect' in Jane Holder and Carolyn Harrison (eds) *Law and Geography* (Oxford University Press, 2003) 13, 20, 21.

abandon 'disciplinary myopia'.[46] He noted that such critical perspectives begin to lay the groundwork for a more nuanced – and necessarily transdisciplinary – account of law, space and power.

Proponents of legal geography have referred to the field as being 'transdisciplinary'[47] or 'post-disciplinary'.[48] Although a number of different definitions and understandings of these terms exist,[49] the term 'transdisciplinary' is typically defined as an advanced form of critical[50] interdisciplinarity where disciplinary approaches and structures are transgressed and transformed;[51] while the closely linked term 'post-disciplinary' is often understood to include a critique of and a break away from disciplinary approaches. This can be seen in some respect as a return to the pre-disciplinary intellectual tradition of polymaths answering large questions and surveying several fields. It is a rejection of the distinctions of modernity: 'the discursive and organisational construction (and worse, the fetishisation) of disciplinary boundaries' which underpins not only the modern university but the education system as a whole.[52] The post-disciplinary vision entails 'the breakdown of these established disciplinary boundaries as well as the rediscovery of space and time as socially constructed, socially constitutive relations'.[53] For Braverman et al, this required a

[46] Nicholas Bromley, *Law, Space and Geographies of Power* (Guilford Press, 1994) 5.

[47] Ibid; David Delaney, *The Spatial, the Legal and the Pragmatics of World-Making: Nomospheric Investigations* (Routledge, 2010) 11.

[48] Irus Braverman, Nicholas Bromley, David Delaney and Alexandre Kedar, 'Introduction: Expanding the Spaces of Law' in Irus Braverman, Nicholas Bromley, David Delaney and Alexandre Kedar (eds) *The Expanding Spaces of Law: A Timely Legal Geography* (Stanford University Press, 2014) 1, 10.

[49] Multidisciplinary work is understood as the juxtapositioning of materials from different disciplines, while interdisciplinary work requires the integration of material from different disciplines. See Russell Sandberg, *Religion, Law and Society* (Cambridge University Press, 2014) 233 *et seq*; and Allen F Repko, *Interdisciplinary Research: Process and Theory* (3rd edition, Sage, 2016).

[50] Within interdisciplinary work, 'instrumental' forms which regard themselves as growing from the foundations provided by the disciplines and regard their function as furthering the needs of the disciplines amid wider social changes, can be contrasted with 'critical' forms which seek to deconstruct disciplinary distinctions, paying particular attention to the implicit values and purposes hidden within such approaches.

[51] The transdisciplinary vision is not the erecting of a new discipline or super-discipline but rather the 'elaboration of new language, logics and concept to permit genuine dialogue': Julie Thompson Klein, 'Prospects for Transdisciplinarity' (2004) 36 *Futures* 515, 516.

[52] Bob Jessop and Ngai-Ling Sum, 'Pre-Disciplinary and Post-Disciplinary Perspectives' (2001) 6(1) *New Political Economy* 89.

[53] Ibid 91.

'move beyond legal geography in a way that both draws on and contributes to broader social and humanities studies'.[54]

Although they noted that there are several examples of post-disciplinary legal geography work,[55] Braverman et al singled out David Delaney's 2010 monograph *The Spatial, The Legal and the Pragmatics of World-Making: Nomospheric Investigations*[56] as having 'a distinctively post disciplinary orientation to legal geography throughout'.[57] Delaney developed a seven-step plan.[58] The first step is 'twisting the split' by seeing worlds and words as shaping one another. The second step involves 'foregrounding performativity' by stressing that discourses have social effect through their performance. The third and fourth steps problematise and deconstruct the spatial and the legal respectively. The third step entails 'rotating the spatial' by 'seeing space as imagined and discursively organized', 'seeing space as performed' and 'rethinking the materiality of space in light of these other critical operations'. Correspondingly, the fourth step rotates the legal by stressing how that too is continuously performed and 'creatively done and redone' – not only by legal actors, but 'by everyone who acts in accordance with (or with transgressive references to) understandings of rules, authority, rights, permissions, prohibitions, duties and so on'.[59] The fifth step – arguably the most important – involves 'braiding'

---

[54]   Irus Braverman, Nicholas Bromley, David Delaney and Alexandre Kedar, 'Introduction: Expanding the Spaces of Law' in Irus Braverman, Nicholas Bromley, David Delaney and Alexandre Kedar (eds) *The Expanding Spaces of Law: A Timely Legal Geography* (Stanford University Press, 2014) 1, 10.

[55]   Braverman et al (ibid 11, 3) mentioned the work of Irus Braverman herself and Andreas Philippopoulos-Mihalopoulos 'in his conceptualization of a genuinely "spatial justice" – and in contrast with conventional *aspatial* notions of spatial justice' (Andreas Philippopoulos-Mihalopoulos, *Spatial Justice: Body, Lawscape, Atmosphere* (Routledge, 2015)). They also noted that Boaventura Santos' 1987 article (Boaventura Santos, 'Law: A Map of Misreading – Toward a Postmodern Conception of Law' (1987) 14 *Journal of Law and Society* 279, 286) provided a very early example of such work. See also the work of Edward W Soja, which is explicitly transdisciplinary, cutting 'across all perspectives and all modes of thought': Edward W Soja, *Thirdspace* (Blackwell, 1996) 3; Edward W Soja, *Seeking Spatial Justice* (University of Minnesota Press, 2010).

[56]   David Delaney, *The Spatial, The Legal and the Pragmatics of World-Making: Nomospheric Investigations* (Routledge, 2010).

[57]   Irus Braverman, Nicholas Bromley, David Delaney and Alexandre Kedar, 'Introduction: Expanding the Spaces of Law' in Irus Braverman, Nicholas Bromley, David Delaney and Alexandre Kedar (eds) *The Expanding Spaces of Law: A Timely Legal Geography* (Stanford University Press, 2014) 1, 10.

[58]   David Delaney, *The Spatial, the Legal and the Pragmatics of World-Making: Nomospheric Investigations* (Routledge, 2010) 12, 14.

[59]   Ibid 19. 'If we restrict our understanding of the legal to the conventional we will think more or less conventional thoughts. If we provisionally try out less conventional

these strands of thinking about the spatial and the legal together 'in a way that highlights the worldly, pragmatic processes of their mutual constitutivity'.[60] Delaney noted that this represented a move 'beyond the domain of law and geography' to focus on how the legal and spatial interrelate with and create one another. The sixth and seventh steps, then, are to politicise and historicise the investigation. This would highlight 'the always political (normatively contested) and historical (dynamic, transformational) character of the pragmatics of world-making and the simultaneously durable and malleable character of the worlds so made'. These seven steps provide a working model that could replicate what Delaney applies to law and space to law and history (or perhaps law and time)[61] or law and religion (or perhaps law and values/ethics).

For some, post-disciplinarity entails rejecting terms such as the term 'legal geography' as reflections of a bygone attachment to disciplinary identities. This led some proponents to devote energy to questions of naming. Soja raised what he saw as 'the interesting little problem of what to call those scholars who are developing this transdisciplinary spatial perspective'.[62] 'Critical human geographers' was dismissed as being 'probably still too narrowly confined'; while the labels 'spatio-analyst', 'spatiologist' and 'geosopher' were all mooted. Others have focused on what to call the object of the inquiry. Delaney offered the term 'nomosphericity';[63] Kedar preferred 'jurispacedence';[64] and, perhaps most influentially, Bromley advocated that 'in thinking about the relation of space and law', we should 'literally run the words together, and refer to the conjunction as a "splice"'.[65] This terminology, he argued, casts critical fire on 'the active, constructed way in which splices are made', which he refers

---

ways of thinking we might think thoughts that had been unthinkable and ask questions that it had not occurred to us to ask. This is the pragmatic attraction of looking at the legal in new ways. However, thinking about the legal in these ways might be asking too much. Maybe a better strategy is to simply call this something else altogether': ibid 20.

[60]   Ibid 23.

[61]   As Emily Grabham and Sian M Beynon-Jones note, there has been 'a flourishing, over recent years, in critical, socio-legal scholarship on law's temporalities. Such scholarship has begun to take seriously time's effects on law and social ordering': Emily Grabham and Sian M Beynon-Jones, 'Introduction' in Sian M Beynon-Jones and Emily Grabham (eds) *Law and Time* (Routledge, 2019) 1.

[62]   Edward Soja, 'Afterword' (1996) 48 *Stanford Law Review* 1421, 1423.

[63]   David Delaney, *The Spatial, the Legal and the Pragmatics of World-Making: Nomospheric Investigations* (Routledge, 2010) 24, 8.

[64]   Alexandre Kedar, 'On the Legal Geography of Ethnographic Settler States: Notes Towards a Research Agenda' in Jane Holder and Carolyn Harrison (eds) *Law and Geography* (Oxford University Press, 2003) 402, 407.

[65]   Nicholas Bromley, 'From "What?" to "So What?": Law and Geography in Retrospect' in Jane Holder and Carolyn Harrison (eds) *Law and Geography* (Oxford University Press, 2003) 13, 30.

to as 'splicing'.[66] Luke Bennett and Antonia Layard regard Delaney's idea of 'braiding' and Bromley's notion of 'splicing' as being more or less identical and as 'the foundational conceptual device in legal geography'.[67] Focusing on splicing reveals how splices 'tend to construct the world in ways that systemically favour the powerful: employers, men, white, property owners and so on. But the apparent neutrality of splices can neutralize or obscure the differential treatment of legal subjects'. For Bromley, 'the complex geographies of law can be made to reveal their culpability, their construction and their contingency'.[68]

Luke Bennett and Antonia Layard noted that legal geographers often have a different starting point from other academic lawyers: beginning with 'an interest in mundane sites' rather than starting with the text, they maintained that the spatial detective 'expands doctrinal legal analysis', exploring the understanding of 'space-talk' or a lack of 'space-talk' in judgments:[69]

> Legal geographers tend to take the analysis wider, considering a wider range of stakeholder and situational influences. This more legal geographically infused doctrinal method echoes the intellectual traditions of the interpretivist turn, which looked to discursive analyses of legal provisions and practice.[70]

Bennett and Layard therefore present the legal geography project as a widely required methodological supplement. The non-institutionalised state of the project, as well as its interdisciplinary nature and post-disciplinary ambitions, enables it to be used as a tool to further legal doctrinal work. This contrasts with law and religion and legal history, whose institutionalised nature as legal sub-disciplines often frustrates such a potential. Reference to legal geography is therefore instructive as an analogy of how law and religion (and indeed legal history) can develop. There is a need to reject the understanding of law and religion as two separate entities and to embrace the approach suggested by Witte. The example of legal geography shows how this can be achieved by an interdisciplinary (or post- or transdisciplinary) approach that transcends the two disciplines to problematise the terms involved and their interaction. This suggests that the whole institutionalised law-based doctrinal-leaning edifices that have been built may need to be destroyed.

---

[66] Ibid 31.
[67] Luke Bennett and Antonia Layard, 'Legal Geography: Becoming Spatial Detectives' (2015) 9(7) *Geography Compass* 406, 409–10.
[68] Nicholas Bromley, *Law, Space and Geographies of Power* (Guilford Press, 1994) 227.
[69] Luke Bennett and Antonia Layard, 'Legal Geography: Becoming Spatial Detectives' (2015) 9(7) *Geography Compass* 406, 413.
[70] Ibid 412.

***

The differing fortunes of legal geography as compared to law and religion and legal history is telling. Legal geography may lack some of the institutional trappings and the status of respectability that legal history in particular enjoys; but the way it is not yoked to law as a discipline has meant that it has become more appealing and has gathered deeper insights. Mariana Valverde has noted:

> The fact that sessions on 'law and space' or legal geography draw large numbers of people at Law and Society Association meetings, whereas legal history is not seen as fashionable or theoretical (even though law schools, institutionally resistant to change, generally employ legal historians not legal geographers), appears to be a fashion trend whose driving forces are mysterious or simply invisible to the very people caught up on it.[71]

These driving forces are neither mysterious nor simply invisible. They reflect the way in which the critical turn has been the central impulse in legal geography which led to it becoming undisciplined by problematising and deconstructing both law and space and how they are entwined. It provides a contrast to and glimpses of a possible future for law and religion (and legal history). Our first two comparators further underscored this. The literatures on gender and race have also been animated by the critical turn and have developed into movements that not only deconstruct but also reconstruct the role that law plays and can play.

The comparators in this section have shown a variety of different ways in which law and religion could develop (and they are by no means exhaustive – there are other inequalities which the law interacts with and other humanities subjects where law can serve as a bedfellow). It is clear, however, that law and religion not only can but must learn from these comparators. At the moment, the adolescent state of law and religion as a field means that it is neither a mainstream influence nor a radical movement. There is a need for change. Having identified the problem and surveyed some comparators, the next part of the book moves onto the main event: how law and religion can be transformed.

---

[71]   Mariana Valverde, *Chronotopes of Law: Jurisdiction, Scale and Governance* (Routledge, 2015) 37.

Excursus II

Meanwhile, in another alternative timeline…

For once, the hype had been justified. The opening of Freedonia University in 2084 transformed the higher education sector in the UK. Replacing most of the existing and ancient universities, Freedonia University ushered in an era of a publicly owned and governed university with dozens of campuses around the country which were no longer in competition with one another. Funded by the taxation of large corporations and the mega-rich, all adults were entitled to attend the university at up to three points in their lives and had constant access to the seemingly unlimited amount of learning and support content available online, thanks to collaboration between the University and a resurgent BBC.

Those who attended or used the University's services were encouraged to draw upon materials, methods, ideas and approaches from a wide range of areas. Talk of academic disciplines was generally discouraged. Some, of course, attended with the desire to specialise and prepare for particular career paths. That was not the only reason, however, why many of the Freedonia University campuses offered law. The ability to understand, question and critique the way in which and the forms by which citizens are governed and interact with one another was considered to be an important part of informed and critical thinking. Indeed, law – often referred to as 'citizenship' or 'justice' – was now a common part of the primary and secondary school curriculum.

The world of work had been transformed in the late twenty-first century thanks to the rise of the machines, the ubiquity of artificial intelligence and public demand for more leisure time. This was reflected in how law was taught at Freedonia University. Of course, this meant that taking part in simulations, writing code and using constantly changing communication forms were central to the student experience. Indeed, these were all now taken-for-granted, everyday occurrences. However, it was not just the methods by which law was taught that differed from the traditional university law schools of old.

At Freedonia University, the focus of the law degree was on the foundations of areas of law and their historical, social, political and economic context. A focus on issues of procedure and the recall of detailed rules was considered superfluous, given that most of the skills that such learning developed were limited to jobs that had long ago been taken over by machines. Yes, lawyers needed to sense check the conclusions reached by algorithms and simulations; but generally, their work was now much more creative and strategic than it had once been. Lawyers still needed an understanding of the foundational areas of law, such as property law, the law of obligations and public law, including crime. But the focus of the law degree was on developing the mindset and skills that would enable them – relying upon ever-evolving electronic means – to address precise issues and questions that came up in disputes. This involved what used to be called 'critical thinking' but was now just known as 'thinking'.

Given the technological advancements, the human dimension of law was more important than ever. Studying law now meant examining questions of history, politics and sociology; and subjecting legal texts – including accounts by legal scholars – to the same level of scrutiny as authors, playwrights, artists, influencers and so on. Voices that had once been marginalised were now at the heart of the curriculum. The gendered and racial dimensions were central throughout the degree, with attention also being paid to a range of other forms of inequality and identity formation. Students asked not only whose values were implicit within the law, but also how they could ensure that their values – and those of wider society – shaped the law going forward.

But one topic was still somewhat neglected. The critical impulse that had now become part of the mainstream was an overwhelmingly secular one. Yes, attention was now being paid to the voices, experiences and needs of what had previously been dubbed 'minority groups'; but the overriding concept here was one of culture, not religion. Religious belief was considered to be a private matter. It was now centuries since religion had controlled and run education and played a pivotal role in the deciding of disputes. It had long been super-seded in such roles by the state; and even though there had been a wobble in those years when neoliberal ideas of privatisation and austerity had held sway, the role of the state was now firmly accepted once again.

The study of law and religion was seen, therefore, as part of legal history. The role of religion in the public sphere was something that society had long grown out of and was considered within that narrative. This meant that religion received considerably less attention in the law degree and other justice-focused courses at Freedonia University than other topics such as gender and race. Law and religion, for the most part, was seen as a curiosity – a medieval throwback.

PART III

Regeneration

In which the benefits of making a pact with the devil are discussed and a change in the scientific underpinning of legal studies is proposed.

14. Systems reboot

Interviewer: In terms of personal qualities, what would you say are necessary for your role within the tribunal?

Interviewee (Catholic Tribunal): I think an ability to blend the two concepts of the judicial and the pastoral because it is an important role within the Church but one has to remember that one cannot, as a religious minister, it's really swimming against the tide by being a purely judicial figure. We can't simply make religion into a system of laws and rules and regulations, Christ himself was very clear about that and he criticised the Pharisees and the Scribes and the lawyers of his day for doing that. So, what one doesn't want to do is to fall into the trap of becoming locked in a legal mindset. You have to have a legal mindset or the ability to adapt to working within judicial structures and disciplines but at the same time you have to retain a pastoral sensitivity and remember that you are also, in your role as a church lawyer, you are trying to help people and you are trying to help people to re-build their lives spiritually speaking and also emotionally and socially after the trauma of the breakdown of a marriage relationship so it requires a certain ability to blend those two skills and to remember that you are a lawyer but you are still a priest and a priest first and foremost.

In 2011, I was part of a team carrying out a study comparing Muslim, Jewish and Christian tribunals (during which we recorded the above exchange).[1] The study followed the furore caused by a scholarly lecture in 2008 by the then Archbishop of Canterbury, Dr Rowan Williams, in which he acknowledged

---

[1] Gillian Douglas, Norman Doe, Sophie Gilliat-Ray, Russell Sandberg and Asma Khan, *Social Cohesion and Civil Law: Marriage, Divorce and Religious Courts* (Cardiff, 2011). For discussion of the findings, see, e.g., Russell Sandberg, Gillian Douglas, Norman Doe, Sophie Gilliat-Ray and Asma Khan, 'Britain's Religious Tribunals: "Joint Governance" in Practice' (2013) 33(2) *Oxford Journal of Legal Studies* 263.

the existence of religious laws and religious tribunals such as shariah councils.[2] The Archbishop's erudite and nuanced lecture – in which he suggested that 'we have to think a little harder about the role and rule of law in a plural society of overlapping identities' – caused uproar.

During our research, I was struck by the above quote from one of the interviewees at the Catholic Tribunal. This was one of the few interviews I had been present at. While the research team's visits to the Shariah Council of the Birmingham Central Mosque and the Family Division of the London *Beth Din* brought them into religious settings that have much in common with modern-day courtrooms, our visit to the Catholic National Tribunal for Wales in Cardiff found us in a much more mundane setting: the front room of a vicarage. Yet despite this domestic setting, it became clear that this too was a location where the religious and the legal were fused. The quote above encapsulates what is unique about religious tribunals: the blurring of the legal and the religious. This is also the underlying reason why religious tribunals are controversial: they offend modern society's expectation that the legal and religious be separated. This also captures the essence of many of the other controversies surrounding the interaction between law and religion in recent years, such as the existence of faith schools and the presence of religious dress and symbols in the public sphere.

Social functional differentiation is understood as being a keystone of modern societies. While in previous eras, religious authorities and their social structures performed a variety of social functions, in modern society a variety of social institutions now perform distinct social functions, with the State playing a central role. The idea of religions performing functions that they previously carried out but which now 'belong' to other social institutions, such as educating children or determining legal disputes, now seems archaic. These are now seen as the preserve of other social institutions – particular forms of the state.

This is especially true in relation to religious tribunals determining legal disputes. Although the fusion of religion and education is controversial, the operation of faith schools is well known and accepted, even by those calling for their abolition. By contrast, religious tribunals have a somewhat shadowy existence.[3] It is commonly assumed that the religious and the legal have long

---

[2]   The lecture was subsequently published as: Rowan Williams, 'Civil and Religious Law in England: A Religious Perspective' (2008) 10 *Ecclesiastical Law Journal* 262.

[3]   This is not to deny that some faith schools also exist in the shadows, particularly unregistered faith schools. This was an issue that the Schools Bill 2022 was to address before it was shelved as a result of the revolving door at Number 10 caused by two prime ministerial resignations in quick succession.

been firmly demarcated. The expansive jurisdictions of the church courts are regarded as a matter of legal history: a curio that sometimes has surprising legacies, which are easily dismissed as anachronistic hangovers. The idea that religious institutions can and should determine disputes – even among their adherents – is often considered extraordinary, controversial and fundamentally inappropriate.

But there is no reason why religious tribunals should be so contentious. It has long been accepted that autonomous and freely informed adults should be able to voluntarily resolve disputes in any way they choose. As Gillian Douglas has noted, given 'the general de-juridification of family matters and the drive to encourage alternative dispute resolution', as furthered by the cuts to legal aid as a result of the Legal Aid, Sentencing and Punishment of Offenders Act 2012, it is difficult:

> to see why religious tribunals should not be as suitable as any other potential medi-ator or arbitrator to assist the parties in reaching a settlement that suits them, even if that settlement is one that reflects cultural or religious norms at odds with those of secular society.[4]

Yes, religious tribunals should cause concern if it is not clear that the parties before them have arrived there wittingly and voluntarily; if there is discrim-ination evident in their practices; or if they become the only place for the resolution of certain disputes.[5] However, their actual existence should be non-controversial – particularly given the move towards private ordering.

The fact that the very existence of religious tribunals is controversial is noteworthy. Indeed, the same is true of faith schools and any signs of religion in the public sphere, which are routinely regarded as aberrations. These are all seen as problems – problems that law and religion scholars have dedicated much ink to. This underscores the way in which the law and religion literature is predicated upon the acceptance of social functional differentiation. Indeed,

---

[4]   Gillian Douglas, 'Who Regulates Marriage? The Case of Religious Marriage and Divorce' in Russell Sandberg (ed) *Religion and Legal Pluralism* (Ashgate, 2015) 53, 61–62.

[5]   This is why the issue of unregistered religious marriages is such a problem. Requirements under marriage law that require religious weddings (other than Anglican, Jewish or Quaker ceremonies) to be conducted in a registered place of worship in order to be legally recognised mean that some religious adherents have little choice but to have religious weddings that are not legally binding. This can mean that where the relationship breaks down, the parties cannot make recourse to the State as they would be able to had they been legally married, and so religious tribunals determining their marital status are no longer forms of *alternative* dispute resolution but are rather their only option. See Russell Sandberg, *Religion and Marriage Law: The Need for Reform* (Bristol University Press, 2021).

our whole society is based on this – and it is entrenched to such an extent that it is often unquestioned. Social functional differentiation is at the heart of social theory. The founding fathers of sociology – Karl Marx, Emile Durkheim and Max Weber – were all concerned, in different ways, by the changes that were occurring following the Enlightenment: the rise of modern society.

They all recognised post-Enlightenment secularisation: the social decline of religion amid the rise of the state and social institutions, that now discharged a number of functions hitherto performed by religion, such as the education and legal systems. They all embraced and perpetuated social functional differentiation. Their work and these assumptions have laid the groundwork ever since – not just for social theory, but much more generally. It is now readily accepted and taken for granted that, while previously in pre-modern society a few social institutions (most notably the Church) performed a range of social functions, in modern society a range of specialist social institutions now discharge specific functions. Religious groups have been left to serve religious purposes only.

***

Although social functional differentiation underpins a number of different forms of macro-sociological theory, it is particularly important within the functionalist tradition that followed Durkheim. Functionalism understood society as operating like the human body, with various parts of society (social institutions) having distinct purposes but working together for the greater good, like parts of the body do, in order to achieve equilibrium. Developed by American sociologist Talcott Parsons in the early twentieth century, functionalism subsequently fell out of favour but received a revival of interest in recent years thanks to the growing influence of German sociologist Niklas Luhmann, who was born in 1927 and died in 1998. Luhmann's theories have attracted increased interest since his death due to the increasing number of translations of his work and the development of his ideas in distinct fields.

Luhmann is a controversial figure. He considered that social theory had taken a wrong turn following the Enlightenment.[6] Luhmann regarded modern sociology as being 'in a profound theoretical crisis',[7] failing to produce 'anything approaching an adequate theory of society'.[8] As Michael King and

---

[6]   As King and Thornhill note, Luhmann positioned his theory 'as an attempt to undermine and critically to refigure the central principles of political and legal reflection deriving from the European Enlightenment': Michael King and Chris Thornhill, *Niklas Luhmann's Theory of Politics and Law* (Palgrave, 2003) 129.

[7]   Niklas Luhmann, *Introduction to Systems Theory* (Polity, 2013) 1.

[8]   Niklas Luhmann, *Theory of Society.* Volume 1 (Stanford University Press, 2012) 2.

Chris Thornhill noted, for Luhmann, social and political theory following the Enlightenment erred in being 'obsessively preoccupied' with the essence or nature of the human being and therefore lacked the means by which it could comprehend 'the social as such'.[9] Luhmann did not abandon the theoretical plan behind the Enlightenment but dismissed 'its claim that people, not systems, are at the origin of social evolution'.[10] Luhmann rebooted sociological theory by resurrecting and redeveloping social systems theory in a significant body of work, including books on his general theory[11] and works dedicated to particular social systems, including religion[12] and the law.[13] Luhmann's social systems theory fits within the functionalist tradition epitomised by the work of Durkheim, which emphasises that society is based on consensus; that social equilibrium is the default; and that social institutions work together like parts of the body to make society as a whole function. It pays increased attention to social functional differentiation and the way in which different social systems (to use his terms) interact with one another.

Like the founding fathers, Luhmann's interest in both law and religion as social institutions formed part of a general social theory. He saw them as two of many separate social systems. However, Luhmann's sociological theories pertaining to law and religion have been understood in isolation from one another. Having noted the potential of Luhmann's social systems theory in *Religion, Law and Society*,[14] I have sought to rectify this. In the last decade, I have examined and returned to his work on several occasions. However, the purpose and length of these pieces have often inhibited the argument that I was attempting to make. This part of the book draws upon and develops this previous work to provide my definitive and possibly last statement on the usefulness of Luhmann's social systems theory to understand law and religion. The next

---

[9] Michael King and Chris Thornhill, *Niklas Luhmann's Theory of Politics and Law* (Palgrave, 2003) 132.

[10] Ibid 133.

[11] Niklas Luhmann, *The Differentiation of Society* (Columbia University Press, 1982); Niklas Luhmann, *Social Systems* (Stanford University Press, 1996); Niklas Luhmann, *Theory of Society.* Volumes 1 and 2 (Stanford University Press, 2012); Niklas Luhmann, *Introduction to Systems Theory* (Polity, 2013).

[12] Niklas Luhmann, *Funktion der Religion* (Suhrkampf Velg AG, 1977), Chapter 2 of which was translated as Niklas Luhmann, *Religious Dogmatics and the Evolution of Societies* (Edwin Mellen Press, 1984); Niklas Luhmann, *A Systems Theory of Religion* (Stanford University Press, 2013).

[13] Niklas Luhmann, *A Sociological Theory of Law* (Routledge, 1985; 2nd edition 2014); Niklas Luhmann, *Law as a Social System* (Oxford University Press, 2004).

[14] Russell Sandberg, *Religion, Law and Society* (Cambridge University Press, 2014) 236, 241.

chapter begins this by elucidating the main elements of social systems theory relevant to law and religion.

15. The lure of Luhmann

Luhmann's social systems theory has a reputation for being overly complex.[1] Yet this is not necessarily complexity for complexity's sake.[2] As Luhmann noted: 'A complex society cannot be understood other than by a complex theory.'[3] Indeed, it is an inevitable by-product of the ambition and interdisciplinary bent of his work: the way in which 'Luhmann weaves together several different strands of theoretical reflection, derived from quite different intellectual disciplines, into his social theory'.[4] It is also a result of the way in which Luhmann's social system theory rejects the 'anthropocentric' assumptions found in almost all sociological studies.[5] For Luhmann, the primary unit of analysis is social systems rather than people.

As we have noted, social systems theory rests upon the notion of social functional differentiation: the way in which, in modern society, a plethora of social systems discharge specific functions, as opposed to the pre-modern tendency for one specific institution to discharge a plethora of functions. For Luhmann, modern society is functionally differentiated into social systems such as law, religion, politics, science and the media. Luhmann saw these social systems as reproducing themselves by communication, rather than following Durkheim and Weber in seeing them as being the product of labour divisions or social action.[6]

For Luhmann, these social systems are 'autopoietic', in that they reproduce themselves – that is, they produce and reproduce their own unity.[7] In other

---

[1]   Richard Nobles and David Schiff, 'Using Systems Theory to Understand Legal Pluralism: What Could be Gained?' (2012) 46(2) *Law and Society Review* 265.

[2]   Michael King and Chris Thornhill, *Niklas Luhmann's Theory of Politics and Law* (Palgrave, 2003) 1.

[3]   Niklas Luhmann, *Law as a Social System* (Oxford University Press, 2004) 67.

[4]   Michael King and Chris Thornhill, *Niklas Luhmann's Theory of Politics and Law* (Palgrave, 2003) 204.

[5]   Ibid 2. Systems theory was previously developed in the sociological work of Talcott Parsons and in biology by HR Maturana and FJ Varela, *The Tree of Knowledge: The Biological Roots of Human Understanding* (Shambhala Press, 1987).

[6]   Michael King and Chris Thornhill, *Niklas Luhmann's Theory of Politics and Law* (Palgrave Macmillan, 2003) 11.

[7]   Niklas Luhmann, *A Sociological Theory of Law* (2nd edition, Routledge, 2014) 281.

words, each social system is autonomous. Social systems define themselves based on self-description and use this to reproduce themselves by distinguishing themselves from other social systems. Law, like any other social system, reproduces itself by communication. It is 'neither structure nor function' that defines what law is.[8] This shifts the focus from debates on the 'true nature of law' towards asking how law defines its own boundaries and where they are drawn.[9] It also means that other systems accept law's decisions as 'social facts'.[10]

***

For Luhmann, social systems are 'operationally closed, but cognitively open'.[11] The unity and independence of each social system are achieved through the concept of 'closure'. As we have just seen, social systems are operationally closed because they are self-referential: their individual operations 'are identified as such by themselves'.[12] Each system has its own form of operational closure: the legal system is 'normatively closed' in that the system itself 'produces its own elements as legally relevant units by the fact that it lends normative quality'.[13] Each system decides, through its own communication, where its boundaries lie: what is included within the social system and what is excluded.

However, crucially, social systems are also 'cognitively open', in that they require 'the exchange of information between system and environment'.[14] Systems confront events and communications from outside, which are then 'transformed or re-constructed' by the particular social system.[15] As Luhmann noted: 'The more systems theory stresses the operative closure of autopoietic systems, the greater the need to establish how the relations between the system and environment are shaped.'[16] The term 'structural coupling' is the label

---

[8]   Gunther Teubner, '"Global Bukowina": Legal Pluralism in the World Society' in Gunther Teubner (ed) *Global Law without a State* (Ashgate, 1997) 3, 14–15.

[9]   Michael King and Chris Thornhill, *Niklas Luhmann's Theory of Politics and Law* (Palgrave Macmillan, 2003) 42.

[10]   Ibid 38.

[11]   Richard Nobles and David Schiff, 'Introduction' in Niklas Luhmann, *Law as a Social System* (Oxford University Press, 2004) 1, 8.

[12]   Niklas Luhmann, *Law as a Social System* (Oxford University Press, 2004) 86.

[13]   Niklas Luhmann, *A Sociological Theory of Law* (2nd edition, Routledge, 2014) 283.

[14]   Niklas Luhmann, *Essays on Self-Reference* (Columbia University Press, 1990) 229.

[15]   Michael King, 'The "Truth" about Autopoiesis' (1993) 20 *Journal of Law and Society* 218.

[16]   Niklas Luhmann, *Law as a Social System* (Oxford University Press, 2004) 381.

Luhmann gave to the links that develop between social systems.[17] This label is used to describe how social systems co-evolve so that one social system includes each other in its environment.[18] For Luhmann, 'structural coupling is a mechanism that both separates and joins'.[19] By evolving links with one another, systems can be both autonomous and coordinated.[20] This is what is meant by saying that they are autopoietic social systems.

***

Social systems theory provides further detail on how this occurs: how social systems become autonomous but linked to other social systems through communication. For Luhmann, each social system produces and reproduces the system, keeping it distinct from all other social systems, by having its own distinct function and binary code. Further, each social system focuses upon 'a specific problem of society'.[21] The bespoke function that each social system fulfils to solve its particular problem provides the means by which each system will self-define and therefore perpetuate itself. Law's function is the 'stabilization of normative expectations' in the face of disappointment.[22] As Luhmann put it:

> Concretely, law deals with the function of the stabilization of normative expectations by regulating how they are generalized in relation to their temporal, factual, and social dimensions. Law makes it possible to know which expectations will meet with social approval and which not. Given this certainty of expectations, one can take on the disappointments of everyday life with a higher degree of composure.

Law alone attempts to fulfil this function. And this is what makes law as a social system distinct from all other social systems.[23] By comparison, the social system of religion alone 'tries to observe the paradoxical unity of

---

[17]   Ibid 385.
[18]   Michael King and Chris Thornhill, *Niklas Luhmann's Theory of Politics and Law* (Palgrave, 2003) 33.
[19]   Niklas Luhmann, *Law as a Social System* (Oxford University Press, 2004) 400.
[20]   Richard Nobles and David Schiff, 'Using Systems Theory to Understand Legal Pluralism: What Could be Gained?' (2012) 46(2) *Law and Society Review* 265, 281.
[21]   Niklas Luhmann, *Law as a Social System* (Oxford University Press, 2004) 93.
[22]   Ibid 147–48.
[23]   Nobles and Schiff note that law is not unique in making communications about what ought to occur. However, law's unique binary code differentiates it from other systems such as morality and religion which contain similar communications: Richard Nobles and David Schiff, 'Introduction' in Niklas Luhmann, *Law as a Social System* (Oxford University Press, 2004) 1, 17.

difference between the observable and the unobservable'.[24] Religion has the 'function of transforming the indeterminable into the determinable'.[25] Social systems become functional insofar as they become 'able to organize communications and disseminate them in ways that they and other communicative systems may make use of them'.[26] This is achieved not only through functional specification but also by means of a 'binary coding'.[27]

For Luhmann, the binary code is 'a guiding distinction by which a system identifies itself and its own relationship to the world'.[28] It is 'the basic distinction that a social system applies in order to communicate'.[29] Each social system applies a code unique to that social system.[30] The code allows the system 'to determine which communications "belong to" the system'.[31] Coding is always binary in nature, 'imposing a distinction between two opposing values and effectively excluding third values'.[32] The only alternative to binary coding is to reject the code, holding that the matter falls outside that social system.[33]

Law's binary code is legal/illegal. Any communications that are based upon this binary code become part of the social system of law. Luhmann notes that this provides a 'widening of the margins of what should be included in the concept of the legal system'.[34] Neither 'law' nor 'the legal system' is defined by institutions, the status of individuals or 'organised legal practice'; rather, law is a system of communications, which 'extends to all those communications that are understood as directly relating to the issue of legality or illegality'.[35] Law is not defined as being part of the state; indeed, for Luhmann, the very concept of the state is 'a paradox or fiction which the political system

---

[24]   Rudi Laermans and Gert Verschraegen, '"The Late Niklas Luhmann" on Religion' (2001) 48(1) *Social Compass* 7, 13.

[25]   Niklas Luhmann, *A Systems Theory of Religion* (Stanford University Press, 2013) 249–50.

[26]   Michael King and Chris Thornhill, *Niklas Luhmann's Theory of Politics and Law* (Palgrave Macmillan, 2003) 9.

[27]   Niklas Luhmann, *Law as a Social System* (Oxford University Press, 2004) 93.

[28]   Niklas Luhmann, *A Systems Theory of Religion* (Stanford University Press, 2013) 45.

[29]   Hans-George Moeller, *Luhmann Explained* (Open Court, 2006) 29.

[30]   Richard Nobles and David Schiff, 'Using Systems Theory to Understand Legal Pluralism: What Could be Gained?' (2012) 46(2) *Law and Society Review* 265, 270.

[31]   Michael King and Chris Thornhill, *Niklas Luhmann's Theory of Politics and Law* (Palgrave Macmillan, 2003) 24.

[32]   Ibid 25.

[33]   For example, matters within politics may subsequently be considered non-political or matters within law may be found to be non-justiciable: ibid 26.

[34]   Niklas Luhmann, *Law as a Social System* (Oxford University Press, 2004) 99.

[35]   Michael King and Chris Thornhill, *Niklas Luhmann's Theory of Politics and Law* (Palgrave Macmillan, 2003) 35, 36.

itself produces (for simplicity's sake)' in order to perpetuate itself.[36] Only law itself can decide what law is.[37]

This same process occurs within other social systems. Each social system uses a particular binary code to differentiate itself and to operate autonomously. Within the social system of religion, the binary code is that of immanence/transcendence, which enables the system to 'perceive what can (and cannot) be adapted as religious communication'.[38] For Luhmann, 'Religion recognizes itself as a religion whenever it refers to anything that can be experienced immanently as transcendence.'[39]

As Teubner noted, this means that 'law' includes any phenomenon which is communicated using the distinction legal/illegal, which has the function of the stabilisation of normative expectations.[40] Any communication that has this function and uses the legal/illegal code becomes part of the social system of law. Any social system that distinguishes itself in the same manner as law is regarded as law. The same is true of religion. Religion includes any phenomenon that is communicated using the immanence/transcendence binary and that has the function of 'transforming the indeterminable into the determinable'.[41]

The binary code enables the system to 'conceal the paradox of its own existence': for a social system to operate, it cannot doubt its own validity.[42] Luhmann noted that 'codes are a precise copy of the paradox that they serve to resolve'.[43] Law cannot doubt the validity of its claim that its decisions are

---

[36] Ibid 77.

[37] This means that it is 'not possible in modern society for legal arguments to be grounded in natural laws, universal truths or even rationality'; paradoxically, and regardless of the ways in which they are presented, legal arguments 'relate only in law's own internal constructions of the external world': ibid 51.

[38] Niklas Luhmann, *A Systems Theory of Religion* (Stanford University Press, 2013) 7.

[39] Ibid 196. Although commentators have been critical of Luhmann's immanence/transcendence distinction (eg, see Rudi Laermans and Gert Verschraegen, '"The Late Niklas Luhmann" on Religion' (2001) 48(1) *Social Compass* 7, 18), Luhmann notes that 'interpretive deficiencies in the coding' are deliberate in order to allow for religious pluralism (Niklas Luhmann, *A Systems Theory of Religion* (Stanford University Press, 2013) 197).

[40] Gunther Teubner, 'The Two Faces of Janus: Rethinking Legal Pluralism' (1991) 13 *Cardozo Law Review* 1443, 1451.

[41] Niklas Luhmann, *A Systems Theory of Religion* (Stanford University Press, 2013) 249–50.

[42] Michael King and Chris Thornhill, *Niklas Luhmann's Theory of Politics and Law* (Palgrave Macmillan, 2003) 21.

[43] Niklas Luhmann, *A Systems Theory of Religion* (Stanford University Press, 2013) 48.

legal.[44] The binary code of legal/illegal requires law to decide between legality and illegality without ever questioning its validity for doing so. Social systems develop programmes to stabilise the application of their codes.

***

Programming fills coding with content.[45] It provides 'the conditions, which that system establishes for when it is appropriate to apply the negative or positive side of the code'.[46] Programming has the effect of concealing the fundamental arbitrariness and contingency of the application of the code. Programming provides 'necessary filters', without which 'the application of codes would appear as crude attempts to reduce everything in the world to simplistic binary propositions'.[47] The content of programming is contingent and can often serve as a distraction. In the social system of law, programming takes the form of legislative provisions and judicial principles 'which make application of the code depend on specific criteria, as opposed to the bare will of the immediate decision-maker'.[48] Programming often takes the form of the 'rules' of law, such as 'the formula of "if-when"'.[49] This means that lawyers, by focusing on the rules of the game, forget that they are working within a system of binary coding.[50] The academic rationalisation of programmes into doctrines and accounts provides further stability.

The paradox at the heart of each social system cannot be overcome through programming; but it can be 'managed' by what John Harrington has called 'deparadoxification strategies'.[51] He observed that:

> Paradoxes cannot be overcome, but only 'managed' by being displaced into the environment of the system or by being made the subject of ever more complex distinctions within it. Either way, these 'deparadoxification' strategies will never be conclusive, but at best only persuasive. To make them plausible is the central task of the judge, or of any other lawyer taking a position on the matter at hand.

---

[44]   Michael King and Chris Thornhill, *Niklas Luhmann's Theory of Politics and Law* (Palgrave Macmillan, 2003) 21.

[45]   Niklas Luhmann, *Law as a Social System* (Oxford University Press, 2004) 203.

[46]   Richard Nobles and David Schiff, 'Introduction' in Niklas Luhmann, *Law as a Social System* (Oxford University Press, 2004) 1, 17.

[47]   Michael King and Chris Thornhill, *Niklas Luhmann's Theory of Politics and Law* (Palgrave Macmillan, 2003) 23.

[48]   John Harrington, 'Of Paradox and Plausibility: The Dynamic of Change in Medical Law' (2014) 22(3) *Medical Law Review* 305, 311.

[49]   Niklas Luhmann, *Law as a Social System* (Oxford University Press, 2004) 197.

[50]   Ibid 203.

[51]   John Harrington, 'Of Paradox and Plausibility: The Dynamic of Change in Medical Law' (2014) 22(3) *Medical Law Review* 305, 306.

Law is presented as concrete and certain when, in reality, every legal decision could actually have 'gone the other way'.[52] Paradoxically, 'law is binding, but provisional; normative, but arbitrary'. Paradox is the 'persuasive and definitive feature of law'. The role of legal actors (including legal academics) is to explain away this paradox. As Harrington has argued in the context of medical law, 'academics and other commentators involve themselves in medical law not as detached experts, but rather as participants in ongoing struggles over how to manage legal paradoxes'.[53] Like judicial decisions, academic narratives restore 'a measure of provisional stability'.[54] As Harrington argued, 'the achievement of the legislator, common law systematiser, and doctrinal scholar is always (only) one of plausibility': providing 'plausibilities' which explains developments within the context of the conventional narratives. Exploring how these 'plausibilities' decline and are replaced over time gives us, argues Harrington, a neat means of mapping and analysing socio-legal change. The next chapter will explore this further in relation to religion, providing our first application of social systems theory to law and religion studies.

---

[52] Ibid 312.
[53] Ibid 306.
[54] Ibid 310.

16. The deparadoxification strategies of religion law

Having sketched out Luhmann's theory, the question arises of how social systems theory applied to law and religion challenges and changes conventional understandings of the field as a whole and issues that have arisen within it. Social systems theory (and indeed social theory generally) indicates that many of the pressure points found in the modern interaction between law and religion are largely a consequence of expectations about the different and discrete functions of law and religion as two separate social systems. The place of religion in the public sphere in all of these controversies is inherently problematic because it offends the expectation of functional differentiation: the notion that religion should perform only religious functions. The operation of religious courts, faith schools and pretty much any presence in the public sphere by religion offends functional differentiation, which sees law and legal adjudication as being the proper business of the legal system only. The moral panics about religious rights and religious authority can therefore be explained as offending expectations about functional differentiation. However, Luhmann's social systems theory allows us to go further than that.

The debates on which law and religion scholarship has focused reflect a fear of what Luhmann calls 'de-differentiation' – the dissolution of processes of differentiation – which he saw as 'the greatest threat to modern society'.[1] This fear of de-differentiation is managed by the social system of law through the development of 'deparadoxification strategies' – to borrow terminology that John Harrington has used in medical law – which are constructed by law to provide stability.[2] In this context, law develops deparadoxification strategies to make sense of and control religion. Paradoxes and instability are managed by displacing religion into the environment of the social system of law;[3] or, to put it more provocatively, faced with the growth and 'de-differentiation' of religion, the social system of law has responded by colonising religion,

---

[1]   Michael King and Chris Thornhill, *Niklas Luhmann's Theory of Politics and Law* (Palgrave Macmillan, 2003) 225.

[2]   Cf John Harrington, 'Of Paradox and Plausibility: The Dynamic of Change in Medical Law' (2014) 22(3) *Medical Law Review* 305.

[3]   Cf ibid 306.

reducing it to something that law can understand and control. Harrington's work in relation to medical law shows how it is possible to identify changing patterns of plausibility. This can be applied and developed in relation to religion. It is possible to identify how these deparadoxification strategies operate and develop over time. Indeed, it may be possible to identify a shift from one deparadoxification strategy to another.

This chapter will attempt to do precisely that as an exemplar of what a social systems theory approach can achieve in the field of law and religion studies. It will suggest that there has been a move from one deparadoxification strategy – which may be called 'liberal tolerated agnosticism' – to another, dubbed 'neoliberal multicultural juridification'. This led to, perpetuated and was then itself perpetuated by the developing field of law and religion. However, neoliberal multicultural juridification has itself now become questioned and this is what law and religion is struggling to come to terms with. The following discussion will explore this in greater depth, focusing first on liberal tolerated agnosticism; next on the rise and main features of the neoliberal multicultural juridification which replaced it; and finally on the main challenges that neoliberal multicultural juridification now faces.

***

The first deparadoxification strategy constructed by law to make sense of its interaction with religion – liberal tolerated agnosticism – was shaped by secularisation. In *Religion, Law and Society*, I identified two waves of secularisation: the first was the result of the post-Enlightenment social functional differentiation, which meant that the Church lost many of the social functions it had hitherto performed; while the second was the death of deference following the 'swinging Sixties', when allegiances to all forms of authority – including the traditional churches – became questioned and eroded.[4] Liberal tolerated agnosticism was the product of the first wave of secularisation. Luhmann's work regarded secularisation as a form of self-description on the part of religion, as part of the system's attempt to understand the effect of functional differentiation.[5] This was true of the first wave of secularisation, which forced the traditional religions to consider their new role as one social system among

---

    [4]   Russell Sandberg, *Religion, Law and Society* (Cambridge University Press, 2014) 171.

    [5]   Luhmann is often primarily regarded as a theorist of secularisation within the sociology of religion: RL Gert Verschraegen, '"The Late Niklas Luhmann" on Religion' (2001) 48(1) *Social Compass* 7, 8–9. For discussion of functional differentiation within the secularisation thesis, see Russell Sandberg, *Religion, Law and Society* (Cambridge University Press, 2014) 64 *et seq*.

others and their new place as 'a partial domain of culture'.[6] This resulted in 'internal secularisation',[7] where 'religious organizations [chose] to apply the codes of other social systems to themselves and their operations'; and 'as a price for influence over society and over systems, [religious organisations were] progressively ... obliged to couch [their] message in terms of a general morality'.[8]

Liberal tolerated agnosticism justified a particular relationship between religion and the law.[9] As Hoffmann J commented in 1993, 'the attitude of the English legislator to racing is much more akin to his attitude to religion ... it is something to be encouraged but not the business of government'.[10] Religion was regarded by law as a benign force for good which was also increasingly part of a private sphere that would seldom bother law. This was perhaps most clearly reflected in English charity law. As Francesca Quint and Peter Hodkin point out, the 'growing tolerance and diversity in the treatment of religions in charity law' rendered questionable the 'original rationale' of recognising religious trusts, which 'was to assist the established (State sponsored) religion, whilst preventing support for heresy and false religions'.[11] This was replaced by a 'modern rationale' which recognised the psychological and social worth of individual religiosity.[12] This change in underlying principle was underlined in *Gilmour v Coats*:[13]

> The law of England has always shown favour to gifts for religious purposes. It does not now in this matter prefer one religion to another. It assumes that it is good for man to have and to practise a religion but where a particular belief is accepted by one religion and rejected by another the law can neither accept nor reject it. The

---

[6]   For Luhmann, 'a new concept of "culture"' emerged in the second half of the eighteenth century: Niklas Luhmann, *A Systems Theory of Religion* (Stanford University Press, 2013) 224–25.

[7]   See further Russell Sandberg, *Religion, Law and Society* (Cambridge University Press, 2014), Chapter 3.

[8]   Michael King, 'The Muslim Identity in a Secular World' in Michael King (ed) *God's Law Versus State Law* (Great Seal, 1995) 91, 97, 105.

[9]   It is worth noting, however, that the law did not become entirely secularised or even-handed. The Church of England remained in a special legal status but its centrality to public life dwindled as it was no longer the automatic vehicle for local government, education and welfare.

[10]   *R v Disciplinary Committee of the Jockey Club ex parte Aga Khan* [1993] 1 WLR 909 at 932.

[11]   Francesca Quint and Peter Hodkin, 'The Development of Tolerance and Diversity in the Treatment of Religion in Charity Law' (2007) 10(2) *Charity Law and Practice Review* 1, 1–3.

[12]   See also *Holmes v HM Attorney General* (1981) *The Times*, 12 February.

[13]   [1949] AC 426.

law must accept the position that it is right that different religions should each be supported irrespective of whether or not all its beliefs are true.

The way that the law represented religion was plausible at the time, given the growing centralisation, welfarism and paternalism.[14] It was also plausible because, for the most part, the accommodation of religion was straightforward. Christianity was prevalent and was intertwined with the 'traditional British values' expressed by the various social systems.

The plausibility that cemented liberal tolerated agnosticism was challenged in the mid-twentieth century by the second wave of secularisation.[15] This period witnessed the decline of certainty regarding gender roles, class distinctions and the UK's place in the world; it saw the opening up of the world via the rise of television, the satire boom and the questioning of authority. In short, as we have seen, the 'swinging Sixties' witnessed the critical turn and the death of deference.[16] And these shifts only escalated in the decades that followed. Following the end of the Cold War and the collapse of Communism, old certainties continued to collapse.

Religious diversity also brought new challenges. As Julian Rivers noted, while ' by the start of the twentieth century, English law had come to accommodate the full range of Christian belief and practice, as well as a significant Jewish minority, with reasonable success', the 'accommodation of other religions, growing primarily through immigration in the second half of the twentieth century, had not been as complete or successful'.[17] The Judeo-Christian legal framework, which treated the Church of England as the norm, was no longer fit for purpose, given the significant presence of non-Christian religious minorities. Diverse forms of religion sometimes sat uncomfortably with 'traditional British values', so social systems could no longer assume that religion

---

[14] As Rivers noted, 'nineteenth-century separation mentality between Church and state did not result in a narrow private conception of spirituality as opposed to a broad notion of state welfare, precisely because social welfare was so obviously a religious function. But as the welfare state grew through the twentieth century, the separation mentality survived, in a model of co-ordination': Julian Rivers, 'The Secularisation of the British Constitution' (2012) 14 *Ecclesiastical Law Journal* 371, 395.

[15] See further Russell Sandberg, *Religion, Law and Society* (Cambridge University Press, 2014), Chapter 5.

[16] Humphrey Carpenter, *A Great, Silly Grin: The British Satire Boom of the 1960s* (Perseus Books, 2000) 238.

[17] Julian Rivers, 'The Secularisation of the British Constitution' (2012) 14 *Ecclesiastical Law Journal* 371, 377.

was a benign force or necessarily a social good.[18] A new justification, a new plausibility, was offered in its place: multiculturalism.

***

Julian Rivers has argued that multiculturalism 'effectively became part of New Labour's constitutional reform agenda', encompassing a 'formal re-commitment to principles of liberty and equality for all'.[19] As we have seen, this was manifested in a rights-based rhetoric, a plethora of new religious rights formulated in statute and the growth of an academic industry that regarded the manifestation of religion and the accommodation of religious difference as a problem to be solved through law. Religion was now seen as just one subjective right among others. The rights-based rhetoric disregarded any notion that religion was more than an identity claim but was rather a way of life, with its own system of norms, laws and morals. Religion was no longer seen as a public good but as a private matter needing to be regulated by the market. As Rivers noted, under New Labour:

> the provision of welfare came to be treated in typical 'third way' fashion as provided privately but regulated publicly. So there has been a new openness to faith-based welfare provision, but the terms on which it is offered have been substantially those of the public sector, with its norms of non-discrimination on grounds of religion.[20]

Religion became seen as a social problem to be solved by law where it offended law's expectations. The fact that religious believers were loyal to forms of authority other than the State was once again seen as a problem. The events of September 2001 changed the way in which the West thought and spoke about not only Islam but religion *per se*. This new context shaped the way in which religions operated in public life. Religion became seen as a social problem and attention was afforded to it. Legislators, judges and doctrinal lawyers embraced the narrative of the 'problematisation of religion' and were complicit in furthering it. This led to the juridification of religion. Although the term 'juridification' is not found in Luhmann's works, Luhmann himself wrote that there 'are now more lawyers and more laws than ever before', and suggested that this has led to an 'ever growing weariness, more complaints

---

[18]   As Davie has noted, the increase in religious pluralism which came as a result of the wave of immigration in the 1990s challenged 'widely held assumptions about the place of religion in European societies': Grace Davie, 'Is Europe an Exceptional Case?' (2006) *The Hedgehog Review* 23, 33.

[19]   Julian Rivers, 'The Secularisation of the British Constitution' (2012) 14 *Ecclesiastical Law Journal* 371, 377.

[20]   Ibid 395.

about the excessive number of legal regulating oppressing every free individual, and demands for deregulation, alternative and dispute resolution and de-bureaucratization'.[21]

A social systems theory approach helps to understand how law dealt with this. In response to the decline of the welfare state and the decay of deference to authority, the social system of law interpreted and colonised other parts of social life in ways that it can understand it. As Michael King and Chris Thornhill put it:

> If one takes a cynical perspective, law could well be seen as constructing a make-believe world which simplifies psychological, political, economic and other 'realities' to enable it to reject all knowledge which threatens to undermine the validity of its normative communications.[22]

Law reconstructed religion in its own terms.[23] Systems theory explains the way in which law reconstructed religion by simplifying religious beliefs into actions which law can understand.[24] Michael King predicted that law would reconstruct religion 'essentially as those customs, rites and rituals which in the public domain come to symbolize statements of faith and holiness … as rights of worship and performance of ritual'.[25] This has clearly occurred, with Article 9 of the European Convention of Human Rights (ECHR) talking of the right to manifest 'in worship, teaching, practice and observance'; and with the charity law definition of 'religion' requiring 'faith in a god and worship of that god'.[26] King's suggestion that law's reconstruction of religion would likely see each religion 'as constituting for law a set of rights' which would often result

---

[21]   Niklas Luhmann, *Law as a Social System* (Oxford University Press, 2004) 272.

[22]   Michael King and Chris Thornhill, *Niklas Luhmann's Theory of Politics and Law* (Palgrave Macmillan, 2003) 54.

[23]   Michael King, 'The Muslim Identity in a Secular World' in Michael King (ed) *God's Law Versus State Law* (Great Seal, 1995) 91, 107.

[24]   For Teubner ,'the juridification of social phenomena' results from the way in which applying law's binary code distorts social realities: Gunther Teubner, 'The Two Faces of Janus: Rethinking Legal Pluralism' (1991) 13 *Cardozo Law Review* 1443, 1455.

[25]   Michael King, 'The Muslim Identity in a Secular World' in Michael King (ed) *God's Law Versus State Law* (Great Seal, 1995) 91, 108.

[26]   *Re South Place Ethical Society* [1980] 1 WLR 1565 at 1572. Note that this definition may be questioned by the new, wider definition of 'religion' under registration law in *R (on the Application of Hodkin) v Registrar General of Births, Deaths and Marriages* [2013] UKSC 77, as discussed in Russell Sandberg, 'Defining the Divine' (2014) 16 *Ecclesiastical Law Journal* 198; and Russell Sandberg, 'Clarifying the Definition of Religion under English Law: The Need for a Universal Definition?' (2018) 20 *Ecclesiastical Law Journal* 132.

in judges 'seeing it in terms of some external authority' such as 'God's law, Islamic law' has proved prophetic.[27] Courts and tribunals have indeed assumed a link between religious doctrine and the behaviour of claimants, and have regarded religions as homogenous groups. The Human Rights Act 1998 and the new laws on religious discrimination have led domestic courts and tribunals to place emphasis upon whether the claimant's actions were obligatory according to the religion in question[28] – a stance that has provoked criticism by the European Court of Human Rights.[29]

This means that law excludes as irrelevant any aspects of religion that do not process a legal character. Luhmann noted that where law 'refers to extra-legal rules', 'these norms attain legal quality only with this reference'.[30] This seems similar to the judgment of Laws LJ in the Court of Appeal decision in *McFarlane v Relate*[31] that 'law may of course protect a particular social or moral position which is espoused by Christianity, not because of its religious *imprimatur*, but on the footing that in reason its merits commend themselves'. The social system of law will only recognise and protect what it recognises in its own terms. This means that discourse needs to be framed in the language of law, and that other social systems are devalued. This has meant that religion has become regarded by law as a legal right – an identity claim that is part of and no greater than any other of the 'secular' human rights canon. This has excluded the notion that religion can act as law. The social system of law does not see religion as its rival. Rather, it downplays religion by presenting it as having a narrower focus. As Rivers has observed:

> The idea that religions command respect on the part of secular government institutions because they consist of, or contain, autonomous systems of law is being lost in the inexorable rise of a dominant state-individual paradigm and the embrace of state regulation.[32]

The focus is on individual subjective religious beliefs rather than on religions as autonomous groups and sources of belonging. The law distorts religions as

---

[27]   Michael King, 'The Muslim Identity in a Secular World' in Michael King (ed) *God's Law Versus State Law* (Great Seal, 1995) 91, 108, 110.

[28]   See, especially, *R (on the Application of Playfoot (A Child)) v Millais School Governing Body* [2007] EWHC Admin 1698 and *Eweida v British Airways* [2010] EWCA Civ 80.

[29]   *Eweida and Others v United Kingdom* (2013) 57 EHRR 8.

[30]   Niklas Luhmann. *A Sociological Theory of Law* (2nd edition, Routledge, 2014) 284.

[31]   [2010] EWCA Civ 880 at para 23.

[32]   Julian Rivers, 'The Secularisation of the British Constitution' (2012) 14 *Ecclesiastical Law Journal* 371, 394.

voluntary organisations, regarding them in the same way as golf clubs or other recreational activities. Believers and adherents are seen as members: autonomous individuals who are always free to terminate their membership; who have a 'right to exit'.[33] The framing and colonising of religion as a subjective right allow it to be balanced and made subordinate to other subjective rights.

Moreover, this protects, increases and perpetuates the role of law. Luhmann regarded the rise of subjective rights as being 'probably the most important achievement of the evolution of law in modern times'.[34] Systems theory regards the rise of subjective legal rights as an internal development functioning as a 'self-description' by law designed to preserve its unity. Subjective rights allow law to overcome what Luhmann referred to as 'the paradox of freedom' – namely, 'the necessity of the limitations of freedom as a condition for freedom'.[35] This refers to the way in which law itself defines freedom by reference to its conditions. Human rights provisions such as Article 9 ECHR provide an example of this: Article 9 defines 'religious freedom' by reference to its limitations in Article 9(2). Crucially, this provides law with a means by which to decide what is protected (and what is not protected) by these provisions without admitting that the process is tautological. As Luhmann put it, this 'juridifies arbitrariness'.[36] The rise of subjective rights perpetuates and increases the domain of the law while furthering the distance between the legal system and society at large, since the framework is increasingly self-referential and so excludes non-specialists.[37]

This can be seen in the way in which law creates binary solutions. King predicted that law's construction of religion would mean that, 'faced with incompatible explanations, individuals ... [would often be] forced to make difficult choices between one or the other'.[38] The restrictive interpretation of

---

[33]   The right to exit argument has been much criticised. See Russell Sandberg and Sharon Thompson, 'Relational Autonomy and Religious Tribunals' (2017) 6(1) *Oxford Journal of Law and Religion* 137, 147. Ayelet Shachar argued that this 'right to exit offers no comprehensive approach at all' because it imposes 'the burden of solving conflict upon the individual' while 'relieving the state of any responsibility for the situation'. As she puts it: 'The right to exit rationale forces an insider into a cruel choice of penalties: either accept all group practices – including those that violate your fundamental citizenship rights – or (somehow) leave': Ayelet Shachar, *Multicultural Jurisdictions: Cultural Differences and Women's Rights* (Cambridge University Press, 2001) 41.

[34]   Niklas Luhmann, *Law as a Social System* (Oxford University Press, 2004) 269.

[35]   Ibid; Richard Nobles and David Schiff, 'Introduction' in Niklas Luhmann, *Law as a Social System* (Oxford University Press, 2004) 1, 30.

[36]   Niklas Luhmann, *Law as a Social System* (Oxford University Press, 2004) 269.

[37]   Ibid 419.

[38]   Michael King, 'The Muslim Identity in a Secular World' in Michael King (ed) *God's Law Versus State Law* (Great Seal, 1995) 91, 112.

religious rights under English law has led to such a situation, which I have termed elsewhere an 'impossible compromise'.[39] The reasoning of the judiciary rests upon a 'binary' understanding of 'either your citizenship rights or your religion', which does not allow the court to consider fully on the merits of the case. As we have seen, prior to the European Court of Human Rights' decision in *Eweida v United Kingdom*,[40] the specific situation rule was relied upon to hold that there is no breach of a person's religious rights where that person can choose to manifest their religion elsewhere – usually outside the public sphere. This same tendency can be seen in relation to religious tribunals, where emphasis has been placed upon the 'right to exit' argument, which provides that the role of the State should be limited to ensuring that at-risk group members can leave if they do not agree with the group's practices. These restrictive approaches wrongly limit people into pre-defined identities, assume an equal playing field in terms of power relations and expect people to act in rational ways. A systems theory approach not only explains this development, but also highlights the change in thinking that is needed. The binary options offered by law need to be understood as part of its fears of de-differentiation.

Neoliberal multicultural juridification held sway and reached its peak during the first decade of the twenty-first century. However, this multicultural rights-based approach has been found wanting as two social systems of law and religion competed with each other for social influence. The first challenge to neoliberal multicultural juridification can be said to have come from religion; the second can be said to come from law.

First, juridification led to changes in the social system of religion as religion fought back against law's colonisation. Like other modern theorists on secularisation,[41] Luhmann contended that religion would prosper if it adapted to the new functionally differentiated society. Under neoliberal multicultural juridification, religion became a social system under fire. This became part of the self-description of religion. Religion's insistence that it has a place in the public sphere and cannot be confined to its social system meant that it could not simply adapt to a functionally differentiated society. Rather, religion adapted to take its place as part of a new functionally re-differentiated society. This entailed the acceptance of and making the argument for religious groups fulfilling functions that have been considered to be the preserve of other social systems and the State. In pre-modern societies, religions dealt with legal disputes religiously. The rise of functional differentiation meant that legal

---

[39] Russell Sandberg, 'The Impossible Compromise' in Russell Sandberg (ed) *Religion and Legal Pluralism* (Ashgate, 2015) 1.

[40] (2013) 57 EHRR 8.

[41] See, e.g., Jose Casanova, *Public Religions in the Modern World* (University of Chicago Press, 1994) and Ulrich Beck, *A God of One's Own* (Polity, 2010).

disputes were dealt with by law and law was seldom concerned with religion – the stance of liberal tolerated agnosticism. Under neoliberal multicultural juridification, by contrast, law began treating religion as law and denying religion a place in the public square. Religion, however, challenged this by dealing with disputes both religiously and legally. The term 'politicisation of religion' can be used to refer to the way in which some religious groups have increased the volume of their voices in the public sphere.[42] This was a response to and challenge to neoliberal multicultural juridification.

Possibly more of a challenge, however, has come from law itself. Law overreached itself and attempted to justify this with a new plausibility which emphasised individual autonomy. This reflected what Charles Taylor and others have referred to as the 'subjective turn'.[43] This concerns the way in which the 'subjectivities of each individual became a, if not the, unique source of significance, meaning and authority'.[44] It describes the increased focus people place upon the construction and reconstruction of multiple personal identities. This postmodernist focus on identity (re)construction perpetuates the framing of religion as an identity claim. This has become problematic not only because it leads to the battle or trumping of rights, but also because – ironically – it has led to the weakening of law. A focus on individualism and autonomy has led to the promotion of private ordering and the privatisation of justice. This was manifest in the increasing localisation of public services where services hitherto provided by the welfare state are provided instead by small groups – often community based, sometimes public in nature and other times private. This development called into question any neat dividing line between the public and the private, so framing the debate as being about the role of religion in the public sphere missed the point and presupposed ideals of differentiation that were now passé.

The rollback of the welfare state has resulted in the retreat of law: cuts to legal aid have resulted in the rise of non-legal means of dispute resolution and/ or an increase in the number of non-law specialists engaged in law work. This challenges law's vision of itself as being a self-contained, all-encompassing and specialist world. The uniqueness of law has been undermined by law's emphasis upon individualism. Emphasising individual autonomy has under-

---

[42]   See Russell Sandberg, *Religion, Law and Society* (Cambridge University Press, 2014), Chapter 5.

[43]   Charles Taylor, *The Ethics of Authenticity* (Harvard University Press, 1991) 26. For discussion see Russell Sandberg, *Religion, Law and Society* (Cambridge University Press, 2014) 161–67.

[44]   Paul Heelas and Linda Woodhead, *The Spiritual Revolution* (Blackwell, 2005) 3–4.

mined the communal nature of law. The struggle continues for a new plausible way that law can represent itself and religion.

This helps to explain the state of law and religion scholarship that this book has highlighted. Law and religion as a legal sub-discipline has played a key role in the deparadoxification strategy that this chapter has referred to as 'neo-liberal multicultural juridification'. Law and religion as a sub-discipline has accepted – largely uncritically – the representations of law and religion that the social system of law has propounded. Scholarship has endorsed and perpetuated a State-centric approach that accepts and glorifies social functional differentiation. The way in which law and religion has developed as a legal sub-discipline has contributed to this deparadoxification strategy. A social systems theory approach underscores that the study of law and religion is part of the social system of law. This legal nature of the academic study of law and religion is reflected in its place within law schools and its legal institutional trappings. This means that the field of law and religion is part of the social system of law's attempt to explain away the tensions between law and religion as two social systems. Accepting social functional differentiation and seeing de-differentiation as a threat have resulted in religion being understood legally; and any attempt by religion to move outside the private domain of religion as a social system has been treated as a problem that law can solve. A social systems approach, therefore, highlights how law and religion as a field has been instrumental in the development of – or at least has been complicit in – the way in which religion has been understood and distorted by law.

17. Religious law as a social system

Until the 2008 speech by the then Archbishop of Canterbury,[1] the law and religion academic community largely ignored religious law. Literatures had emerged to varying extents dealing with the laws of particular religious communities – the Ecclesiastical Law Society and the LLM in Canon Law at Cardiff University notably leading to the production of a significant literature on the law of Anglican churches – but little attention was paid to religious law generally and the extent to which it interacted with the law of the State.

A systems theory approach provides an explanation for this and for the focus that emerged following the Archbishop's lecture, which centred on the conflict of religious law and civil law and on the question of enforcement of religious law by State authorities. The explanation for both of these arises once again from what Luhmann calls 'de-differentiation'. The fear of shariah (and other religious legal systems) arose from a perception that religious adjudication offended functional differentiation, which sees law and legal adjudication as the proper business of the legal system only. This resulted in the legal system's failure to regard religious law as law and its attempt to manage the issue through the lens of State law. Once again, the social system of law colonised the issue and reinterpreted it in its own terms, reasserting the primacy of law and the norm of social functional differentiation.

However, systems theory not only provides the diagnosis to the problem of the neglect and misunderstanding of religious law; it also provides the cure. The following discussion will begin by exploring how a systems theory approach recognises religious law as law, and will then outline how systems theory can explain and justify the operation of religious adjudication not as evidence of de-differentiation, but as a further process of differentiation whereby religious legal systems are seen as autopoietic systems in their own right. Though derived from the work of Luhmann, this argument advances his theory, in that it does not adopt his forward-moving evolutionary model of history.

***

---

[1]   Rowan Williams, 'Civil and Religious Law in England: A Religious Perspective' (2008) 10 *Ecclesiastical Law Journal* 262.

Luhmann's theory emphasises the pervasiveness of law. The opening paragraph to *A Sociological Theory to Law* underscores not only the legal dimension of social life but also the way in which all social systems have a legal dimension:

> All collective life is directly or indirectly shaped by law. Law is, like knowledge, an essential and all-pervasive fact of the social condition. No area of life – whether it is the family or the religious community, scientific research or the internal networks of political parties – can find a lasting social order that is not based on law. Collective social life embodies normative rules which exclude other possibilities and lay to be binding with a degree of success. This is always so, although the degree of technical formulation and the extent to which behaviour is determined vary from area to area. However, a minimum amount of legal orientation is indispensable everywhere.[2]

Luhmann's understanding of law is, therefore, not limited to State law.[3] It accepts legal pluralism: the notion that 'it is normal for more than one "legal" system to co-exist in the same social arena'.[4] Indeed, for Luhmann, law 'is not confined to communication occurring within legally regulated procedures, but also includes that of daily life insofar as it raises legal questions or otherwise registers or repudiates legal claims'.[5] A systems theory approach to legal pluralism therefore transforms the concept of legal pluralism.[6]

Brian Tamanaha has argued forcibly that the concept of legal pluralism is 'fundamentally flawed' despite its popularity.[7] He criticised the legal pluralist literature as a whole on the basis that scholars have tended to hold 'essentialist assumptions' about law: they have assumed that law consists of a singular phenomenon which can be defined but have then failed to agree

---

[2]　Niklas Luhmann, *A Sociological Theory of Law* (2nd edition, Routledge, 2014) 1.

[3]　Several critics, however, point out that Luhmann's concept of law is 'openly parasitic upon the state law model', given that the operation of the binary code rests upon common legal centralist ideas about the notion of law: Brian Z Tamanaha, *A General Jurisprudence of Law and Society* (Oxford University Press, 2001) 103. See also Martha-Marie Kleinhans and Roderick A Macdonald, 'What is a *Critical* Legal Pluralism?' 12(2) (1997) *Canadian Journal of International Law and Society* 25, 39.

[4]　Brian Z Tamanaha, *A General Jurisprudence of Law and Society* (Oxford University Press, 2001) 171.

[5]　Niklas Luhmann, *The Differentiation of Society* (Columbia University Press, 1982) 122. For Luhmann, the very concept of the State is 'a paradox or fiction which the political system itself produces (for simplicity's sake)' in order to perpetuate itself: Michael King and Chris Thornhill, *Niklas Luhmann's Theory of Politics and Law* (Palgrave Macmillan, 2003) 77.

[6]　See also Richard Nobles and David Schiff, 'Using Systems Theory to Understand Legal Pluralism: What Could be Gained?' (2012) 46(2) *Law and Society Review* 265.

[7]　Brian Z Tamanaha, *A General Jurisprudence of Law and Society* (Oxford University Press, 2001) 171.

upon a definition of 'law', meaning that their work suffers 'from a persistent inability to distinguish what is legal from what is social'.[8] This has meant that even the founders of modern legal pluralism have seemingly turned their backs on the term.[9] John Griffiths has argued that the word 'law' should be 'abandoned altogether for purposes of theory formation in sociology of law', with the terms 'normative pluralism' or 'pluralism in social control' as his preferred candidates to replace 'legal pluralism'. Sally Falk Moore has written that distinctions must be made between governmental and non-governmental norms of social control.[10] The failure of legal pluralism is that, while it asserts the normality of there being more one 'legal' system co-existing in the same social arena, it does not provide a means whereby such 'legal' norms can be identified and distinguished from other forms of social control.[11]

Luhmann's great contribution is to overcome the failure of legal pluralism. As Gunther Teubner pointed out, applying systems theory, legal pluralism is 'defined no longer as a set of conflicting social norms in a given social field but as a multiplicity of diverse communicative processes that observe social action under the binary code of legal/illegal'.[12] Systems theory therefore provides a methodology for the distinction and description of law as opposed to other social or doctrinal norms. A social systems approach shows that we can recognise legal pluralism but still distinguish law from social norms. As law defines itself through its own communications, law as a social system perpetuates itself. A systems theory approach means that social norms can be distinguished from legal norms. It allows the definition of law to be kept in line with social change without either having to resort to an external objective definition with set criteria or a wholly subjective approach that allows individuals to define

---

[8]   Ibid 171, 174. See, however, Victor M Muñiz-Fraticelli, *The Structure of Pluralism* (Oxford University Press, 2014) 135–36. Muñiz-Fraticelli agrees that the legal pluralist tradition has 'failed to provide criteria either for distinguishing legal from non-legal phenomena or for recommending for or against the recognition of a normative system as law': ibid 139.

[9]   Brian Z Tamanaha, 'Understanding Legal Pluralism: Past to Present, Local to Global' (2008) 30 *Sydney Law Review* 375, 393.

[10]   John Griffiths, 'The Idea of Sociology of Law and its Relation to Law and to Sociology' (2005) 8 *Current Legal Issues* 49, 63–64; Sally Falk Moore, 'Certainties Undone: Fifty Turbulent Years of Legal Anthropology, 1949–1999' in Sally Falk Moore (ed) *Law and Anthropology: A Reader* (Wiley, 2005) 346, 357.

[11]   For further discussion, including the appropriateness of objective and subjective approaches to the definition issue, see Russell Sandberg, 'The Failure of Legal Pluralism' (2016) 18 *Ecclesiastical Law Journal* 137.

[12]   Gunther Teubner, 'The Two Faces of Janus: Rethinking Legal Pluralism' (1991) 13 *Cardozo Law Review* 1443, 1451.

what is law on a case-by-case basis.[13] As Richard Nobles and David Schiff point out, a focus on coding has more potential to extend the study of what is legal beyond a focus on formal sources than does an approach that identifies as 'law' only what a significant number of participants, if questioned, would describe as 'law'.[14]

This transforms the discussion of religious law. It moves it on from the question of *whether* religious law is law (a discussion invariably shaped by a State-centralist account) to the question of *when* religious law is law; or, more accurately, when religious communications are legal. The question of what is 'religious law' is not answered by reference to institutions but is rather dependent upon the particular communication. Religious decision-making bodies – whether the Governing Body of the Church in Wales, a shariah tribunal or a Quaker meeting – all produce legal as well as non-legal kinds of communication. Whenever they produce communications based on the binary code legal/illegal, that – according to systems theory – is law.

***

A systems theory approach allows us to take a further step. Applying Luhmann's theory, it can regard religious legal orders as autopoietic social systems in their own right.[15] They can be regarded as social systems that

---

[13]   For subjective approaches, see, e.g., Tamanaha's 'social theory of law' (Brian Z Tamanaha, *Realistic Socio-Legal Theory* (Oxford University Press, 1997), Chapters 5 and 6; and Brian Z Tamanaha, *A General Jurisprudence of Law and Society* (Oxford University Press, 2001) 162 *et seq*); the 'critical' legal pluralist' approach of Martha-Marie Kleinhans and Roderick A Macdonald ('What is a *Critical* Legal Pluralism?' (1997) 12(2) *Canadian Journal of International Law and Society* 25); and Amy R Codling's concept of 'subjective legal pluralism' (Amy R Codling, 'A Critical Pluralist Analysis of *R (on the application of Begum) v Headteacher and Governors of Denbigh High School*' (2012) 169 *Law & Justice* 224; Amy R Codling, 'What Do You Believe? Taxonomy of a Subjective Legal Pluralism' in Russell Sandberg (ed) *Religion and Legal Pluralism* (Ashgate, 2015) 199); and Amy R Codling, *Thinking Critically About Law: A Student's Guide* (Routledge, 2018) 90–92).

[14]   They point out that, unlike Tamanaha's theory, 'Systems theory proceeds on the basis that the process of inclusion within a functional social subsystem is not established through consensus (the number of individuals who express a similar view) but through the operations of that system': Richard Nobles and David Schiff, 'Using Systems Theory to Understand Legal Pluralism: What Could be Gained?' (2012) 46(2) *Law and Society Review* 265, 274–76.

[15]   For discussion of the meaning of the term 'legal order', see Maleiha Malik, *Minority Legal Orders in the UK* (The British Academy, 2012) 22–24. She contended that a legal order can be said to exist where there are legal norms (ie, where an individual can point to distinct norms that regulative normative social order and which are 'sufficiently distinct, widespread and concrete to ensure that they are distinguishable from general social relationships') that are applied though 'some additional mechanism, for

simultaneously apply both legal and religious codes. Religious legal systems combine the binary coding and functional specifications of the two social systems of law and religion.[16] The notion that social systems could produce further systems is recognised in Luhmann's theory, which stated that 'we have to presuppose it is possible to form further autopoietic systems within autopoietic systems'.[17] He wrote that 'differentiations become conditions for further differentiations', and that religious organisations provided an example of 'autopoietic systems that operate on their own'.[18]

However, to date, there has been no discussion of this idea that religious legal systems could operate as social systems. Rather, it is assumed that the

---

exercising authority through decisions, interpretation and implementation'. For Malik, the term is said to 'exclude diffuse mechanisms for normative regulation even if their adherents insist that these are "law"'. She calls for an 'objective criterion' to determine whether the mechanisms are diffuse, but it is unclear what criterion would be used; Malik assumes that this is implicit in her definition. Although it is possible to identify such standards (eg, using the 'five basic techniques' by which law discharges social functions identified by Robert S Summers and/or Karl Llewellyn's four 'law-jobs' or basic functions of law (see Robert S Summers, 'The Technique Element in Law' (1971) 59 *Californian Law Review* 733 and Karl N Llewellyn, 'The Normative, the Legal and the Law Jobs: The Problem of Juristic Method' (1940) 49 *Yale Law Journal* 1355), the use of objective standards is questionable given that such conditions are prone to suffer from three defects. First, they may be overly conservative, understanding legal mechanisms by precedent so that mechanisms are seen as legal only if they are similar to existing legal mechanisms and thus excluding novel or different mechanisms. Second, they may be culturally specific, perpetuating a Westernised notion of law. Third, they may fail to take into account changing understandings of what people regard as law. This would include failing to take into account or at least being slow to take into account social change. It is also unnecessary to exclude 'diffuse mechanisms'. The difference between norms and orders is simply that between the existence of an obligation and the enforcement of an obligation. Malik is correct to exclude obligations that are not enforced by 'decisions, interpretation and implementation'. However, there is no reason why such obligations need to be 'distinct, widespread and concrete'. A preferable approach would be to conclude that in order to become a legal order (rather than a mere norm), all that is needed is that norms are enforced. The work of Liam Murphy may be instructive here. Murphy has observed that: 'While the availability of coercive enforcement cannot be seen as a necessary condition for a normative order counting as a legal order, I do believe that when it is law we are talking about (rather than, say, morality or etiquette), we hold that coercive enforcement is in principle appropriate' (Liam L Murphy, *What Makes Law* (Cambridge University Press, 2014) 5). This would be in line with a systems theory definition of 'law'.

[16] This develops the argument that religious law is necessarily and by definition both religious and legal: Russell Sandberg, *Law and Religion* (Cambridge University Press, 2011), Chapter 9.

[17] Niklas Luhmann, *Law as a Social System* (Oxford University Press, 2004) 467.

[18] Ibid; Niklas Luhmann, *A Systems Theory of Religion* (Stanford University Press, 2013) 165.

continued operation of religious legal systems is a sign of de-differentiation. It is assumed that the end point in a purely functionally differentiated society is that religious institutions simply should not use the communications of another social system such as law. This is why shariah councils and other forms of religious tribunals are treated with ill ease, as shown by the reaction to Rowan Williams' 2008 lecture on religious law.

Understanding religious legal systems as autopoietic systems in their own right would rebut perceptions that regard them as a throwback to pre-modern undifferentiated society. Rather, than being signs of de-differentiation, religious legal systems should be seen as evidence of 're-differentiation'. This would represent a further stage of functional differentiation where the voluntary organisations (religious and non-religious) perform functions which it was thought had become the preserve of the State. This approach would question Luhmann's implicitly forward-moving model of history by showing how further differentiation can occur in a less centralised way.

The neoliberal rollback of the State, manifested in the form of legal aid cuts and the increased reliance upon voluntary organisations rather than State institutions, can be understood in systems theory terms as a process of re-differentiation where functions are differentiated further but backwards: specific functions returned from centralised State-centric social institutions (such as law) to social systems which formerly performed such functions (such as religion). The difference is that the latter (religion) is now expected to behave like the former (law), and thus develops in a way that is outside its core function. This explains the existence and increasing use of religious legal orders. In an undifferentiated society, religions routinely dealt with all matters of adherents' life, including any adjudicative functions. In a differentiated society, adjudication passes to the legal system and to the State. In a re-differentiated society, the legal system/State abrogates responsibility for adjudication on certain matters, so those matters fall back to the religious systems (alongside other new systems), which develop ways to charge these functions in a way that blends religious and legal discourses and behaviours. This insight transforms the way in which religious legal systems are regarded and places them firmly in the context of the privatisation of disputes.

Re-differentiation should transform not only how religious law is understood, but also how law and religion is understood. The plausibility narratives constructed by the social system of law seek to cement law's own autonomy and deny re-differentiation, seeing it as a breach of de-differentiation. Focusing on re-differentiation stresses that religious legal systems are not throwbacks. Rather, they are adapting to a new situation (the neoliberal rollback of the State and State-funded mechanisms) and operating in new ways that fuse the religious and the legal. This was shown in the Cardiff study of religious tribunals: all three systems emulated elements of the modern legal system in how they operated. They fused the religious and the legal – often in awkward ways, as the interviewee at the Catholic Tribunal quoted at the beginning of Chapter 14 underscored. The interviewee suggested that Church lawyers (as he called them) needed 'to have a legal mindset or the ability to adapt to working within judicial structures and disciplines', while at the same time retaining a 'pastoral sensitivity' – neatly highlighting the fusion of the legal and the religious that religious tribunals exemplify. This is why Luhmann's systems theory is useful in understanding them – and the response that other institutions have had to them.

Like other social theories, social systems theory underlines the importance of social differentiation, which explains why religious tribunals are treated with unease and seen as 'throwbacks' that do not fit within modern society. The work of Luhmann allows us to understand this more clearly: the social system of law cannot understand the existence of religious tribunals; religious forms of adjudication offend and question the very underlying ideas that law uses to perpetuate and differentiate itself. De-differentiation is particularly challenging for law as it exposes the paradox at its core: that law itself decides between legality and illegality, but can never question its validity for doing so. If religious forms of adjudication are deciding between legality and illegality using religious values, this poses the question that should never be asked about what values law is using to make such decisions.

However, regarding religious legal orders as autopoietic social systems does not result from a straightforward application of Luhmann's social systems theory. Rather – much like the last chapter, which used the work of Harrington to identify the deparadoxification strategies utilised in religion law – this chapter has developed and deviated from social systems theory. In particular, it has shown the need to move away from Luhmann's implicitly forward-moving model of history. As the next chapter will discuss, system theory's acceptance and perpetuation of what Robert Gordon famously referred to as the 'dominant vision of evolutionary functionalism' – whereby 'an objective, determined progressive social evolutionary path' is naturally followed[19] – is one of the main problems with the theory that needs to be overcome.

---

[19] Robert W Gordon, 'Critical Legal Histories' in Robert W Gordon, *Taming the Past: Essays on Law in History and History in Law* (Cambridge University Press, 2017) 220, 226–27.

18. Systems upgrade

'I am the Lucifer of social theory,' declared Niklas Luhmann on what would be his last visit to London. Commentators have said that as he spoke, 'his face glowed with a mischievous smile' and that the comment was made 'not without some relish'.[1] How seriously he meant his comment is open to doubt. Yet it underscores that my suggestion that law and religion scholarship make a pact with this devil is a controversial one. Although his work has attracted a significant degree of scholarly attention, Luhmann remains a controversial figure in his own native Germany and much further afield. The mere mention of his name or reference to his social systems theory can provoke negative and hostile reactions. His theory is often dismissed as an overly complex meta-theory that allows no room for alternative explanations. However, such denouncements are often based upon somewhat caricatured versions of the theory. The significant delay in translating many of his works into English and French,[2] the number of different interpretations that have evolved in the now vast secondary literature[3] and the dynamic nature of his work – which underwent a self-professed 'paradigm change'[4] – have all contributed to the ill reputation of social systems theory.

---

[1]   Francisco Carballo, 'Niklas Luhmann as a Theorist of Exclusion: A Journey from the Greek *Polis* to the Brazilian *Favelas*' (2019) 14 *Transtext(e)s Transcultures: Journal of Global Cultural Studies* [Online] para 1; Michael King and Chris Thornhill, *Niklas Luhmann's Theory of Politics and Law* (Palgrave, 2003) 203.

[2]   On which see Martin Albrow, 'Editor's Introduction' in Niklas Luhmann, *A Sociological Theory of Law* (2nd edition, Routledge, 2014) xxxii; and Richard Nobles and David Schiff, 'Introduction' in Niklas Luhmann, *Law as a Social System* (Oxford University Press, 2004) 3.

[3]   Jiri Priban, '(Review of) *Niklas Luhmann: Law, Justice, Society* by Andreas Philippopoulos-Mihalopoulos' (2010) 73 *Modern Law Review* 893. There is a need to distinguish the work of Luhmann from those who have developed his theory. In the legal context, this is particularly true of the work of Gunther Teubner; on which see Andreas Philippopolous-Mihalopoulos, 'Introduction: Gunther Teubner's Foundational Paradox' in Gunther Teubner, *Critical Theory and Legal Autopoiesis: The Case for Societal Constitutionalism* (Manchester University Press, 2019) 1.

[4]   Niklas Luhmann, *Social Systems* (Stanford University Press, 1995) 1. In terms of his legal writings, there is a clear shift between the first edition of *A Sociological Theory of Law* (Routledge, 1985) and *Law as a Social System* (Oxford University Press, 2004). The development of his thought was shown by the new conclusion he added to

Yet Luhmann's notoriety was neither unexpected not accidental. Luhmann's work explicitly represented a significant break with (and therefore a challenge to) longstanding sociological orthodoxies. As Moeller pointed out, Luhmann's basic claim that 'society does not consist of human beings can be seen as shocking, as going against common sense, or as absurd'.[5] Many critics of Luhmann would accuse it of being all three.[6]

However, such criticisms are overstated.[7] Luhmann's theory is not anti-human; it is no more so than the grand theories of Marx or Durkheim. The thing to remember is that, like those theories, it is a social theory: a theory of society rather than of psychological-organic systems.[8] For Luhmann, people are '"living systems", which exist as bodies and bodily parts, and "psychic systems", which produce meaning through consciousness'.[9] These can be contrasted with society, which 'consists of interdependent social systems which make sense of their environments through their communications'. A system and how it develops can be analysed while simultaneously recognising that the system is a human construct and that it is being constantly shaped by the actions of individuals. It is perfectly possible to talk and analyse the legal system or systems within the legal system while recognising that the system is the product of humans thinking and litigating.[10] As Nobles and Schiff noted,

---

the second edition of *A Sociological Theory of Law* (Routledge, 2014). In terms of religion, this shift can be found after the publication of *Funktion der Religion* (*Funktion der Suhrkampf*, 1977), culminating in his posthumous publication *A Systems Theory of Religion* (Stanford University Press, 2013).

[5]   Hans-George Moeller, *Luhmann Explained* (Open Court, 2006) ix.

[6]   For discussion see, e.g., Roger Cotterrell, 'The Representation of Law's Autonomy in Autopoiesis Theory' in Jiri Priban and David Nelken (eds) *Law's New Boundaries: The Consequences of Legal Autopoiesis* (Ashgate, 2001) 80, 95–98.

[7]   Michael King, 'The Radical Sociology of Niklas Luhmann' in Reza Banaker and Max Travers (eds) *Law and Social Theory* (2nd edition, Hart, 2013) 59, 62.

[8]   Niklas Luhmann, *A Sociological Theory of Law* (2nd edition, Routledge, 2014).

[9]   Michael King and Chris Thornhill, *Niklas Luhmann's Theory of Politics and Law* (Palgrave, 2003) 7.

[10]   Criticisms to the contrary often operate with a narrow and restrictive understanding of the concepts used by systems theory. Amy Codling has written that my call to adopt social systems theory 'rests on three key misunderstandings'. The first is that law is 'meaning and not machinery': 'Concepts such as the "state", "society" and "community" are shaped by the knowledge, they inherit, create and share with other subjects.' Yet there is nothing in my reading and application of social systems theory that contradicts this. Legal communications clearly produce meaning and this develops organically, both within the social system of law and through interactions with other social systems in much the way that Codling describes. The second misunderstanding she identifies is that 'unrealistic power is granted to communication (or legal systems)' in a way that risks abandoning the power and control of humans to control and change the system. This again seems confused. Systems theory does focus on communications but

a systems theory analysis simply takes a different focus: 'its hermeneutics are rooted not in the intentions of human actors, but in the meanings generated by those actors through their participation as communicators.'[11] A more pressing criticism, however, relates to the sociological tradition within which social systems theory developed. The problem, in short, is that the devil wears Durkheim.

∗∗∗

Luhmann took what was already an often derided social theory – the functionalist perspective epitomised by Durkheim and extrapolated by Parsons in his general systems theory[12] – and developed it to focus more on systematic processes than on the collective effect of social behaviours. The functionalist tradition presupposes that the default nature of the social order is consensus, and that social institutions work with one another for the sake of the whole in the same way that parts of the human body function separately but also

---

in doing so emphasises rather than denies that they are the product of human agency. All sociological theories group people together, focusing on social action in the most part but here on communication. That does not deny human agency. It simply operates not as a psychological theory but as a sociological one. Codling's third misunderstanding focuses on the charge that the theory is 'anti humanist because it focuses on phenomena or essences rather than the creativity of the human imagination'. I would counter that paying attention to social systems in all their complexity actually illustrates human creativity since the systems are the product of human thought and endeavour. Codling finds my argument that social systems theory does not deny human agency to be 'unconvincing' on the basis that 'the creative capacity of the human mind enables even the most rigid of social systems to be bent, broken or defeated'. This again operates from a very different understanding of systems theory that sees systems as being impenetrable and immovable. This is not my reading of Luhmann's thesis. Indeed, such a static approach would be of very limited use. It is a shame that, while Codling begins by seeing her preferred approach as being similar to social systems theory, she then dismisses the application of social systems theory by presenting a caricatured and basic version of the theory that exhibits 'key misunderstandings' that are of her creation: Amy R Codling, *Thinking Critically About Law: A Student's Guide* (Routledge, 2018) 90–92.

[11]   Richard Nobles and David Schiff, 'Using Systems Theory to Understand Legal Pluralism: What Could be Gained?' (2012) 46(2) *Law and Society Review* 265, 266–67.

[12]   Rudi Laermans and Gert Verschraegen note that the 'general aversion to systems theory in the post-Parsonian age was probably also responsible for the striking lack of interest' in Luhmann's theory within the sociology of religion: Rudi Laermans and Gert Verschraegen, '"The Late Niklas Luhmann" on Religion' (2001) 48(1) *Social Compass* 7, 9. Parsons' work has also been afforded little attention in the sociology of law: Reza Banaker and Max Travers, 'Systems Theory' in Reza Banaker and Max Travers (eds) *Law and Social Theory* (2nd edition, Hart, 2013) 53. See, however, Kenneth C Bausch, *The Emerging Consensus in Social Systems Theory* (Springer, 2001) for a full discussion of the field of systems theory.

collectively in order for the body as a whole to function. A functionalist approach presumes equilibrium as the default and regards any turbulence as being fleeting or a perversion; a dysfunction. The functionalist approach understands societies as having universal and specific needs which 'operate both as pressures and constraints': they are 'motors driving the society to find means for their fulfilment' and setting 'the limits on the possibilities of social experimentation'.[13]

Functionalist social theory is countered by the critical theory that has developed from the Marxist tradition and which informed the critical movements we discussed in the second part of this book. Such approaches see society predicated upon conflict rather than consensus and point to the inequalities and power imbalances that are inherent and perpetuated in order to sustain the status quo, which favours the powerful. Yet although critical theories are more fashionable than functionalism in terms of social theories, it is functionalist ideas that are otherwise prevalent. Legal historian Robert Gordon referred to 'evolutionary functionalism' – the idea of linear progress – as the 'set of background assumptions ... about the course of western History, that American legal scholars tended to take for granted'.[14] It is not only Americans, and not only legal scholars, who unquestionably accept evolutionary functionalism; it is the prevalent unthinking backdrop most of the time – the expectation of linear progress is entrenched.

For Gordon, evolutionary functionalism comprises five threads when applied to law:[15] first, law and society are separate categories and law is autonomous; second, societies have needs which drive them and limit the possibilities of social experimentation; third, societies follow an objective, determined, progressive social evolutionary path and law assumes this; fourth, legal systems are described and explained in terms of their functional responsiveness to social needs (whether have satisfied, or failed to satisfy, the functional requirements of each stage in social development); and fifth, the legal system adapts to changing social needs in that, although legal changes can be dysfunctional for short periods, adaption is the normal course. This is reflected in the ideas that the 'common law over time tends to work itself pure'; that legal doctrine has become 'ever more certain and predictable as well as more adaptable to social needs'; and that the law has 'become more and more efficient'.[16]

---

[13]   Robert W Gordon, *Taming the Past: Essays on Law in History and History in Law* (Cambridge University Press, 2017) 225.

[14]   Ibid 221.

[15]   Ibid 223–29.

[16]   Ibid 229.

Gordon observed that the critical approach counters evolutionary functionalism. A critical approach argues that this representation obscures the way in
which these processes are actually manufactured by people.[17] Legal forms and
practices are political products that arise from the struggles of conflict. A critical approach shows that the course of historical development is not determined
by any uniform evolutionary path. There is no necessary link between social
and legal change ('Comparable social conditions (both within the same and
across societies) have generated contrary legal responses, and comparable
legal forks have produced contrary social effects'). This means that law is
neither an objective response to objective historical processes nor a neutral
technology adapted to the needs of that particular society. Gordon insisted that
law and society are 'inextricably mixed'.[18] As he put it, 'it is just about impossible to describe any set of "basic" social practices without describing the legal
relations among the people involved'.[19] Indeed, 'legal categories affect social
perceptions' to such an extent that law persuades that 'the world described in
its images and categories is the only attainable world in which a sane person
would want to live'. This hides the extent to which law is 'founded upon
contradictions' and the chief job of law is 'to keep those oppositions from
becoming too starkly obvious'.[20] Legal scholarship written in the evolutionary
functionalist mode seeks to hide and/or normalise this. By contrast, legal
scholarship written in the critical mode seeks to highlight and question this. As
Gordon put it, critical legal historiography becomes 'the intellectual history of
the rise and fall of paradigm structures of thought designed to mediate contradictions'.[21] A critical approach, then, reveals what John Harrington referred to
as 'deparadoxification strategies'.[22] This focus on programming and how the
paradoxes of law are concealed by legal communication gives a glimpse of
how a critical approach can be applied to Luhmann's work.

***

However, a critical approach to social systems theory needs to go further than
that. There is a need to question, deconstruct and reconstruct the assumptions
and values that underlie social systems theory. Indeed, so ubiquitous are these
functionalist underpinnings and so routinely are they perpetuated by legal

---

[17]   For a fuller discussion of the seven 'partial critiques' which inform critical
approaches, see ibid 261.
[18]   Ibid 266.
[19]   Ibid 262.
[20]   Ibid 273.
[21]   Ibid 274.
[22]   John Harrington, 'Of Paradox and Plausibility: The Dynamic of Change in
Medical Law' (2014) 22(3) *Medical Law Review* 305, 306.

communications to preserve law's stability that questioning, deconstructing and reconstructing the foundations of social systems theory simultaneously involves doing the same for law as a whole. Building on the work of Gordon, in *Subversive Legal History: A Manifesto for the Future of Legal Education*,[23] I contended that lawyers – we could say the social system of law – had applied the wrong scientific paradigm to understand legal change.

I have suggested that, rather than the dominant assumptions of 'evolutionary functionalism', the development of law is actually characterised by 'entropic complexity'.[24] The concept of entropy denotes the gradual decline into disorder. Such an approach would see such chaos – uncertainty, nuance and flexibility – as normal. This rejects the functionalist aspect of evolutionary functionalism. It also rejects the evolutionary aspect. The concept of complexity disregards the idea of linear progress that is so commonplace and perpetuated by what Gordon referred to as:

> determinist teleologies, whose elemental parts – the 'extension of the market,' the 'breakdown of traditional communities and status hierarchies,' the 'shift from ascribed to achieved social status,' the 'triumph of the middle class,' the 'revolution of production in the factory system,' the 'rise of the administrative state,' and the 'development of the multi-divisional form of corporate organization' – are all linked together in a master process of social evolution.[25]

In its place, law is understood as being 'untimely':[26] it operates in neither linear nor progressive ways. This means that rather than focusing on origins or end points, there is a need to explore the intellectual history of the ebb and flow of legal ideas.

---

[23] Russell Sandberg, *Subversive Legal History: A Manifesto for the Future of Legal Education* (Routledge, 2021).

[24] Ibid 123 *et seq*. This draws upon three different but complementary literatures: social entropy theory, chaos theory and complexity theory. It explicitly drew upon three works that have applied these theories in the context of law: David Collins, 'The Chaos Machine: The WTO in a Social Entropy Model of the World Trading System' (2014) 34(2) *Oxford Journal of Legal Studies* 353; Robert E Scott, 'Chaos Theory and the Justice Paradox' (1993) 35 *William & Mary Law Review* 329; and Jamie Murray, Thomas E Webb and Steven Wheatley (eds), *Complexity Theory and Law: Mapping an Emergent Jurisprudence* (Routledge, 2019). For identification and discussion of the seven characteristics of entropic complexity, see Russell Sandberg, *Subversive Legal History: A Manifesto for the Future of Legal Education* (Routledge, 2021) 133–34.

[25] Robert W Gordon, *Taming the Past: Essays on Law in History and History in Law* (Cambridge University Press, 2017) 226–27.

[26] Kathryn McNeilly, 'Are Rights Out of Time? International Human Rights Law, Temporality, and Radical Social Change' (2019) 28(6) *Social and Legal Studies* 817.

A complex system exists where there is emergence. This concept of emergence represents the notion that the whole is more than the sum of its parts, and that something new has been created which has an autonomous life of its own: a system. This is where entropic complexity can be fruitfully combined with social systems theory.[27] Applied to the context of law, an approach based on entropic complexity underscores that equilibrium is not the default but is rather a facade. Law is a complex system, and the natural result of a complex system is entropy. This reverses the usual approach to the common law, which:

> assumes that although the law may appear to be irrational, chaotic and particularistic, if one digs deep enough and knows what one is looking for, then it will soon become evident that the law is an internally coherent and unified system of rules.[28]

The social system of law counters its complex reality by insisting upon and promoting the opposite view. Law cannot accept the chaotic reality since that would reveal the paradox at the heart of the social system: that law itself is the pragmatic and biased decision-maker of what it recognises and what it does not. The social system of law must conceal this and does so through promoting evolutionary functionalist ideals. Judgments and legal writings suggest that law has a basic harmony and humane purpose; particular issues are cast as specific controversies that do not require consideration of broader change.

***

Entropic complexity, therefore, bridges critical approaches with social systems theory by discarding the functionalist underpinning of Luhmann's theory. This upgrade replaces equilibrium with chaos, evolution with entropy, progress with inequality and cohesion with complexity. It provides a means by which we can take a step back and analyse the 'deparadoxification strategies' of law

---

[27] Entropic complexity emphasises the dynamic interconnectedness of systems and shows how complex social systems – such as law – are self-organising but not fully autonomous. They have an open and contested interaction with other systems. This underscores that legal and the non-legal cannot be adequately distinguished from one another but are interpenetrative. Cf Roger Cotterrell, 'Why Must Legal Ideas be Interpreted Sociologically?' (1998) 25 *Journal of Law and Society* 171, reprinted as Roger Cotterrell, *Law, Culture and Society* (Ashgate, 2006), Chapter 3.

[28] David Sugarman, 'Legal Theory, the Common Law Mind and the Making of the Textbook Tradition' in William Twinning (ed) *Legal Theory and the Common Law* (Blackwell, 1986) 26.

as a social system.[29] As Jamie Murray, Thomas E Webb and Steven Wheatley have noted:

> Complexity theory understands law as an emergent, self-organising system in which an interactive network of many parts – actors, institutions and 'systems' operate with no overall guiding hand, giving rise to complex collective behaviours that can be explore observed in patterns of law communications.[30]

This stresses the need to examine individuals and systems – overcoming the often unfair criticism of Luhmann's theory that it excluded people. Like other critical approaches we have examined, an approach based on entropic complexity underlines the importance of agency of individuals and their social groups. Attention also needs to be paid to how complex systems grow from the actions of individuals and social groups. Rather than excluding people, a focus on communication underscores the power of individuals and the development of groupthink, showing how complex systems such as law develop their own artificial intelligence: how they emerge and develop a life of their own which equates to more than the sum of their parts. Law is a complex system and communications within that system need to be an object of study. Rather than accept and regurgitate, the role of the legal scholar is to uncover the chaotic and unpredictable behaviour that is hidden by the dominant discourse and to expose that strategy. As Murray, Webb and Wheatley noted, this can involve revealing:

> The unpredictability of legal systems; the idea of the law system as emergent, the result of the interactions between law actors; the ability of law to adapt to changes in its external environment and the functioning of other law systems; the importance of context to understanding law; the unclear, contested and open nature of law system boundaries and the way they interface with society; and the fact that practitioners and scholars cannot avoid ethical responsibility in their work.[31]

***

However, developing social systems theory in a manner such as this has proved controversial. Murray, Webb and Wheatley have argued that their complexity theory 'is qualitatively different from' social systems theory and 'significantly

---

[29]   Cf John Harrington, 'Of Paradox and Plausibility: The Dynamic of Change in Medical Law' (2014) 22(3) *Medical Law Review* 305, 306.

[30]   Jamie Murray, Thomas E Webb and Steven Wheatley, 'Encountering Law's Complexity' in Jamie Murray, Thomas E Webb and Steven Wheatley (eds) *Complexity Theory and Law: Mapping an Emergent Jurisprudence* (Routledge, 2019) 3.

[31]   Ibid 11.

enhances' the study of law.[32] For them, 'complexity theory is better science', in that in while social systems theory simply drew upon the work of Maturana and Varela,[33] complexity theory is 'well established in physics, chemistry and biology, and the literature has drawn on a wide range of sources in these disciplines'.[34] Yet, as Richard Nobles and David Schiff have responded, the issue is not which theory is 'drawn from more categories of science than the other, but which of them best informs the object to be observed, which in this case is society, and law within society'.[35] This is surely correct. Nobles and Schiff are right to say that the two theories have much in common and are complementary.[36] Combining the two would enable 'seeing the primary unit of society not as human actors, but as communications, and seeing how humans become constituted as actors, alongside organisations, and perhaps other entities within systems of communication'.[37] They concluded that social systems and complexity theory have much in common, and that this included the acceptance of entropy:

> Neither theory presumes that the systems to be analysed are causally closed. Neither theory denies thermodynamics – all systems expend energy, and require ever increasing amounts of energy in order to achieve increased complexity. Both theories acknowledge that a system is affected by its environment (remembering that a system's environment includes other systems). Both theories are directed to systems that do not have a simple input/output relationship with their environment, whereby the same input always leads to the same output, which would allow a given input from the environment to determine the output of the affected system.[38]

Nobles and Schiff have argued that much of the criticism made of systems theory in terms of its functionalist mindset applies more to earlier functionalist theories than to Luhmann's work. This underscores the value of bringing together the two approaches. Complexity theory can be used to reject Luhmann's progressive account of history.

Entropic complexity can therefore serve as a corrective to systems theory, limiting its functionalist bent. However, this can also underscore how com-

---

[32]   Ibid 6.

[33]   HR Maturana and FJ Varela, *The Tree of Knowledge: The Biological Roots of Human Understanding* (Shambhala Press, 1987).

[34]   Jamie Murray, Thomas E Webb and Steven Wheatley, 'Encountering Law's Complexity' in Jamie Murray, Thomas E Webb and Steven Wheatley (eds) *Complexity Theory and Law: Mapping an Emergent Jurisprudence* (Routledge, 2019) 3, 6.

[35]   Richard Nobles and David Schiff, 'Taking the Complexity of Complex Systems Seriously' (2020) 83(3) *Modern Law Review* 661, 668.

[36]   Ibid 661.

[37]   Ibid 677.

[38]   Ibid 674–75.

plexity theory too is in need of remedial action. In demonstrating the compatibility of social systems theory with complexity theory as understood by Murray, Webb and Wheatley, Nobles and Schiff ironically highlighted how functionalist ideas also underpin complexity theory. They noted that the way in which both approaches have a shared onus on 'the necessity for problem solving if a particular system within modern complex society is to reproduce' means that complexity theory and social systems theory 'adopt a similar attitude to functionalism'.[39] This 'similar attitude' embracing a forward-moving account of history is objectionable.

Given how pervasive the problematisation of religion is within law and religion scholarship, this underscores the importance of rooting out and rejecting functionalist ideas and assumptions. The focus on entropy as opposed to the traditional functionalist focus on equilibrium provides some help in this respect.[40] However, there is a need to go further still by embedding a critical, subversive approach.

The controversy between social system and complexity theories is not to be solved by favouring one over the other. Rather, it points to the need for both theories to inform each other. Luhmann's work is valuable in developing the idea of social functional differentiation and exploring how complex systems operate. However, Luhmann's theory needs to be shorn of its evolutionary functionalist assumptions. Applying it to the context of law and religion can help with this, as shown by the focus on the 're-differentiation' of religion in previous chapters, which provides a significant step forward and highlights the potential of what can be achieved by a social system theory predicated upon entropic complexity. A developed critical – you could say, subversive – social systems theory also highlights what is being concealed by the deparadoxification strategies being carried out by legal communications. This challenges and changes the role of legal academics and commentators. Rather than being complicit in the concealment strategy found within the social system of law, the role of scholars is to expose it. This requires a subversive approach to the analysis of law, recognising that the artificial intelligence of law is constructed and shaped by particular people with their own biases, assumptions and values. Rather than dismissing people (as Luhmann's critics would have it), this approach disturbs the way in which we see the system by focusing on agency – especially the agency of those who have previously been marginalised. It also requires the questioning, deconstruction and reconstruction of concepts, ideas

---

[39] Ibid 674.

[40] Kenneth D Bailey asserted that 'the limitation of functionalist systems theory stem largely because it is based upon the isolated-system equilibrium theory ... rather than on ... entropy analysis': Kenneth D Bailey, *Social Entropy Theory* (University of New York Press, 1990) 71.

and boundaries, including those around areas of study. It requires us to subject everything to critical scrutiny, rejecting the assumptions, values and biases that we have been socialised in. In short, it requires us to begin again.

19. Rewriting history

Every generation thinks that the challenges they face are unique. This is a reflection of historical illiteracy. Evolutionary functionalist ideas are now taken for granted. Narratives of progress are entrenched. Social functional differentiation is taken as the norm. This has had a significant impact upon legal academia generally, and in particular upon the development of law and religion as an area of study in England and Wales. The subject has been constrained by the endemic secularised framework in which law schools operate. Law and religion has been relegated to the margins since it is regarded as a medieval throwback. The very presence of religion in the public sphere offends our cultural and social mindset. It is instantly seen as a problem that law ought to fix. A social systems account provides a means of analysing this, showing us how law operates as a social system to colonise and deny the claims of religion to operate outside its own narrow social system. Such a theory, however, is itself imbued with evolutionary functionalism and so needs adapting. The linear conception of time and progress that results in fear of de-differentiation needs to be replaced. The default of equilibrium needs to give way to that of entropy. Progress and linear models of evolution need to be superseded by theories of complexity and chaos. The claims being made by the social system of religion – manifest in the operation of religious tribunals, the existence of faith schools and the presence of religion in the public sphere – need to be reconceptualised as re-differentiation; something new.

To the extent that law and religion has developed as an academic sub-discipline, it has done so by accepting and perpetuating the very set of assumptions that has marginalised it. Transcending this requires not only acts of deconstruction – highlighting and dismantling the edifices built in the name of law and religion and those who have created and sustained them – but also, crucially, acts of reconstruction. This entails changing the lens from the prevalent legalistic approach that problematises religion towards something new. It involves questioning – and where necessary debunking – accepted and prevalent orthodoxies. Nothing about the study of law and religion is sacred; it has all been constructed and so can be taken down and rebuilt.

This does not always mandate the need to begin again with a blank sheet of paper. That will sometimes be necessary, especially in relation to matters that have hitherto been neglected or ignored. Yet in other instances, the deconstructed rubble – once stripped of the reverence previously bestowed upon it

– can be used to forge its replacement. We can learn lessons from our mistakes. This is true in relation to my last two full-length books on law and religion.[1] Although there is much found in their pages that I hope is still of value, there is also a lot that I would now repent of. Both books were underpinned by a conviction that law and religion was and should develop as a legal sub-discipline. As we have seen, this led to the kind of institutional trappings that ironically constrained the development of law and religion by rendering it inherently legalistic and by leading to the development of a ghetto of scholarship. That was a mistake. This, however, was not the only sin committed in those earlier publications. The taint of evolutionary functionalism can also be felt throughout. This is particularly so in relation to the chapter on the historical development of the interaction between religion and the law in the first book. This chapter will revisit that discussion to show how endemic evolutionary functionalist ideas are and also to suggest how this can be corrected.

$$***$$

Chapter 2 of *Law and Religion*, 'Historical Development', began by noting that what followed would be 'illustrative rather than exhaustive, seeking to place the significant legal changes that have occurred in the twenty-first century into their historical context'.[2] This underscored how the historical account being given reflected and perpetrated the agenda of the book. The opening paragraph stated that the chapter posed the question of 'whether these new laws are best seen as providing historical continuity to what went before or a substantial shift in the way in which law and religion interact'. However, the answer to the question was predetermined. The whole book rested on the answer being that of change rather than continuity, especially in relation to what was being routinely referred to as the 'new' legal framework. This answer was arrived at in the chapter by identifying 'four broad overlapping but conceptually distinct phases'. Such a periodisation was by no means unique. As the footnote to the paragraph noted, it was 'largely derived' from a paper which Norman Doe had delivered at the European Consortium of Church and State Research in the late 1990s.[3] Moreover, just after I had written the chapter, Julian Rivers published a book that also included a chapter on 'The Changing Law of Church and

---

[1]   Russell Sandberg, *Law and Religion* (Cambridge University Press, 2011); Russell Sandberg, *Religion, Law and Society* (Cambridge University Press, 2014).

[2]   Russell Sandberg, *Law and Religion* (Cambridge University Press, 2011) 17.

[3]   Norman Doe, 'National Identity, the Constitutional Tradition and the Structures of Law on Religion in the United Kingdom' in *Religions in European Union Law* (Proceedings of the European Consortium of Church and State Research, Luxembourg 1997) 93, 109–10.

State', which identified six periods.[4] This told a similar story to my chapter – a story that focused on change rather than continuity and which perpetuated a narrative of progress.

The first period I identified was the 'temporal–spiritual partnership'. This began around the Norman Conquest and ended with the Reformation. This followed the template of most legal history accounts that follow Maitland to begin at around 1066, exploring the position immediately before the Battle of Hastings.[5] The importance of the Anglo-Saxon period and the effect of the Norman Conquest are matters of debate among legal historians, and this starting point is especially odd when looking at the history of the interaction between law and religion. The common law or any notion of the State did not exist at this time and there was also no national religion: the Church was part of the Catholic Church based in Rome. 1066 was not a turning point in terms of the regulation of religion. Christianity originally came to England when it eventually became accepted by the Roman Empire; but when the Roman troops left Britain in 410, pagan religion once again asserted its supremacy. The following centuries witnessed the slow re-emergence of Christianity and after the Synod of Whitby in 663, England became fully a part of the world-wide Catholic Church. It could be said that the starting point should be well before 1066. The impact of 1066 upon Church law was also minimal. One innovation under the Normans was the separation of the ecclesiastical courts from the courts of land, the shire courts and the hundred courts.[6] Yet it is questionable whether this separation of the ecclesiastical jurisdiction ought to be the starting point for the history told in *Law and Religion*.

Moreover, my first period from 1066 to the 1530s treated as exceptional tensions between the Church and the Crown, epitomised by what I underplayed as 'the dispute between Henry II (1154–1189) and Becket, the Archbishop of Canterbury, over whether clergy who had broken the King's peace should be tried in the King's Court as well as the Courts Christian'.[7] This was a significant simplification which normalised the growing centralisation of the State in

---

[4]   'The First Millennium'; 'From the Norman Conquest to the Break with Rome'; 'Reformation and Revolution'; 'Establishment and Toleration'; 'Religious Pluralism'; and 'Towards the Modern State': Julian Rivers, *The Law of Organized Religions* (Oxford University Press, 2010).

[5]   Frederick Pollock and Frederic W Maitland, *The History of English Law* (2nd edition, vol 1, Cambridge University Press, 1968 [1898]). For discussion see Russell Sandberg, *A Historical Introduction to English Law: Genesis of the Common Law* (Cambridge University Press, 2023), Chapter 3.

[6]   See ibid 68.

[7]   Russell Sandberg, *Law and Religion* (Cambridge University Press, 2011) 22. See Russell Sandberg, *A Historical Introduction to English Law: Genesis of the Common Law* (Cambridge University Press, 2023) 86–88 for a fuller account.

a narrative that used the term 'partnership' to cover what was actually subservience. The story being told is a typical 'top-down' narrative of evolutionary functionalism, where the development of a more sophisticated and therefore better legal system is at the forefront of the narrative. The dates chosen and the labels used can and should be contested: the choices made can be shown as being precisely that – choices that further a particular narrative and a specific agenda. It is also a Christian-centric history, as shown by the unforgivable omission of the discussion of the anti-Semitism and ethnic cleansing that culminated in the expulsion of the Jews in 1290.[8]

The whiff of evolutionary functionalism continued to pollute the second period I identified: 'discrimination and intolerance', dating from the Reformation of the sixteenth century.[9] Again, a 'schoolboy's history' approach was taken with reliance upon developments that are ingrained in the national psyche. While the first period relied upon and perpetuated the fixation with 1066, the close of that period and the beginning of the next did the same in relation to the Tudors and Henry VIII in particular. Unlike with the Norman Conquest, it is clear that the Reformation marked a distinct turning point in the history of law and religion. Yet here too, periodisation simplified and distorted. The re-establishment following the restoration of the monarchy was skimmed over, since that did not fit the story being presented of the Tudor legacy.[10] Again, my focus was on the posture of the State towards religion. And once more, voices of dissent were silenced as the benefit of hindsight meant that the spotlight was shone on the winners and the powerful.[11]

This was true even of the third period I identified: 'religious toleration', which followed from the Glorious Revolution of 1688–89.[12] There it became clear that the narrative was now being painted in even broader strokes: 'Over the course of the seventeenth, eighteenth, nineteenth and twentieth centuries, most of the legal disabilities against alternative religions were removed.' And for the first time, there is recognition (albeit slight) that the real story may not be linear. Yet although the text warns that 'the process was slow, piecemeal, uneven and sometimes contradictory',[13] the story given remains defiantly one of progress. The law is seen to be cleansing itself of previous biases.

---

[8]   For discussion see ibid 121–23.

[9]   Russell Sandberg, *Law and Religion* (Cambridge University Press, 2011) 23.

[10]   This has now been rectified in Russell Sandberg, 'The Restoration and Re-Establishment: 1660–1701' in Norman Doe and Stephen Coleman (eds) *The Legal History of the Church of England* (Hart, 2024) 95.

[11]   Rebecca Riedel, 'A Critical Legal Study of the Prevent Duty: The Religious Dimension' (PhD thesis submitted to Cardiff University, 2023).

[12]   Russell Sandberg, *Law and Religion* (Cambridge University Press, 2011) 26.

[13]   Ibid 27.

A number of Acts of Parliament are cited out of context with no discussion of their rationale, let alone the motivations for their enactment. They are then collectively praised for representing progress because they meant that 'by the late nineteenth century, alternative religion was not only lawful but was often facilitated by the law'.[14] There was also a whiff of presentism to the discussion: a dividing line is drawn and all that has previously been discussed is classified and dismissed as history. This was shown in the penultimate sentence that 'the identification between Church and State became more of a historical anachronism than a sociological fact'.[15]

It is the fourth and final periodisation, however, which was the most crucial to the book's argument: 'positive religious freedom'. This discussion normalised the book's claim that the legal framework concerning religion in the twenty-first century was new by erecting a firm dividing line. It drew a distinction between 'religious toleration and the legal right to religious freedom' and asserted that 'English law has now moved beyond toleration'.[16] It conceded that 'it is difficult to pinpoint a date when this occurred' but offered two options: the building of the international human rights system after the Second World War or the juridification of religion in the early twenty-first century.[17] However, it is simply not the case that only two views can be taken. A range of possible dates could be adopted. It would be possible to look further back and see provisions that are described as toleration as giving religious rights. Moreover, the evolutionary emphasis of the text, with its focus on change, is lamentable.

While periodisation was presented as a supposedly neutral way of structuring the chapter, it was actually grounding and normalising the argument of the book that there was now a new legal framework concerning religion. Ironically, a historical discussion was being used to justify the book's ahistorical focus. The book relegated history to one chapter, where it could be both dismissed as being distinguished from the present and used to underscore the novelty of the distinct new framework. It is possible to argue that the Human Rights Act 1998 and the laws that followed – particularly those which outlawed discrimination on the grounds of religion or belief – marked a turning point in how English law regulated religion. However, that claim is precisely that: an argument. The use of periodisation in that chapter normalised and presented an assertion as a description. It also adopted a standpoint imbued with particular values and expectations: a Christian-centric account that accepted secularisation

---

14 Ibid 28.
15 Ibid 29.
16 Ibid 30.
17 Ibid 30–31.

and social functional differentiation. The problem with the chapter is that it presented a particular story as *the* story. More than that, it presented it as if it were not even a story but rather fact.

***

Having deconstructed the historical development chapter in *Law and Religion*, the question arises of how this can be reconstructed. Two areas that I have focused on in recent years – how religion interacts with marriage and education law[18] – highlight well the limits of progress narratives such as that relied upon in *Law and Religion*, and how an alternative understanding can be developed that moves away from the conventional approach, that fetishes social functional differentiation and evolutionary functionalism.

When law and religion writers comment on marriage law and education law in England and Wales, they typically embrace the endemic narrative of social functional differentiation. They tend to recount how these laws still show evidence of their Christian past but point out that, although the Christian fingerprints are still visible on the law, they have somewhat faded. The account given is typically an example of what Charles Taylor has called 'subtraction stories':[19] accounts of things that the historical churches used to do where their impact was reduced over time. In most of these subtraction stories, no distinction is made between the different branches of Christianity, let alone of other religions or beliefs. Rather, the perceived declining social and legal power of the established Church of England is considered to be synonymous with the perceived decline of Christianity. And the underlying assumption is that the Christian hold on such laws will and should weaken further as differentiation and secularisation run their course.

The history of English and Welsh law on marriage and education would look very different if the base assumptions of evolutionary functionalism were replaced by those of entropic complexity. Contrary to the schema I presented in *Law and Religion*, neither the Norman Conquest nor the Reformation had much effect on the development of marriage or education law.[20] In relation to marriage, the Church courts had exclusive jurisdiction over marriage and divorce from the mid-twelfth century, applying Roman Catholic canon law. Although there were some minor amendments, chiefly through the enactment

---

18   Russell Sandberg, *Religion and Marriage Law: The Need for Reform* (Bristol University Press, 2021); Russell Sandberg, *Religion in Schools: Learning Lessons from Wales* (Anthem Press, 2022).

19   Charles Taylor, *A Secular Age* (Harvard University Press, 2007) 22.

20   Russell Sandberg, *Law and Religion* (Cambridge University Press, 2011) Chapter 2. This book did not include discussion of marriage law and was only interested in the current law on religion in schools.

of the Canons Ecclesiastical 1603–04, it was not until the Marriage Act 1753 that significant reform occurred. That Act consolidated the monopoly of the Anglican Church – the Reformation statutes had little to do with it. Marriage had developed as something that the Church did. It was not really the concern of the State. The Reformation identified Church and State more explicitly but did not change the practice. This was largely because the practice was, if not in the shadow of the law, then at arm's length away from it. The same was true in relation to education. Primary and secondary education grew out of the work of the Church. Literacy was for centuries tied up with the Church.[21] The earliest schools that we know of, dating back to the Anglo-Saxon period, were linked to the Church; as were Oxford and Cambridge Universities, which were established in the early medieval period.[22] Again, the Reformation changed very little in terms of law – largely because law rarely, if at all, concerned itself with education. Education, like marriage, was something left to what we would today call the voluntary sector.

Similarly, marriage and education law does not fit the periodisation of toleration I identified in *Law and Religion*; but these areas of law do underline my comments about the process being uneven and contradictory. The experiences during the centuries following the Reformation were notably different in these two areas and neither saw a process of toleration. In terms of education, the fusion of Church and State did not lead to any form of education by the State or the State Church, so there was nothing to relax. Instead, the demand for education gradually grew in the centuries that followed but it remained within the voluntary sector. The churches played a crucial role in this but they did not monopolise it.[23] The bulk of educational provision before the nineteenth century 'had been built up by charitable endeavour and private initiative'.[24]

---

[21] Gareth Elwyn Jones and Gordon Wynne Roderick, *A History of Education in Wales* (University of Wales Press, 2003) 5.

[22] However, as Elwyn Jones and Wynne Roderick pointed out, 'it is mistaken to regard late medieval education as the province only of the monasteries and the Church – there was sufficient demand to foster the creation of grammar schools': ibid 13.

[23] From the very start, education took various different forms: from guilds that were developed in many trades to dissenting academies which were unofficially set up following the Reformation to Sunday schools and later on to developments that took place under the auspices of the Poor Law. About three-quarters of all working-class children were registered in Sunday schools run by both the Church of England and other churches: William Cornish et al, *Law and Society in England 1750–1950* (2nd edition, Hart, 2019) 420.

[24] Ibid 411. The motivation for the provision of education 'remained religious, a matter for philanthropy rather than the state': Gareth Elwyn Jones and Gordon Wynne Roderick, *A History of Education in Wales* (University of Wales Press, 2003) 27.

By contrast, 'central and local government played no significant role in the running of schools'.

By contrast, in marriage law, the centuries following the Reformation saw the exact opposite of toleration. The Marriage Act 1753 gave the established Church a monopoly. It provided the foundations of the modern law on marriage. It imposed the canon law requirements upon all weddings except for those of Jews and Quakers: all marriages were to take the form of a public ceremony in the parish church at which a clergyman would officiate according to authorised rites and marriage had to be preceded by banns or licence. Breach of any of these requirements, which had previously made a marriage irregular, would now render it void. Although it was not the first attempt to regularise the performance and registration of marriage, the enactment of the Marriage Act 1753 is often regarded as a pivotal moment, providing certainty as to who was married and stopping marriages taking place in ways that the State was unaware of. This was problematic because marital status bestowed certain legal rights and social attitudes at the time saw children born out of wedlock as being illegitimate. Although it is now questioned whether the Act largely reinforced existing social conventions rather than stamping out a serious and prevalent problem of marriages being conducted in various and unusual ways,[25] the effect of the legislation was nevertheless clear. The emphasis upon marriage taking place in a religious building open to the public continues to underscore the current law. The Act imposed uniformity. The monopolisation of the Church of England over marriage, therefore, was not the result of the Reformation but was only formally consolidated by the 1753 Act.

Significant reforms to both areas of the law took place in the nineteenth century. However, again, these changes do not observe and therefore question the general template of ongoing toleration. In *Law and Religion*, I described how the ad hoc recognition of alternative religion led by the nineteenth century to some evidence of a distancing between Church and State and to the Church of England developing a greater level of autonomy as a result. On the face of it, there is some evidence of marriage law following this toleration template. The Marriage Act 1836 made provision for 'civil marriage', permitting marriages to take place in register offices following a civil ceremony in the presence of a registrar and witnesses. That Act also provided that buildings registered as places of religious worship could be registered for solemnising marriages therein. This was a key component of the piecemeal toleration of other forms of religion. The foundations of the modern law of marriage were now fully laid out. Yet the picture is more complex than that. Rebecca Probert has argued

---

[25]   Rebecca Probert, *Marriage Law and Practice in the Long Eighteenth Century* (Cambridge University Press, 2009).

that there is a need to question the common perceptions about the 1836 Act whereby it is 'seen as an important liberalizing measure' and the 'story told about it has 'generally been ... a positive one ... that ... recognised the religious (and irreligious) diversity of nineteenth-century England and Wales'.[26] Probert noted that there is 'a tendency in at least some of the scholarship to exaggerate the extent to which the 1836 Act liberalised the law': many 'imply that it allowed couples to be married in any chapel and by any minister of religion'. In fact, she observed, 'the exacting criteria for places of worship to be registered for weddings meant that many were not'.[27] She highlighted that, above all else, how any given couple could marry depended very much on local factors. Probert further argued that the category of civil marriage has been misunderstood. The term 'civil' was not defined in the Act and the register office weddings were not envisaged as being the default. Rather, the 'option of getting married in a register office was intended for that small subcategory of dissenters who regarded marriage as a civil contract'. Moreover, 'civil' was not originally synonymous with 'secular'. It was not until the Marriage and Registration Act 1856 that religious content became prohibited in civil ceremonies. The effect of the Marriage Act 1836 has often been overstated as part of a narrative of progress. It did not sever the monopolistic assumptions that had previously been consolidated by the 1753 Act.

The situation in relation to education law was also messier than talk of toleration and religious autonomy often suggests. Religious rivalry was often a catalyst for change and State involvement increased gradually, usually in a pragmatic way. The turning point came with the Elementary Education Act 1870.[28] The Act established local school boards in areas where there were insufficient voluntary schools. Their function was to build and manage schools to fill up the gaps in the system provided by the denominations and charities to ensure that education was provided up to the age of 13. The Forster Act, therefore, 'saw a move from state subsidiary of voluntary education to state supplementation of voluntary education'.[29] It proved contentious

---

[26] Rebecca Probert, *Tying the Knot: The Formation of Marriage 1836–2020* (Cambridge University Press, 2021), Chapter 1.

[27] The Act required a separate building for all but Catholics and 20 householders had to certify that it was their usual place or worship. Furthermore, it was not until the Marriage Act 1898 that registered places of worship were permitted to appoint their own 'authorised person' in place of a registrar. And even today, 'many registered places of worship have not appointed their own authorised person and remain dependent on a registrar attending and registering any weddings that take place there'.

[28] Often known as the 'Forster Act' after William Edward Forster, who was responsible for education in Gladstone's government.

[29] William Cornish et al, *Law and Society in England 1750–1950* (2nd edition, Hart, 2019) 422.

among religious groups: while the Church of England 'wished to preserve and even to extend its grip on education', the 'Non-conformists fiercely opposed any additional financial support for Church schools'.[30] The question of religious teaching 'dominated' the passage of the Bill through Parliament.[31] Parliamentarians considered whether the Act should require compulsory religious instruction; whether it should 'not be used or directed in favour of or against the distinctive tenets of any religious denomination'; and whether there should be a conscience clause allowing a right to withdraw from this.[32] In the end, a compromise was reached that limited how denominational religious instruction in the new schools could be, but did not mean that schools could not teach their religious ethos. The situation was worsened by the fact that the Act applied only to the new elementary schools, which were only built where there was no existing sufficient provision; and by the fact that a grace period was provided to allow churches to set up new schools before the new system came into effect.[33] As Anthony Howard noted:

> The result, inevitably, was a typically British compromise – or more bluntly, muddle – in which some parents could choose between secular and denominational education while others, mainly in rural villages, had no choice but to send their children to schools in which the dogmas of the Established Church formed a specific part of the curriculum.[34]

These nineteenth-century developments, culminating in the Forster Act, saw the State take an interest in education for the first time and attempt to bring it within the purview of State law. They can therefore be regarded as the educational equivalent of the Reformation legislation or indeed the Marriage Act 1753. However, the Forster Act did not lead to anything like the monopolisation of the Church of England that occurred under those other two developments. It was also not an act of toleration or of secularisation. Rather, it was an example of the State working alongside the existing provision provided mostly by the churches. Yet this pragmatic response was never completely stable. Both marriage and education law were the object of significant legislation in the mid-twentieth century; but while the Marriage Act 1949 largely con-

---

[30]   Gareth Elwyn Jones and Gordon Wynne Roderick, *A History of Education in Wales* (University of Wales Press, 2003) 79.
[31]   William Cornish et al, *Law and Society in England 1750–1950* (2nd edition, Hart, 2019) 422.
[32]   See the House of Commons discussion at Committee stage: HC Hansard (30 June 1870) columns 1236–63.
[33]   William Cornish et al, *Law and Society in England 1750–1950* (2nd edition, Hart, 2019) 422.
[34]   Anthony Howard, *RAB: The Life of R A Butler* (Jonathan Cape, 1987) 111.

solidated the existing law, the education legislation was to prove much more controversial. As Howard commented, following the Forster Act:

> The seeds for the last great battle fought on behalf of the historical forces of Dissent in Britain had been sown. So firmly were they planted that they defied the successive efforts of Governments of differing political complexions over the next seventy years to uproot them.

This battle, however, was completely omitted from the account in *Law and Religion* which, like much related scholarship, paid little attention to dissent and radicalisation.[35] My focus on the juridification of religion at the turn of the new millennium meant that insufficient attention was afforded to the significant reforms of the twentieth century, which – contrary to the 'subtraction stories' often told about the perceived secularisation of the law – actually clarified, consolidated and then reinforced the hold of Christianity.

The Education Act 1944 – known as the 'Butler Act' – revolutionised both the position of the voluntary church schools that existed alongside State schools and the teaching of religion in both types of school.[36] It has been noted that under the Butler Act, 'the role of Anglicanism within education was not only secured but enlarged'.[37] Butler, the Education Minister, devoted a considerable amount of time to negotiating with religious leaders themselves.[38] In

---

[35] Rebecca Riedel, 'A Critical Legal Study of the Prevent Duty: The Religious Dimension' (PhD thesis submitted to Cardiff University, 2023).

[36] The Education Act 1902 was also significant. It replaced the school boards with local education authorities (LEAs) and brought the voluntary schools under their control. Such schools were now supported by the rates and in return LEAs appointed one-third of the managers/governors of the school. The 1902 Act therefore formally recognised the 'dual system' whereby 'denominational schools run (but no longer wholly paid for) by the Churches lived cheek-by-jowl with schools both administered and supervised by the State'. The passage of the Act led to civil disobedience from some dissenters who refused to pay their rates knowing that they would fund the Church of England school. Parental choice was respected by means of a conscience clause but the nature of religious instruction remained undefined: Anthony Howard, *RAB: The Life of R A Butler* (Jonathan Cape, 1987) 112.

[37] William Cornish et al, *Law and Society in England 1750–1950* (2nd edition, Hart, 2019) 454.

[38] This built upon developments already underway. As Butler noted in his memoirs, in Cambridgeshire in 1924 a committee of Anglicans, Free Churchmen and teachers had met and had drawn up a syllabus of religious instruction for use in the county's schools. By 1942 the Cambridgeshire syllabus was in use in over 100 LEAs. Butler noted that 'because of this, many Anglican managers were willing to hand over their schools to the local authorities in return for Christian teachings on these lines': Lord Butler, *The Art of the Possible: The Memoirs of Lord Butler* (revised edition, Penguin, 1973) 100.

the end, he presented a solution that comprised 'an offer of two alternatives'.[39] There were to be two categories of voluntary schools – voluntary controlled schools and voluntary aided schools – with the difference between the two being dictated by control and financing. This built upon the existing category of voluntary schools but crucially brought all schools within the system.

The Education Act 1944 followed this schema and also made collective worship and religious instruction statutory obligations.[40] It also provided that local education authorities would have the power to 'constitute a standing authority council on religious education [SACRE] to advise the authority'.[41] These provisions further entrenched the position of the Church of England, since the Church had its own committee (on the SACRE), which had a deciding vote.[42] The Butler Act made no further comment on the content of religious instruction or worship; in the House of Lords, Lord Selborne maintained that it was not necessary to explicitly state this, because the Act's provisions on the composition of the SACRE meant that 'it will be a syllabus which the Church of England can accept, and the Church of England is not going to accept a syllabus which is not in accordance with the Christian faith'.[43]

The Education Reform Act 1988 tightened rather than loosened the provisions on religion. The original Bill introduced the National Curriculum

---

[39]   Ibid 102.

[40]   Gary McCulloch, *Educational Reconstruction: The 1944 Education Act and the Twenty-First Century* (Woburn Press, 1994) 39. Section 27 stated that in voluntary controlled schools, religious instruction would also be given in accordance with the agreed syllabus unless parents requested that their children receive religious instruction in accordance with the school's trust. Under Section 28, the religious instruction given at a voluntary aided school was under the control of the managers or governors of the school and was to be in accordance with the school's trust deed or, where provision was not made in the trust deed, 'in accordance with the practice observed' in the school. However, arrangements were to be made for religious instruction in accordance with the agreed syllabus adopted by the LEA where this was requested by parents and where pupils could not 'with reasonable convenience' attend a school where that syllabus was in use, unless there were 'special circumstances' that made it 'unreasonable' for this to be accommodated.

[41]   Such bodies were optional under the Act and there is evidence of similar bodies existing before the Act.

[42]   Schedule 5 stated that a conference would be convened to prepare any agreed syllabus and this would consist of four committees: the first of these was to consist of the representatives of religious denominations that the LEA considered ought to be represented 'having regard to the circumstances of the area'; the second, in England, was a committee of representatives of the Church of England; the third was to be a committee of teachers; and the fourth of representatives of the local authority. The LEA was to have regard to any unanimous recommendations made to them; Section 29.

[43]   House of Lords Hansard (21 June 1944) volume 132, Column 362.

and did not focus on religious matters.[44] However, the Bishop of London successfully tabled amendments to ensure that, as he saw it, the Bill did not represent a move towards secularism or away from traditional Christian values.[45] The Act as amended by the House of Lords actually reinforced the place of Christianity. It stated that daily collective worship[46] had to 'be wholly or mainly of a broadly Christian character', and that this would be satisfied 'if it reflect[ed] the broad traditions of Christian belief without being distinctive of any particular Christian denomination'.[47] It was further specified that the agreed syllabus 'shall reflect the fact that the religious traditions in Great Britain are in the main Christian whilst taking account of the teaching and practices of the other principal religions represented in Great Britain'.[48] The rationale was to 'reinforce' the Butler Act.[49] However, the 1988 Act clearly went beyond the Butler Act.[50] At the very least, the Act made explicit what had previously been implicit – and what may have been implicit and taken for granted in the 1940s was no longer uncontroversial in Thatcher's Britain. This applied not only to the idea that Christianity in general and the Church

---

[44] On the Act generally, see, e.g., Leslie Bash and David Coulby (eds), *The Education Reform Act: Competition and Control* (Cassell, 1989); Denis Lawton (ed), *The Education Reform Act: Choice and Control* (Hodder & Stoughton, 1989); and Michael Flude and Merril Hammer (eds), *The Education Reform Act 1988: Its Origins and Implications* (Falmer Press, 1990).

[45] In the House of Lords debate, he stated that these amendments were based upon five main principles: 'We have sought to provide a framework for worship which, first, maintains the tradition of worship as part of the process of education, giving proper place to the Christian religion; secondly, maintains the contribution of the collective act of worship to the establishment of values within the school community; yet, thirdly, does not impose inappropriate forms of worship on certain groups of pupils; fourthly, does not break the school up into communities based on the various faiths of the parents, especially in that it makes some groups feel that they are not really part of the community being educated in the school; and, lastly, is realisable and workable in practical terms of school accommodation and organisation': House of Lords Hansard, 7 July 1988, Column 434.

[46] Which could be 'a single act of worship for all pupils or separate acts of worship for pupils in different age groups or different school groups': Education Reform Act 1988, Section 6.

[47] However, every act of collective worship did not need to comply with this provision, as long as, 'taking the school term as a whole, most such acts that take place in the school do comply': Section 7. Powers were given to SACREs to determine whether it was not appropriate for the rule to 'apply in the case of a county school or in the case of any class of description of pupils at such a school'.

[48] Education Reform Act 1988, Section 8.

[49] House of Commons Hansard, 15 December 1987, vol 124, column 439W.

[50] For aurther analysis, see Edwin Cox and Josephine M Cairns, *Reforming Religious Education: The Religious Clauses of the 1988 Education Reform Act* (Kogan Page, 1989).

of England in particular were the norm, but also to the notion that local areas were largely mono-creedal. The growth of religious diversity and pluralism rendered quaint the idea that each locality could determine its own unique and distinct religious makeup and so, as with marriage law, the disconnect between the law and the social reality became a constant theme in the literature.

The current domestic law governing religious observance in schools in England[51] can now be found in the Education Act 1996 and the School Standards and Framework Act 1998. These provisions continue to be broadly the same as the settlement reached in 1944, as amended by the 1988 Act. However, this leads many accounts to assume that the current law is archaic and reflects a historical reality that has been relaxed over time but is itself ingrained. This is not so. The supposedly archaic law is actually very recent in origin. In place of the usual subtraction stories, which highlight the perceived decline of influence of the Church, the reality is a much less straightforward picture whereby legal change is often the result of pragmatic and unpredictable compromise, and the letter of the law often exists in a different reality from the social practice.

The same is true of marriage law, where – by contrast to education law – the twentieth century saw comparatively little change. The Marriage Act 1949 consolidated the much older law and did not adjust the legal framework on getting married. It differentiated between marriages solemnised according to the rites of the Church of England/Church in Wales and marriages otherwise solemnised. This latter category included civil marriages in a register office or in approved premises; marriages 'according to the usages of the Society of Friends'; marriages 'between a man and a woman professing the Jewish religion according to the usages of the Jews'; and marriages in any place of worship registered under the Places of Worship Registration Act 1855 and Section 41 of the Marriage Act 1949. On the surface, therefore, the Act allowed for the legal recognition of religious marriages. However, the way in which it deals with religions differently has bred confusion and disadvantage. The fact that three religious groups are specifically named in the legislation has led to some confusion.[52] The problem is not that other religious marriages cannot be legally recognised under the Act. It is rather that the requirements required for such recognition indirectly discriminate against some religions: the requirements that religious weddings (other than Anglican, Jewish and Quaker ceremonies) be inside a registered place of worship and that a pre-

---

[51]   There has been recent reform of the law on religious education in Wales, as documented in Russell Sandberg, *Religion in Schools: Learning Lessons from Wales* (Anthem Press, 2022).

[52]   Law Commission, *Getting Married: A Consultation Paper on Weddings Law* (Consultation Paper 247, 2020) paras 5.25 *et seq.*

scribed choice of words be used do not fit with some religious traditions.[53] The legal framework completely excludes weddings conducted by belief organisations, which simply cannot be legally binding in their own right. Couples who have such weddings are not married in the eyes of the law unless and until they also undergo a civil ceremony. Accounts of marriage law also tend to present these legal obstacles as being longstanding. Yet the Marriage Act 1949 simply reflects compromises reached. Marriage law has historically been the subject of pragmatic reform. The longevity of the Marriage Act 1949 is the anomaly. The current law is not a stump of a once magnificent tree that has been chopped away at over time, but rather the product of historical quirk based on grubby compromises and an unwillingness – if not downright refusal – to consider comprehensive reform. This in itself recasts the debate as to reform. Seeing the present law as the often accidental consequence of tweaks that were politically possible at particular times, rather than as some received wisdom passed down and 'improved' as societies advanced, not only makes the need for reform more compelling but also means that such reform can and should be more radical. Moreover, the picture should be rendered more complex by adjusting the focus away from majority interests, shedding light on the lived experiences of adherents and paying attention to non-Christian religions and non-religious beliefs.

***

Recasting the history of religion's interaction with marriage and education law rejects the four phases of development I identified in *Law and Religion* and debunks the usual linear account of a secular 'progress'. In its place, it reveals a pragmatic and often chaotic trajectory whereby law slowly, inelegantly and often inadequately tried to regulate aspects of an activity that was previously largely, if not completely, dealt with by the voluntary sector. The picture is not one of the voices of the churches declining but rather of the State attempting – not entirely successfully – to gain a foothold. This is not the picture that we are usually presented with. That is because social functional differentiation is so ingrained. The conventional subtraction stories, predicated upon the idea that religious involvement is a historical throwback, are parts of the deparadoxification strategies used by the social system of law to perpetuate its own autonomy.[54] These strategies are so ingrained and so successful that they frustrate

---

[53] This leads to religious marriages taking place that are not legally recognised, which can prove problematic on relationship breakdown where the redress and support provided by the State for those separating and divorcing are not available to those who are not legally married.

[54] John Harrington, 'Of Paradox and Plausibility: The Dynamic of Change in Medical Law' (2014) 22(3) *Medical Law Review* 305, 306.

the reform movement. They focus our attention on the experience of majorities and present the historical foundations of the law as being firmer and older than they are. This conceals the extent to which the legal rules are actually the result of grubby compromises fit for purpose at the time in which they were made, but which can now be remodelled to suit today's social situation. The fact that the direction of travel has been far from linear, definitely not inevitable and absolutely not irreversible highlights the capacity for legal change and the fact that reform can be achieved on a pragmatic basis.

This chapter has singled out my own work for critique in order to show how endemic evolutionary functionalist ideas are. At this point in the book, you have probably already made up your mind as to whether such self-flagellation is an exercise in autoethnography or self-indulgent navel gazing. Yet the ubiquity of implicit narratives of progress and acceptance of societal functional differentiation in my textbook on law and religion shows how, ironically, the assumptions upon which that sub-discipline is based have led to its current predicament. The decline of law and religion has arisen not only due to its institutionalisation. A deeper cause can be identified. Law and religion, by accepting conventional narratives, has problematised not only its subject matter but also its existence as an area of academic enquiry. To overcome this, it needs to challenge these narratives.

Excursus III

Meanwhile, in yet another alternative timeline...

Millie and Ncuti were among the last delegates to arrive at the 'History of Legal Scholarship' conference. It was being held at the Upper Temple, the new Inn of Court that had ironically been built underground during the 2180s. Passing past a display on the history of criminal law scholarship entitled 'From Glanvill to Glanville Williams', Millie's eyes alighted upon a book that was over 100 years old.

'Ah – that one is from the heyday of legal publishing,' Ncuti commented, 'from the days before it all went online. They say that you used to be able to walk down corridors of books in libraries finding books on the shelves next to the ones that you wanted to read that were related to the one you wanted. Imagine that. I bet it even has actual footnotes rather than hyperlinks.'

Millie was too afraid to pick up such a delicate-looking object. She believed that it used to be called a 'hardback', which she thought was odd given that the front looked as robust as the back did. The words on the front said, 'The Legal Framework of the Church of England' and said that the author's name was Norman Doe.

'It's one of the texts that were part of the revival of ecclesiastical law', she noted. 'The golden age.'

Ncuti nodded. He, after all, had undertaken some research on the rise and fall of law schools in the early twenty-first century. 'Wasn't that one of the early law and religion books?' he pondered.

Millie took this as an invitation to provide a mini-lecture: 'Yes, from the late twentieth century/early twenty-first century. The so-called "war on terror" led to increased interest in religion and a literature developed – not just on ecclesiastical law, but also on international and national laws affecting religion. What a time that was. Scholars writing about human rights law; the Orwellian titled Equality Act, which was basically about discrimination; new criminal offences – a whole new legal framework.'

'Yes,' Ncuti interrupted in the hope that the conversation could be brought to a close and he could join the queue for coffee, 'but then it kind of dried up.'

'It wasn't that the place of religion in the public sphere became less controversial, but other topics took over as the concerns of the day,' replied Millie, clearly warming to her theme. 'Academics stopped paying attention to religion. The topic also wasn't widely taught, especially as law schools became more and more influenced by the legal profession and the fear of the machines. So the field began to shrink almost as soon as it had begun.'

'Absolutely,' agreed Ncuti, now giving up hope of any caffeine-based refreshment. 'Some of those who researched in the field expanded their focus and then found that their work no longer fitted in the specialist law and religion book series and journals.'

Millie nodded and then continued: 'But their work laid the seeds for the revival. New voices; new perspectives. Work that explored religion alongside other forms of inequality such as gender, race and class. Non-religious beliefs began to be more of a focus. Interdisciplinary and comparative research explored beliefs alongside questions of time and place.'

'Yes – it became less State-centric and more critical,' Ncuti reflected. 'More creative – subversive, even – but taking both law and religion seriously and challenging ways in which they were understood and how they understood themselves. Some say it was the second golden age. Just imagine if that had never happened; if law and religion had just died.'

Millie shuddered, noticed the time on the hologram clock and headed to the coffee stall, where she managed to obtain the final cup.

PART IV

Conclusion

20. So what

The ten years since the publication of *Religion, Law and Society* have been a tumultuous decade.[1] We have all been affected by the uncertainties perpetuated by Brexit, the Covid-19 pandemic and the increasingly aggressive culture wars. Economic fears, the bogeyman of artificial intelligence and war on the European continent have unsettled us. All of these things and much more have been perverted by the pervasiveness of fake news and the creation of false devils. We increasingly feel lost. It has also been a tumultuous decade personally. In terms of my writings, my sharp focus on law and religion has given way to a growing canvas of interests. These new adventures have caused me to reflect upon law and religion as a field of studies and my role in its creation and paralysis. My response has increasingly been one of concern: lamenting and pillorying my previous work, scribbling that it now seems to belong to a simpler time.

This book has sought to bring together and rework the observations I have made during the last decade. They reflect the backdrop of the prevailing culture. Optimism often seems to be in short supply. Yet in revisiting and remaking those arguments on the larger canvas provided by a full-length book, I hope that sufficient attention has been given to solutions. In legal academic writings, providing a diagnosis is easy; providing a cure is much more difficult. It is easy – and in step with the culture of the last decade – to lament shortcomings; to suggest that law and religion is not flourishing in the way in which my previous work thought that it might – indeed, in a way that I thought it would. It is easy to overlook what has been achieved in the last decade; to hold it against an impossible idealised standard and denounce it. It is much more difficult to address what should and what can be done about it.

This is not to deny that the task of deconstruction is important. There is a need to question, to crack open assumptions and to demolish. This often requires asking uncomfortable questions about biases, assumptions and other limitations. Yet such work on its own is not even an effective post-mortem. The criticism that such work constitutes mere navel gazing is often astute. This applies to some of the short pieces I have penned over the last decade: their

---

[1]   Russell Sandberg, *Religion, Law and Society* (Cambridge University Press, 2014).

length has meant that I have been unable to move beyond deconstruction, so their worth is limited.

Perhaps, then, the anonymous peer reviewer was right. Perhaps some of the pieces that fed into this book did include 'an element of navel gazing over a minority interest'. The same may be true of parts of this book, or even the book as a whole. But I hope that the previous chapters have proved that this is not the case. I hope that this book has demonstrated not only the need to rethink law and religion, but also how law and religion can be rethought and the potential benefits of doing so. This final concluding chapter will attempt to reflect upon these matters. It will begin by briefly recapping the main arguments of the book and will then go on to show what can be learned from these insights through a spot of time travel. I will reflect upon what I would do differently now if I could return to the beginning of my career and how I would rewrite my book on *Law and Religion* in light of what I now know (and think).[2]

***

Our attempt to rethink law and religion has comprised three stages. However, before recapping each stage, it is important to remember what we have been rethinking. This book has focused on the legal sub-discipline of law and religion as it has developed in law schools in England and Wales. In the same way as the relationship between law and religion differs greatly over time and space, so too does the study of law and religion. Even if we limit our focus geographically and temporally, identifying the object of our study remains difficult and inherently subjective. There is no fixed objective, all-purpose definition of any academic field. Yes, there are criteria that can be applied; and this is easier in some fields, such as those concerning specific legal actions. But even with a field such as criminal law or tort law, there are questions of where boundaries are to be drawn. These questions become more difficult in fields to do with relationships with law such as family law, media law or sports law; and they are more difficult again in less well-established fields, such as law and religion. In short, this book has tried to rethink what I understand to be 'law and religion'. Your definition might – and probably will – differ. This is just one of many reasons why this has proved to be a very personal book; an exercise in autoethnography; an act of repentance.

Repentance was the first of the three stages explored here. It was my first and perhaps overriding purpose in writing it. In a sense, it has been therapeutic to return to what I considered to be unfinished business and to properly reflect not so much on what did not happen but rather on why this was so. Rather than dwelling upon the limitations of the field (as I see them), I have

---

    Russell Sandberg, *Law and Religion* (Cambridge University Press, 2011).

concentrated more upon how my work and actions have been responsible for limiting the growth of law and religion. In the first stage of the book, it became clear that the problem was that law and religion grew too quickly, obsessed and constrained by the high-profile legislation, litigation and public debate of the day. This led to a legalistic approach being taken. Ironically, attempts to develop the field further made this worse. The institutional trappings that we sought in order to develop law and religion as a legal sub-discipline ended up creating a ghetto. Law and religion grew to the size where the field was large enough for those within the field to have conversations among themselves, but their impact outside the field was limited and this detrimentally affected the visibility and reputation of the field. It remained marginal at best within law schools; the volume of institutional trappings – such as book series and specialist journals – was at odds with how the field had developed in terms of its teaching and its place within the legal mainstream.

A major theme of the autoethnographical reflections in this book has been the influence of others: the role models who have inspired me, invariably by showing other ways of thinking, questioning and researching. This is also true of law and religion as a field in England and Wales. We can look to places and people elsewhere where law and religion is in healthier spirits for guidance. The work of John Witte Jr and his research centre at Emory is particularly helpful in this respect. Their work shows what ambition law and religion can have and what it can achieve. And, as we have seen, Witte's own reflection on the nature of law and religion in the US can show what is missing in the UK (as well as where UK scholarship is leading the way). In particular, his definition of law and religion studies as including 'the study of the religious dimensions of law, the legal dimensions of religion and the interaction of legal and religious ideas and institutions, norms and practices'[3] highlights the extent to which law and religion scholarship in the UK has largely focused on 'the legal dimensions of religion'. It has been mostly a legalistic analysis that regards the place of religion in the public sphere as a problem for law to solve. This focus also explains the waning power of law and religion in England and Wales, given that concerns about the place of religion in the public sphere are not as common as they once were. Interest in studying religion legally has declined given that the new religious rights are no longer that new and also because they have been narrowly interpreted, with Article 9 of the European Convention on Human Rights (ECHR) becoming a paper tiger.[4] The narrow understanding of

---

[3]   John Witte, Jr, 'The Study of Law and Religion in the United States: An Interim Report' (2012) 14 *Ecclesiastical Law Journal* 327.

[4]   Cf Frank S Ravitch, *Advanced Introduction to Law and Religion* (Edward Elgar Publishing, 2023) 77.

law and religion as being mostly the study of religion law with some focus on religious law is no longer fit for purpose. The creation and perpetuation of that distinction and the development of the institutional trappings that led to law and religion becoming a legalistic disciplinary-bound specialist area of study are my contributions – which, although well meaning, have served to undermine the very cause I intended to achieve: the healthy long-term development of law and religion.

Witte's account also highlighted how the study of law and religion should inherently be an interdisciplinary endeavour, since it involves examining religion from the perspective of law and exploring law from the perspective of religion. *Religion, Law and Society* lamented how law and religion in the UK was not as interdisciplinary in focus as it should have been by exploring the way in which it could interact and learn from the sociology of religion. In this book, however, a different approach has been taken. While my previous books tried to group law and religion with legal sub-disciplines concerning social relationships such as family law and sports law, here we have rethought which areas law and religion can be associated with. This was the second stage of our analysis: reappraisal.

First, law and religion was compared with other areas of law based on inequalities. It was clear not only that the literatures on law and gender and law and race are more developed than law and religion, but also that they act as critical movements. There is no equivalent to feminist or critical race theory approaches in law and religion. This means that the status quo is rarely questioned and the legalistic, state-centred lens is seldom challenged. Second, law and religion was placed within the law and humanities literature – again, a placing that seems obvious but which is rarely made. Here, comparison with law and history showed the dangers that could come if law and religion continued on the path to become a legal specialism. By contrast, law and geography showed the freedom and potential that came from eschewing institutional trappings and pursuing an inter- or even transdisciplinary approach. This reinforced the findings of the law and gender and law and race comparisons by showing how this approach was enabled and reflected a critical approach to law. The reappraisal stage therefore underlined that law and religion was lacking inspiration from the critical turn.

The third and final stage – regeneration – is where perhaps our study took a controversial turn, in that it recommended applying the work of Niklas Luhmann. Although increasingly featured in works of socio-legal theory, Luhmann's theory is notorious for its complexity and its bold focus on social systems rather than upon human agency. Yet his theory helps us to unpack further the nature and importance of social functional differentiation: the idea that while in pre-modern societies, a few social institutions – such as the Church – discharged a multitude of social functions, in modern society, a multitude of social institutions – such as the legal, education systems, the family and so on – each discharge specific functions. While social functional differentiation forms part of many sociological theories and accounts of secularisation, Luhmann's social systems theory is particularly helpful as it enables us to see and scrutinise how law and religion both operate as social systems; and how many of the controversies discussed in the law and religion literature – such as the operation of religious courts, the existence of faith schools and any presence of religion in the public sphere – offend the autonomy of law as a social system. The way in which law frames such matters reflects this. Law seeks to understand religion only in law's own terms. It sees any legal functions discharged by religion as an attack on law's autonomy that must be dealt with. The discharge of such legal functions by religion is seen as a historical throwback and a dangerous act of de-differentiation.

Luhmann's social systems theory, therefore, sharpens our diagnosis. It shows why law and religion has focused on 'the legal dimensions of religion'. The social system of law sees religion as a threat and has sought to neutralise it by understanding it and subjecting it to its own framework. Law and religion as an academic field has often been complicit in achieving this. The rights-based framework has sought to understand and limit religion legally – hiding this through the presence of paper tigers. It has treated religions performing legal functions as being inherently problematic. Academic analysis has been complicit in the 'deparadoxification strategies'[5] that the social system of law has used to attempt to conceal the inherent paradoxes at the heart of law – that law cannot question the validity of its claim that its decisions are legal. Being aware of this allows us to question it. It allows us to take a step back and see not only how law regulates religion, but also how law understands and manipulates religion and to what end.

In this way, Luhmann's social systems theory helps point towards a cure. This is especially true if Luhmann's theories are modified and if critical ideas are introduced, ushering in what may be styled a subversive social systems theory.[6] Crucially, this develops social systems theory so that the discharging of legal functions by religion is seen not as evidence of de-differentiation but rather as re-differentiation. Religious legal systems can be seen as social systems in their own right that blend legal and religious functions. This is a significant revision of social systems theory, which is a functionalist approach that

---

    5   Cf John Harrington, 'Of Paradox and Plausibility: The Dynamic of Change in Medical Law' (2014) 22(3) *Medical Law Review* 305, 306.

    6   This label may be useful in distinguishing the attempt made here from other work that applies a critical approach to social systems theory such as that of Gunther Teubner, *Critical Theory and Legal Autopoiesis: The Case for Societal Constitutionalism* (Manchester University Press, 2019).

tends to adopt a forward-moving, linear, progressive understanding of history. This is unsurprising given that systems theory developed in the functionalist tradition in social theory. This points the way for further revisions. Although what Gordon referred to as 'evolutionary functionalist ideas' underpin social system theory as they do wider thinking in general,[7] they can be removed if we change the underpinning scientific idea from evolution to entropy. Blending chaos, complexity and social entropy theories allows us to question and reconstruct the stories that we are told about legal change. For instance, in relation to how religion interacts with education and marriage law, such an approach radically alters our understanding by replacing the 'subtraction stories'[8] that assume that differentiation and secularisation are inevitable and possibly even natural with an account instead that sees protracted conflict between the legal and religious social systems where law attempts, pragmatically and often chaotically, to strengthen its foothold and to attain a monopoly.

Social systems theory, then, once its functionalist underpinning is decontaminated, provides a way of thinking through Witte's conceptualisation of law and religion as being about understanding the 'dialectical interaction' between law and religion[9] – the way in which the two co-constitute, challenge and complement one another, and how an absolute line cannot be drawn between the two. The interdisciplinary study of law and religion can therefore be understood as involving the study of law as religion and of religion as law – and crucially, this includes how the religious and legal social systems interact with and interpret each other (or, to put it another way, fight with, colonise and misrepresent each other). This suggests that there are important directions in which law and religion as a field of study in England and Wales needs to grow. This is true even in the context of areas where law and religion scholarship has focused on: there needs to be a move beyond the current legalistic approach, which focuses just on how the State regulates religion, to see what this reveals about the priorities of law and what is being concealed. In short, a critical approach – I would say a subversive approach – needs to be taken both to how law regulates religion and to how this is presented through academic works. Law and religion in this sense can lead the way for other areas of law by being more self-aware and self-critical. There is a need for more rather than less navel gazing in law schools: we need to question and problematise the intellectual development of legal ideas and the construction of areas of law. We need to pay more attention to what I have called the 'common lore': the

---

[7] Robert W Gordon, *Taming the Past: Essays on Law in History and History in Law* (Cambridge University Press, 2017) 221.

[8] Cf Charles Taylor, *A Secular Age* (Harvard University Press, 2007) 22.

[9] John Witte, Jr, 'The Study of Law and Religion in the United States: An Interim Report' 14 (2012) *Ecclesiastical Law Journal* 327, 327–28.

development of legal concepts principles and ideas in legal writings that then become ingrained and unquestioned.[10]

***

Reading the above, you might be thinking along the lines of Lord Denning's comment about the ECHR: 'As so often happens with high-sounding principles, they have to be brought down to earth.'[11] This final section will attempt to do just that. It will time travel back to the start of my law and religion journey and will reflect upon what I would have done differently in light of the findings of this book. In particular, it will reflect on how I would have approached writing *Law and Religion* in light of what I now know (and think).[12]

The short answer to this is that I would remove the focus on developing law and religion as a legal sub-discipline akin to family law or sports law; or perhaps recast it as a discussion of the different ways in which law and religion can be understood, critiquing the dominant legalistic State-centric approach. As the last chapter discussed, I would also revise the account of historical development to attempt to remove or at least challenge the evolutionary functionalist underpinnings. However, these revisions would just scratch the surface and do not fully show what is required. More than minor revisions are required.

If *Law and Religion* were written today, it would not have that title. It has now become clear that the focus of that book is on just one aspect of law and religion studies. This is not to say that the book ought to include all aspects, being an interdisciplinary and critical exhaustive guide to how law and religion interact and the consequences of this. That agenda is probably too ambitious for just one book, possibly too demanding for one author and beyond the purpose of producing a work that primarily serves as a textbook for undergraduates. The book, therefore, while recognising the various aspects of law and religion that can and should be explored, needs to be selective in its focus. If I were writing a book along the lines of *Law and Religion*, it would be more likely to be titled something along the lines of *Freedom of Religion or Belief*. To move away from the argument that a body of law exists called 'religion law', the book would explicitly focus on how different areas of law interact with religion or belief. This would open up the analysis to other legal fields rather than promote the idea of law and religion as a specialist ghetto.

---

[10]   See further Russell Sandberg, *Subversive Legal History: A Manifesto for the Future of Legal Education* (Routledge, 2021) 202 *et seq*.

[11]   *Ahmad v Inner London Education Authority* [1978] QB 36 at 41.

[12]   Russell Sandberg, *Law and Religion* (Cambridge University Press, 2011).

This would also be reflected in a move away from looking at general principles in separate chapters at the start of the book, which assumes that there are common stories and approaches in all the various ways in which different areas of law regulate religion. Rather than having chapters on the historical development and legal definition of 'religion', these matters would be included and discussed in each substantive chapter. Chapters on religion and belief in international law, constitutional law, charity law, education law, marriage law, criminal law and so on would each include a discussion of the pragmatic ways in which those areas of law have understood, interacted with and regulated religion and belief over time. They would focus on how law has constructed religion: what has been included and what has been excluded. The inclusion of belief in the book's title would also be reflected in its contents. In each chapter, there would be a need to pay equal attention to both religion and belief by exploring the extent to which similar treatment is currently provided and should be provided to non-religious beliefs, examining whether reform is needed to ensure that laws are compatible with international human rights standards and to adequately protect non-religious beliefs. This would expose the way in which law understands and interprets the terms 'religion' and 'belief', which would include analysis of how and why law does this and what the ramifications of this would be.

Suggesting revisions to just one book by outlining what would be done differently if it were being rewritten today may seem unambitious and under-whelming. It may also be dismissed as a clear example of self-indulgent navel gazing. However, the differences between *Law and Religion* as it was written and the version speculated about here underscore the benefit of rethinking the field. Being self-reflective and self-critical enables diagnoses to be made and alternative trajectories to be identified. Identifying mistakes – or at least realising that what was achieved previously is unlikely to be appropriate and satisfactory now – allows lessons to be learned. Following a decade character-ised by pessimism and plagued by uncertainty, writing this book by collating and rethinking the contributions on the topic I have made during this time has actually made me more optimistic about the future of law and religion as an area of study, and of legal studies generally. For me, it has underscored that we can be more ambitious if we not only seek to describe and scrutinise what law does but also ask why. The words 'so what' need to be our constant response.[13] Law and religion scholarship needs to take both law and religion seriously and examine them critically. This can be achieved by regarding law and religion as two social systems in a constant dialectical and often competitive interaction.

---

[13] Focusing on the 'so what' question was one of the very many useful pieces of advice offered by Professor Nigel Lowe throughout the early period of my career.

Other fields show how this can be achieved. An interdisciplinary approach is needed, so we need to move beyond the current legalistic focus.

This does not necessarily mean scrapping the institutional trappings that current exist, but it does mean reforming them and opening out law and religion as a field. As with the discussion of how my *Law and Religion* textbook should be rewritten, this may necessitate changes to titles and labels – but the more important changes are to the ambition and approach of the scholarship. Rather than seeing this as a criticism of what has come before, however, the opportunity to rethink should be viewed in a much more positive light. It is an opportunity to regroup, recharge and prepare for the resurgence of the field. Rethinking is an important initial step but the revolutionary changes it inspires means that in its wake there is much work to be done. The fact that a number of excellent pieces of recent scholarship have questioned the nature or assumptions of law and religion scholarship or have sought to position themselves outside the field, either explicitly or implicitly is encouraging;[14] but it also shows the need for a critical – or subversive – law and religion scholarship that can include such work. A critical interdisciplinary approach to law and religion will reveal much not only about religion but also about law; this is why it will be important for what law schools do, but also why it cannot be limited to being a law school activity. The benefit of rethinking law and religion is that the field can include and grow from the constructive criticisms and reflections that are made. It is not a question of undermining the phenomenal achievements that led to the development of law and religion in the first decade of the twenty-first century, but rather of developing new and improved ways of doing law and religion scholarship which will match and further the successes of the recent past to develop scholarship that makes a significant and transforming contribution to the future. I do not think that such work would amount to 'navel gazing over a minority interest'; but if a certain amount of navel gazing is needed to rethink and recharge the field in order to achieve greater things, then in my view, that navel gazing has been more than justified. Now, however, there is a need to move beyond rethinking law and religion to rebuilding law and religion (or whatever we want to call it). It will be interesting to see what the next decade brings.

---

14   Eg, Javier Garcia Oliva and Helen Hall, *Religion, Law and the Constitution: Balancing Beliefs in Britain* (Routledge, 2018); Méadhbh McIvor, *Representing God: Christian Legal Activism in Contemporary England* (Princeton University Press, 2020); Patrick S Nash, *British Islam and English Law: A Classical Pluralist Perspective* (Cambridge University Press, 2022); Caroline K Roberts, *Freedom of Religion or Belief in the European Convention on Human Rights: A Reappraisal* (Cambridge University Press, 2023); Rebecca Riedel, 'A Critical Legal Study of the Prevent Duty: The Religious Dimension' (PhD thesis submitted to Cardiff University, 2023).

To be continued…

Index